TOWN NORTH NATIONAL BANK

Photograph by Hans Zielke

WHERE CREDIT IS DUE
A History of the Credit Union Movement in Texas, 1913-1984

By BILL SLOAN

Research by Lana Henderson

All rights reserved.
Library of Congress Catalog Card Number:
84-050230

International Standard Book Number: 0-9613232-0-5

Printed by Taylor Publishing Company, Dallas, Texas

Table of Contents

PART III:

Reaching for Tomorrow (1960-1984)

Acknowledgements

Although a single individual may be listed as its author, no book of this type is the work of one person alone. This particular book is the product of many months of effort by a great many people, each of whom deserves a measure of gratitude from the writer. While it is impossible to recognize each of these contributors individually, it would be inexcusable not to single out a few people without whose help there would have been no written or published history of the credit union movement in Texas.

TCUL Public Relations Vice President Dick Williamson offered invaluable and continual assistance all along the way, both personally and through his staff. His assistant, Rebecca Richardson, was never too busy to help dig out an elusive piece of information, spend her weekends and evenings correcting the manuscript, photocopy a mountain of research material or assist in any number of other ways.

In helping to piece together the story of the League over the past three or four decades, a number of present-day employees offered vital assistance, including Mary Ogden, Jim Vest, Ted McGehee, Allen Hudson, John Dunagan, John Arnold, Ron Liles, Carol Luebke, Walt Bondies, Tony Gehring, Betty Danyluk, and, of course, President Jack Eaker, to name a few. Former Assistant Managing Director Paul Mullins graciously welcomed us into his home and shared his memorabilia and priceless photographs with us, as did former League President Jack Mitchell. Former Managing Director Jim Barry was always as near as the telephone when we needed to check a particular historical point, and so was Phil Davis.

Other important input came from such past and present League leaders as R.C. Morgan, Jimmy Parker,

Bessie Heard, the late W.S. MacKinnon; his wife, Helen Wood MacKinnon, the late John Quinlan and others. State Credit Union Commissioner Pete Parsons offered indispensible help in interpreting and tracking down various pieces of credit union legislation. And a special word of thanks is due Jerry Burns, historical librarian at CUNA headquarters in Madison, Wisconsin, who kept a steady stream of historical tidbits headed in our direction—material to which we would never have had access otherwise.

Finally, I want to express my deep appreciation for the outstanding job of research and editing carried out by my partner in this long and involved project—my wife, Lana Henderson. She spent countless hours organizing incomprehensible masses of material into easily digested files, interviewing principal figures in this history, traveling with me to Madison and numerous points in Texas and backstopping me for errors in the working manuscript.

To the many others who rendered assistance in one form or another, I am also grateful. You know who you are, even if I have neglected to mention you here by name. My thanks and best wishes!

Bill Sloan
Dallas, Texas
October, 1984

PART I:

The Formative Years (1913-1936)

Then And Now

Just over a half-century ago, credit unions were virtually unknown to the average citizen of Texas, even though the concept behind them had been used with some degree of success in other parts of the world for decades. Centered around the ideal of cooperative thrift and credit, the "people's banks" as credit unions were sometimes known, had attracted the interest of political figures, religious leaders and social theorists for upwards of 150 years. In isolated instances, the concept had worked well long before the dawn of the Twentieth Century, but even by the late 1920s, it remained largely untried in the Southwest.

The concept had sounded good enough more than 70 years ago to persuade a rural-dominated Texas Legislature to attempt to give it its first test in the region by enacting one of the earliest credit union laws in the United States. Unfortunately, though, that original enabling legislation was seriously flawed, and the Texas farmers whom it was intended to benefit were unable to put it to practical use. For 16 years, the law languished on the books, accomplishing little beyond gathering dust. As a result, as recently as 1929, the credit union concept had still managed to attain neither form nor substance insofar as Texans were concerned.

Then, aided by timely changes in the law just as Texas and the rest of the nation were stumbling under the financial calamities of the Great Depression, the credit union concept suddenly captured the public imagination and blossomed into a powerful grassroots movement all across the country. Within the space of a

1

few years, it became a driving socio-economic force, a godsend for countless hard-pressed wage earners, and an innovation that not even the highest levels of the national political power structure could fail to notice. It was an idea whose time had come. As President Franklin D. Roosevelt noted in a memo to Secretary of the Treasury Henry Morgenthau Jr. in June 1934: "I really believe in the usefulness of these credit unions."

So did a growing number of Texans. At about that same time, Congress passed the original Federal Credit Union Act, under the sponsorship and guidance of two key Texas political leaders—Senator Morris Sheppard and U.S. Representative Wright Patman. Not coincidentally, the first federal credit union in the entire nation was chartered before the end of 1934—in Texarkana, Texas.

Despite such progress and recognition, however, life was no bed of roses for the early Texas credit unions and their members. They faced a tremendous uphill struggle for solvency and survival. Some were formed with assets of only a few-score dollars, and yet they clung tenaciously to life and managed somehow to gain strength. A surprising number of them lived to see better days. In fact, of the eleven original Texas credit unions chartered in 1929, five are still flourishing today.

Paralleling the growth of the credit union movement in Texas over the past fifty years has been the growth and development of the Texas Credit Union League (TCUL), formed in that same eventful year of 1934. As was the case with most of the state's pioneer credit unions, the League began inauspiciously and without much fanfare. It grew out of the need to coordinate credit union activities, to communicate mutual concerns over the vast expanses of the Lone Star State, most of which were then very sparsely populated, and to protect the interests of all credit unions and their shareholders at a time when their number was rapidly proliferating.

2

Credit union leaders from all over Texas gathered in Fort Worth in October of that year for the organizational meeting of the TCUL, at which they elected a slate of officers and appointed a managing director. On the day of its birth, League officials counted 63 credit unions scattered across the state, with a combined total of just 8,048 members and only $535,000 in assets—or about $66 per member.

For the next few years, the League existed in little more than name only, without so much as a place to call home. It was not until 1941 that the League's first headquarters—a cramped one-room office in Houston—was opened. A few years later, after World War II, the League moved its official residence to equally unpretentious quarters situated first in one side of a rented duplex, then upstairs from a well-known beer bar at the corner of Knox Street and Cole Avenue in Dallas.

From these humble beginnings, the credit union movement in Texas has grown into an economic giant that embodies both the "can-do" spirit of the Lone Star State and its traditional reverence for the individual. Today, that movement encompasses a network of about 1,200 credit unions with a combined membership of more than 3.5 million—or one of every five Texans—and total assets of more than $7.5 billion.

Meanwhile, the Texas Credit Union League and its Affiliates, which represent and serve fully 95 percent of all credit unions in Texas, have also grown at a phenomenal pace. Today's TCUL is symbolized by the gleaming, twelve-story Texas Credit Union Center towering above LBJ Freeway in the heart of North Dallas' fabulous "Golden Corridor." Opened in 1980, the center serves as home both for the League and its affiliated institutions—Members Insurance Companies and TCUL Services, Inc., and the various other service groups, including Town North National Bank and Southwest Corporate Federal Credit Union, that support Texas credit unions.

Each day, more than 800 employees report to work at the center to carry out the myriad functions of TCUL and Affiliates.

What lies between those primitive beginnings of yesterday and the resounding successes of today is much more than a story of mere buildings, budgets and balance sheets. It is a story of people—people of resolve, foresight, wisdom, energy, and courage—who have led the Texas Credit Union League and the millions of individual credit union members it represents through five momentous decades of change and challenge to the proud plateaus of the present.

This book is intended to commemorate the accomplishments of the past fifty years and to salute all of those people—living and dead—who have made these accomplishments possible.

A False Start

It is incredibly difficult for a resident of one of Texas' large urban centers of today, especially someone who has lived in the state for only a decade or so, to comprehend the differences between the Texas of the mid-1980s and the remote, raw-boned land of seventy years ago. You will not find much of this land—or the attitudes that grew out of it—in present-day Houston, Dallas-Fort Worth, San Antonio, or other major cities. In the smaller cities and towns, traces may still be noticed, but it is actually necessary to drive past the abandoned, tumbledown farmhouses of the old East Texas cotton belt, through the endless green fields of the irrigated High Plains, or into the rugged ranchlands of the Edwards Plateau to begin to understand the character and mentality of Texas in the pre-World War I era.

In the spring of 1913, when one of the nation's first state credit union laws was enacted in Austin, Texas was still an agricultural society. The majority of its people and the bulk of its vast territory remained virtually untouched by the Industrial Revolution. Where there was sufficient water to support dry-land crops, small, non-mechanized farms dotted the landscape. And on the dusty ranges of West Texas, giant herds of cattle still grazed on the short grass across mile upon empty mile of prairie. All in all, most of the State of Texas could hardly have presented a more vivid contrast with the booming, populous, wealthy, industrialized, urbanized, frenetic, sophisticated atmosphere of today.

Then, as now, Dallas and Harris Counties boasted the state's largest populations. But, even so, the federal census of 1910 had found only 135,000 and 115,000 persons living in the two counties, respectively, at that time. There was nothing remotely resembling the sprawling metropolitan complexes of today. There were a few large towns, but no really big cities, and almost three out of every four Texans lived in rural areas, drawing their livelihood directly from farming and ranching. Often, it was a tenuous livelihood at best. Even successful farmers suffered through periodic "hard times," as drouths, floods, storms, unseasonal freezes, and other erratic Texas weather conditions contributed to crop failures. Texas farmers were also trying to expand their production capabilities to feed and clothe a rapidly expanding population. This involved buying expensive modern equipment, building lakes and ponds for water storage, clearing more land, and utilizing new types of hybrid seeds and fertilizers. And all of this required either cash or credit—usually at a time when the farmer had neither. The typical farm family often went for months without seeing any "hard cash," except what they were able to put aside at harvest time after all expenses were paid. Given this scenario, it is not difficult to understand why their elected representatives in Austin were seeking, in that long-ago spring of 1913, to do something to alleviate the farmers' annual plight. One answer, they hoped, might be a law permitting the establishment of rural credit unions.

But even then, revolutionary changes were afoot in Texas—changes that would dramatically affect the lives of every Texan within the next few decades, but changes that were often beyond the comprehension of either the farmers or the legislators of the period. At the turn of the century, agriculture still dominated everything in Texas, and neither manufacturing nor mineral development had yet had any significant impact on the economy. But as early as 1901, when the great Spindletop gusher blew in near Beaumont and triggered the most colossal oil boom in history, Texas had been flashed a signal of things to come. The accidental discovery of a second huge oilfield near the West Texas town of Electra in 1911 made Texas the undisputed focal point for the nation's fledgling oil industry. By 1913, Texas was already producing about 15 million barrels of oil annually. This, of course, was a mere drop compared to what would come later, as an insatiable world appetite for "black gold" made it the most sought-after substance since the dawn of civilization. But the vast oil industry that would become synonymous with Texas by mid-century was alive and kicking—and growing stronger by the day.

The arrival of the railroads in the 1870s had been another important turning point for Texas. Although their main appeal at first had been as a means to get the state's great agricultural bounty to the nation's markets, the railroads also made cities such as Dallas important distribution centers for manufactured goods of every description, brought tremendous economic wealth pouring in, and allowed Texas-made non-farm products to compete in the mainstream of the American marketplace. Furthermore, rail transportation now made it feasible to process home-grown agricultural products within the state for shipment elsewhere. Beef cattle no longer had to be driven across country in herds to a railhead in Kansas. Now they could be slaughtered and processed right here at home. Consequently, several large meat-packing plants were built in Fort Worth, and other agricultural processing facilities began to appear rapidly in various locations.

In 1913, tensions in Europe were leading inexorably toward world conflict. Before the next six years had passed, more than 200,000 Texans would see military service in World War I. But of even more lasting importance insofar as the economy of Texas was concerned, the war would bring tens of thousands of ruralities crowding into the cities—where many would remain permanently—and it would help increase the rate of industrialization in the Lone Star State to fever pitch.

In that relatively tranquil year, however, few in Texas could envision what lay just ahead. No one had yet been given cause to wonder "How you gonna keep 'em down on the farm?" The lonely windmill, the barbed-wire fence, the cotton gin, the one-room schoolhouse, and the general store were as symbolic of the Texas of that era as the oil drilling rig, the skyscraper and the spacecraft would become in the future. On the surface, there was little to suggest the monumental changes lurking just over the horizon. At the moment in Texas, there were no paved highways, no electric lights outside the cities, no television or radio broadcasts, no airplanes except for a handful of experimental military craft. And although more and more "tin lizzies" were snorting and sputtering along Texas streets and roads, even the automobile was a decided and disruptive rarity in the countryside. Its raucous racket frightened the horses, and in the pastoral, agricultural Texas of 1913, nothing had yet replaced the horse—and nothing moved much faster than a horse could pull it.

For the most part, Texans of the period were content to be part of an insular society that had little interest in what the rest of the world was doing. Texans believed in the rural ethic of "minding your own business." They were, for example, far more concerned over the incursions of bands of Mexican outlaws across the Rio

Grande than about the festering, age-old animosities underlying the powderkeg of Europe. These so-called Mexican "revolutionaries," led by the legendary Francisco "Pancho" Villa and others who hoped to overthrow an unstable regime in Mexico City, frequently terrorized the South Texas countryside and even raided some small towns.

Another matter of deep concern was the debate raging over Prohibition. A referendum in 1908 had shown a slight majority of Texas voters (but a vast majority of those in rural areas) favoring a constitutional amendment to prohibit the sale of alcoholic beverages all over the country. By failing to act on the issue, the State Legislature had aroused the ire of church people from border to border and put considerable pressure on the administration of Governor O.B. Colquitt. But the governor was occupied with other matters besides the public's drinking habits—matters directly linked to Texas' emergence from a land-bound economy of cotton farms and cattle ranches to a diversified industrial-commercial society. The Colquitt administration was notable for its passage of such legislation as the first eight-hour labor law, the first law regulating the number of hours worked by women, a child labor law, a workmen's compensation act, and a home-rule act for cities of more than 5,000 population. It was *not* notable, however, for passing a workable credit union law.

Regardless of how ill-conceived it may have been, the 1913 law was certainly well-intentioned. There had been, for several years, a great and growing interest in American government in finding some means of adapting the principles behind the cooperative rural credit associations of Europe for use in the United States. Outside the highly industrialized Northeast, many other states shared Texas' rural, farm-based character, along with the problems of credit and cash flow that had long been inherent with farming. Just a year earlier, in 1912, no less a personage than President William Howard Taft had written letters to the governors of all the states, urging them to work for credit union legislation at the state level. The letters had been accompanied by copies of a lengthy report to the President from Myron P. Herrick, U.S. ambassador to France, detailing the success of credit associations in rural areas of Europe.

And only three years prior to that, in 1909, Massachusetts had become the very first state in the Union to pass a general state credit union act. Impetus for the Massachusetts legislation had come from a 1908 conference in Boston, attended by such early credit union enthusiasts as Canadian journalist Alphonse Desjardins, Massachusetts Banking Commissioner Pierre Jay, and wealthy Boston merchant Edward A. Filene. These men and others like them considered credit unions the economic wave of the future for farmers, tradesmen, small businessmen, and other "common folk." But the growth of the movement came with painful lack of speed at first, even in Massachusetts, where only a few credit unions were formed under the law, mostly around Boston. Virtually no progress in following the Massachusetts example had been made in other states until President Taft issued his plea to the various governors in 1912.

Why Texas became one of the first states to respond with its own legislation is not entirely clear. Some reports say that Governor Colquitt drafted the original 1913 bill himself, apparently acting in direct response to President Taft's request (although by this time Woodrow Wilson had succeeded Taft in the White House). Other accounts indicate that the author was State Banking Commissioner W.W. Collier. As far as can be determined, the Legislature enacted the bill substantially as it was submitted and practically without debate. When it was passed on March 31, 1913, the law—styled Senate Bill No. 458—was approved by a vote of 27-0 in the State Senate and by a voice vote in which no formal count was made in the House. It was part of a small avalanche of financial and banking-related legislation enacted by the 33rd Legislature in its regular session, all of which became effective as of July 1, 1913.

It was a lengthy law, containing no less than 25 sections, and probably was not well understood by most of the lawmakers who voted on it. It was described, in its own introduction, as: "An Act providing for the formation and incorporation of rural credit unions or cooperative associations for the purpose of promoting thrift among their members, and to enable the members thereof, when in need, to obtain for productive purposes moderate loans of money for short periods and at reasonable rates of interest..."

Without doubt, there were leaders in Texas at the time who understood—as well as any of their contemporaries—the potential importance of such a law. One such Texan, S.A. Lindsey, served as vice chairman of a group known as the American Commission, established in 1913 and authorized by President Wilson to investigate and study cooperative rural credit unions in European countries. This commission, made up of representatives from 29 states and the District of Columbia, as well as four Canadian provinces, also included among its Texas delegation Clarence J. Ousley, editor of *The Fort Worth Record*, Charles B. Austin of Austin, W.W. Dexter, J.S. Williams, and Francis W. Wozencraft. In addition, Governor Colquitt appointed N.A. Shaw of Texarkana, Howard Bland of Taylor, and Peter Radford of Fort Worth as an advisory committee to work in conjunction with the American Commission in determining the agricultural needs of the state where credit unions were concerned.

In spite of all this scurrying about, however, neither the Texas credit union law nor the entire concept of rural credit associations seemed to hold water. While, in one sense, enactment of the law could fairly be called the birth of the credit union movement in Texas, it could also be branded a tragic abortion, under which not one single credit union ever achieved long-term success. It would, in fact, be 16 long years before membership in a credit union would actually begin to come within reach of the average Texas citizen. And even then, most of those who would actually obtain benefits from credit unions would be workers in industry, professional people, and employees of large commercial enterprises— rather than the long-suffering farmers for whose relief that original law was intended.

That the ineffectiveness of the 1913 Texas law took a good while to sink in was evidenced by the enthusiastic greetings it received in some quarters. For instance, an article published in the May 24, 1913 (or almost two months after the law was passed) issue of a publication of the Cooperative Finance League known as the *Orange Judd Farmer* was headlined: "Texas Leads in Rural Credit Law." The article went on to exult as follows:

> "Texas is the first state to enact any standard rural credit law for personal loans... It follows closely our standard bill for cooperative finance, which is based upon the credit union law enacted in Massachusetts in 1909. The comparatively few changes made adapt the measure to conditions prevailing in Texas... We congratulate the Lone Star State upon having this excellent law, and share Governor Colquitt's hope that it may be a great help to tenant farmers and beginners at farming. The Cooperative Finance League worked diligently for this measure, and its co-workers join the public in Texas and throughout the country in hoping that full advantage will be taken of the new system. The league has furnished Governor Colquitt with a full set of forms and blanks for organizing rural credit unions under the new law."

The Cooperative Finance League could have saved its forms and blanks, however. They would not be necessary because the law, as it turned out, had not been adapted to "conditions prevailing in Texas" at all. It was, in fact, practically worthless and destined to be a sore disappointment to its framers, supporters, and would-be users. As R.C. Morgan, president of the Government Employees Credit Union of El Paso and a pioneer leader in the Texas credit union movement, who has served both as president of the TCUL and the Credit Union National Association (CUNA), recalls it, Senate Bill No. 458 was "a lousy law" and one that "wasn't practical at all" where the organization of credit unions in Texas was concerned.

According to Morgan, only two credit unions were ever established under the 1913 act. "One never conducted any business at all and was soon liquidated," Morgan recalled in an interview many years later. The other did not survive for very long, either, but is worth mentioning in some detail here for several reasons.

It is significant that this second credit union formed under the "rural" credit union law of 1913 was not rural at all, but was intended to serve Galveston employees of one of the Southwest's major companies—the Santa Fe Railway. It is also significant that Joseph Collerain, later a president and board member of the Texas Credit Union League and one of the best-known leaders of the movement in Texas during the first half of this century, served as treasurer of that short-lived credit union. Collerain recalled years later that the credit union was conceived in order to advance small sums of money to the railroad's employees, who were paid only once a month at the time and who often had difficulty surviving for 30 days at a stretch between paychecks. The situation "made it sweet for the high rate money lenders," he recalled. The credit union was used primarily as a check cashing service and small loan facility, Collerain said. Most loans were for no more than 15 days, or just long enough to tide workers over until payday arrived. Eventually, the employees prevailed upon the railroad to pay them twice a month. Soon afterward, they decided that they had no further use for their credit union, and it was liquidated. Although its death was premature and its success strictly limited, the experiment was a milestone of sorts and a harbinger of things to come. Unfortunately, it would be the summer of 1929 before anyone in Texas managed to achieve more lasting results with a similar organization.

As the Santa Fe incident helped to illustrate, the overriding problem with the 1913 law may have been the simple fact that it was aimed at the wrong audience. It was conceived as a purely rural instrument, one whose primary concern was to provide credit to farmers during the lean periods between crops. It did not forbid city dwellers from organizing credit unions, but those responsible for its creation had no conception that it could have equal, if not greater, value in an urban setting.

But in retrospect it is also easy to find basic flaws in the legislation that rendered it inoperable where ordinary people—whether small farmers, small wage-earners or small businessmen—were concerned. The first three sections of the law provide strong clues about these flaws:

> "SECTION 1. In this Act the words 'rural credit union' shall mean a co-operative association formed for the purpose of promoting thrift among its members, and to enable them, when in need, to obtain for productive purposes moderate loans of money for short periods at reasonable rates of interest. The capital stock of rural credit unions organized under the provisions of this Act shall be divided into shares of twenty-five dollars. Entrance fees of rural credit unions may be fixed by the board of directors at such an amount as may be prescribed by the by-laws.

> "SECTION 2. A rural credit union may receive the savings of its members in payment for shares; may lend to its members at reasonable rates of interest not to exceed six percent, per annum, or invest as hereinafter provided the funds so accumulated and may undertake such other activities relating to the purposes of the association as its by-laws may authorize.

> "SECTION 3. Ten or more citizens of this State may associate themselves together, by articles of agreement, and form a rural credit union, and upon the approval of the State Banking Board may become a corporation upon complying with such provisions of the Act regulating State banks as may be applicable to the transaction of the business herein authorized to be done. . ."

To simplify the legislative jargon, the law stated that, before a credit union could be established, a minimum of ten persons in a rural community were required to put up $25 each in order to purchase the original shares in the credit union, thereby endowing it with $250 in startup capital. In the grossly inflated financial structure of today—when a restaurant meal or a tank of gasoline can easily cost $25—this may sound like "chicken feed." But where the farmers of 1913 were concerned, it was anything but a negligible amount. At that time, many employed persons worked long hours for $50 or less per month, and many Texas farm families did not see more than $200 to $300 in cash in the course of an entire average year. Under the circumstances, the requirement was ridiculously high. At this point in time, the reasoning behind this requirement can only be guessed. Since the law was undoubtedly patterned to a great degree after the Massachusetts law, it could have been as simple as the difference between the availability of $25 in the industrial Northeast and in the rural Southwest. On the other hand, it could have been some sort of veiled attempt to keep the credit unions safely in the hands of the wealthier individuals—just as the banks and other financial institutions were. Whatever the reasons for it, the wording of the law raises some obvious questions as we look back on it from the vantage point of today. As John "Pete" Parsons, now credit union commissioner of the State of Texas, put it nearly seven decades later: "Where were you going to find ten farmers in any one community with $25 each to spare? It might as well have been $25 million."

Small wonder, then, that the law failed, or that the only "rural credit union" that ever succeeded in functioning under the terms of the law was made up not of farmers, but of railroad men. But the theory that the credit union concept should be limited mainly to rural localities and to those who earned their living in agriculture was destined to die hard—not only in Texas, but across the United States. After all, the examples which the credit union supporters of North America were attempting to follow had been set in Europe over a period of many years. And for the most part, they had been set in just such rural locales, where other types of savings facilities and loan resources were frequently very scarce, if not non-existent.

Birth of a Concept

In the second decade of the Twentieth Century, credit unions were still considered a revolutionary— and, as far as some wealthy financiers were concerned, downright dangerous—concept. Except for experiments in a handful of states, they remained, as we have seen, largely untested in the U.S., and most of those who were in the business of lending money would just as soon they had remained so. In Europe, however, cooperative credit organizations had already been successfully utilized for many years.

The idea of cooperative credit began to develop in the mid-1700s, scattered records reveal, as an outgrowth of the breakdown of the feudalistic system which had kept most farmers landless and impoverished for centuries. As onetime serfs became landowners for the first time, the need for credit among European farmers greatly increased. Likewise, in the cities and towns, small shopkeepers and tradesmen encountered similar needs as they tried to establish their own businesses under the emerging ideal of private enterprise.

John Wesley, one of the founders of the Methodist Church, is credited with helping to establish a credit society to assist struggling businesses in England as early as 1746. Wesley later wrote to a friend about the results: "It is most incredible, but it manifestly appears from their accounts, that with this inconsiderable sum (50 pounds), 250 have been assisted within the space of a year..." The society apparently flourished for a number of years, making three-month loans ranging from a few shillings to five pounds, but seems not to have inspired many imitators in Eighteenth Century England.

Some claim that the term "credit union" was first used in Belgium in 1848 in connection with a bank-style enterprise launched by one M. Francois Haeck. But other historians point out that Haeck's experiment involved primarily wealthy individuals and, therefore, played no major role in extending the ideal of cooperative credit to those who could have derived the most benefit from it—the working classes.

In France, meanwhile, cooperative associations for cabinetmakers and goldsmiths were founded between 1832 and 1834 by Frances Buchez. And in 1848, Louis Blanc persuaded the French government to contribute the equivalent of $500,000 to create national cooperative workshops for the unemployed. It was at about this same time that Pierre Joseph Proudhon proposed a "Bank of the People" in France. Although it was not a true cooperative, Proudhon's proposal reflected a growing demand for changes in the system of banking, currency, and credit in general use at that time.

Despite all these early, unrelated efforts, most historians credit Germany with being the true birthplace of the credit union movement as we know it today. In 1844, a German economic reformer named Victor Aime Huber began publicizing and interpreting the cooperative experiments taking place in England and France. Huber's writings on the subject of economic self-help for workers and small proprietors became highly influential, but it was left mostly to others to implement the ideas that Huber put on paper.

Herman Schulze, a young lawyer, developed the first practical cooperative credit societies in Germany in the late 1840s. In 1846, following a massive crop failure, Schulze formed a local committee to buy grain at wholesale prices, grind it into flour, and then bake bread for distribution to the needy. Later Schulze entered politics and changed his name to Schulze-Delitzsch (for the village where he was born). His political career ended in disaster, but this may have been a godsend for the cooperative credit concept. After being charged with treason by his political enemies, he was acquitted, but nevertheless lost his position in the government. Subsequently, he turned his full attention to the cooperative credit movement, organizing a cooperative purchasing society for shoemakers and another to provide insurance for craftsmen. In 1850, he founded his first cooperative credit society with initial capital of just $140. He spent most of the rest of the decade traveling extensively in Europe as a sort of "economic missionary" spreading the gospel of cooperative credit, and by 1859, he had been instrumental in organizing 183 "people's banks" with approximately 18,000 members.

Despite the work of Schulze-Delitzsch, however, the man usually identified as the father of the modern-day credit union movement was Friedrich Wilhelm Raiffeisen, who was equally possessed of missionary zeal and who spent the better part of forty years developing German credit cooperatives. As mayor of the small town of Flammersfeld, Raiffeisen became alarmed by the economic plight of his rural community. More and more families were being victimized by high interest rates, crop failures and the loss of their livestock and farmlands to unscrupulous moneylenders. Raiffeisen organized his first cooperative credit society in 1849, but it was really more of a charitable venture than a true cooperative. Although this first venture was strikingly similar to Schulze-Delitzsch's societies, it had one important difference: Raiffeisen concentrated on helping the struggling, starving farmers around him, rather than urban craftsmen and proprietors. If the American credit union pioneers of a half-century later had identified more closely with Schulze-Delitzsch, they might have adapted their movement more to the urban setting where it eventually found widespread success. Instead, they sought to emulate Raiffeisen's rural example—without much immediate success, as we have seen.

Raiffeisen's dedication to the cause of cooperative credit, and the religious fervor with which he worked to achieve his goals, won him international admiration and laid the groundwork for a movement that would spread throughout the Western World. Motivated by devout love for his neighbors, he spent fifteen years, after founding his first agricultural cooperative, experimenting with and perfecting the cooperative concept. In 1864, he organized the first credit union to be set up along the lines now used by most modern credit unions. It differed from his earlier cooperatives in two key respects: (1) its objective was to serve its members only, rather than everyone in a given area; (2) it was governed by a set of bylaws which defined for the first time the limits of members' rights, obligations, earnings and losses.

Two years later, in 1866 Raiffeisen published his classic work, *The Credit Union,* which was destined to become a sort of unofficial "bible" of the international credit union movement. Credit union services and techniques have, of course, changed significantly since that time, and so has the scope of the credit union movement. But the Christian principles and the spirit of brotherly love that guided Raffeisen continue today to inspire the movement he helped originate.

By the time of Raiffeisen's death in 1888, 425 of his societies had sprung up in rural areas of Germany and his ideas had crossed the Atlantic and had begun to take root in North America. Late in his life, he spelled out his own conclusions about the importance to mankind of the movement he had set in motion when he wrote: "It is my firm conviction that there is only one way to improve social, and particularly the economic conditions, and that is to put the Christian principles (of course without consideration of denomination) into action in free cooperatives."

As early as 1864, meanwhile, forerunners of today's credit unions were cropping up on this side of the Atlantic. Before the end of the Civil War, several cooperative credit organizations had been established among followers of Schulze-Delitzsch in New York. By 1870, Samuel M. Quincy, a Boston attorney, had introduced the concept into Massachusetts, and the following year, Quincy's nephew, Josiah Quincy, introduced enabling legislation for a "people's bank" into the Massachusetts Legislature. The move failed, however, and there would be no further attempts to legally institute the credit union concept at the state level in the U.S. for more than 35 years. Most other efforts to "Americanize" the credit union movement before the end of the Nineteenth Century were equally unsuccessful. As a nation, it seemed the United States simply was not ready yet. And when the concept of cooperative credit was eventually imported into this country on a large scale it would be by way of Canada, rather than directly from its German originators.

In the late 1890s, Canadian journalist Alphonse Desjardins became perhaps the most enthusiastic supporter of credit union ideals in North America. After studying all the material he could find on the European experience, he called a group of friends together in his hometown of Levis, Quebec, in December 1900 and established the continent's first functioning credit union or "people's bank".

The following year, Desjardins organized a second credit union, followed by a third in 1905. Gradually, his work became known across the border in New England, where it drew the interest of several Catholic priests. At the invitation of one of these, a Monsignor Hevey, Desjardins visited Manchester, New Hampshire, and established the first credit union in the U.S. there in 1909 to serve the parishioners of St. Mary's Church. A few months later, Desjardins was called to another parish in

Lynn, Massachusetts, where he founded a second U.S. credit union.

Ironically, at about the same time Desjardins was organizing the first Massachusetts credit union, a Boston department store tycoon, who had already demonstrated an abiding interest in humanitarianism and public welfare, was returning from a "dream" trip around the world with some important ideas of his own about cooperative credit. His name was Edward Albert Filene, and with the help of Desjardins and others, he was about to launch a movement in the United States that would make credit unions as familiar as sliced bread to millions of Americans who followed.

In a period often characterized as the era of the "robber baron" in American business, Filene was a breed apart. He was a genuine idealist who strongly believed that all Americans should have a share in their own economic destinies—not merely in the form of wages and salaries paid by an employer, but through cooperative ownership of the sources of capitalism. He looked forward to the day when his own Filene and Sons store in Boston would be employee-owned. At the time he sailed away on his world cruise in 1907, however, there is no indication that Filene had ever heard of a credit union or a "people's bank."

It was far away, in poverty-ridden India, where he first encountered agricultural cooperative banks and was amazed at the services they were able to perform among the destitute Hindu peasants, who, he wrote "can save nothing, and if the harvest fails, famine kills more than a million." En route home, Filene visited the Philippines, then an American protectorate, where provisions were in place for an agriculture bank, but where strict requirements made loans inaccessible to most farmers.

Filene came home to Boston in the fall of 1907 convinced that agriculture cooperative banks were the only answer to the widespread suffering and destitution among the kind of peasant farmers he had observed in the Far East. A short time later, he discussed his feelings in a conversation with President Theodore Roosevelt, and in February 1908, at the President's invitation, he wrote him a lengthy letter urging that an effective system of cooperative banking be introduced in the Philippines to help prepare the Filipinos for self-government.

Apparently, it did not immediately occur to Filene that "people's banks" might also be an answer to inadequate credit and excessive interest rates affecting the average citizens of Massachusetts. But the interest aroused by Filene's proposal helped convince the state's commissioner of banks, Pierre Jay, to look into the idea. Jay soon visited Desjardins in Canada, and Desjardins returned the favor by coming to Boston to meet with Jay and a group of interested citizens—one of whom, by this time, was Edward Filene.

From this point on, the pieces quickly fell into place in Massachusetts. A credit union bill was drafted, with Jay and Desjardins as its chief authors, and was introduced in the Legislature early in 1909. In April of that year, Massachusetts became the first state in the U.S. to enact a credit union law. With both President Roosevelt and his successor, President Taft, deeply interested in ways to help the nation's farmers, the stage was set for other states to follow the Massachusetts example, as Texas attempted to do four years later, in 1913.

But to the chagrin of Filene and other pioneers in the U.S. credit union movement, it was not to be that easy. The first battle had been won, but a long, exhaustive war still lay ahead.

A 16-Year Hiatus

If it is difficult for the average Texan of today to visualize what life in general was like in his state some seven decades ago, it is even more difficult to imagine the kind of existence endured by the typical farm family of that time. In the years since World War II, home ownership has become the norm in Texas for both its urban and rural residents, and low-interest federally backed mortgage loans have made owning one's own home an achievable goal for the vast majority of Texas families. But in the Texas of seventy years ago, such was not the case—far from it.

In the first place, most Texas farmers of the time were tenants, who rented small parcels of land—usually 150 acres or less—from a few big landowners. Thus, although feudalism had never been practiced *per se* in Texas since it won its independence from Mexico, most of those who depended on agriculture for a living in Texas were not much better off than their European ancestors had been. In lieu of rent, the tenant farmer mortgaged a portion of his crop to his landlord. Then, likely as not, in order to keep such staples as flour, coffee, and sugar on his table, provide shoes and clothes for his children, and obtain other essential goods that he could not produce himself, he mortgaged yet another portion of his crop, either to his landlord or to a supply merchant in the nearest town. Interest rates on these crop mortgages could be virtually anything the landlord or merchant wanted to charge, but they probably averaged around 25 percent. At harvest time, whatever was left over after these mortgages were paid belonged to the farmer, but in the event of a crop failure, the farmer not only had nothing left, he also found himself hopelessly in debt.

It was almost impossible to stay solvent, much less get ahead, under such circumstances. Yet every tenant farmer's dream was to own a house and a few acres of his own, and somehow a few managed to make their dream a reality against long odds. Those who did were required to pay from one-fifth to one-quarter of the purchase price down and to retire the note on the rest over a mere five-year term. And, although a good small farm could be purchased in those days for about

$10,000—a sum that sounds ridiculously low by today's standards—many farm families were lucky to earn a dollar or two a day, even during the best of times. And trying to save $2,000 to $2,500 for a down payment from such an income was a long, bitter struggle.

Texas Congressman Hatton W. Sumners squarely addressed this situation in the fall of 1914 when he spoke to the twelfth annual convention of the American Institute of Banking in Dallas. Although his audience was presumably less than totally friendly to the idea of rural credit cooperatives, Sumners told them bluntly: "We need a system of rural credits in the country that will give to the honest man, willing to make a fight for his home, the cheapest money on the face of the earth . . . Every man that gets him a home in this country strengthens the foundation of the government that we love."

Sumners was concerned at the time with a dwindling farm population and what he considered a dangerous drop in food production because of it; and although his fears were to prove greatly exaggerated on this score (as mechanized farming allowed fewer and fewer people to produce more and more foodstuffs), he was correct in assailing the higher interest rates which farmers of the era were forced to pay.

"Not only is it true that when the farmer and the manufacturer bid against each other for the brains and activity of men and the farmer is paying a higher rate of interest than the manufacturer, that the farmer is at a disadvantage . . . ," he said, "but . . . when that ten percent (interest paid by farmers, as opposed to six percent being paid by manufacturers at the time) is passed on, it falls as a burden upon the poor people of this country, upon the average family."

Making the situation even more ruinous, from a credit standpoint, was a homestead law which had been on the statute books in Texas for many years and which made it unlawful for a small landowner to mortgage his homestead once it was paid for. Thus, the farmer was

23

forbidden to use the one tangible asset he might manage to obtain in order to buy needed equipment, make necessary improvements to his land, or to acquire additional acreage.

Given this situation, it is small wonder that the Texas Legislature was anxious to find legal means to alleviate the farmer's plight at the time it approved the original 1913 credit union law. Washington was also concerned at that time with the issue of rural credit—or, more correctly, the lack of it. The following exerpts from the transcript of a joint congressional subcommittee hearing held in the nation's capital on March 3, 1914, feature the testimony of Colonel Clarence Ousley, editor of the *Fort Worth Record* and a member of the American Commission which had traveled to Germany the previous year to study that country's cooperative credit associations. Under questioning by Senator Henry F. Hollis of Indiana, the subcommittee chairman, Ousley's comments about conditions faced by farmers in Texas at the time paint a graphic and disturbing picture, but they also help to explain why the rural cooperatives of Europe were not readily adaptable to the situation in Texas:

> Senator Hollis: You went abroad with the commission, did you not?
>
> Mr. Ousley: Yes, Sir.
>
> Senator Hollis: And you had some chance to see what was done there with cooperative credits among farmers, did you not?
>
> Mr. Ousley: Yes, sir.
>
> Senator Hollis: Do you think that is likely to prove successful in Texas?
>
> Mr. Ousley: Not in Texas.
>
> Senator Hollis: Why not?
>
> Mr. Ousley: For the reason that our tenant class is composed of men of unstable habits of mind. They shift about from place to place. They are not fixed to the soil, like the people are in Germany and other European countries. They go and come. They are moved by the prospects of better conditions somewhere else. And besides all that, they do not live in the village communi-

ties like they do in the European countries, where every man knows his neighbor's affairs and their history and their dependability. They are more aloof. Our farmers live on their farms. In the European countries they cluster largely in villages, and it makes a different social condition; it makes a different family condition, so that a man does not object to endorsing for his neighbor. But among the tenants we have, where a man is not well-acquainted with his neighbors a mile or a half a mile away, he does not feel that social interest in them; there is not that neighborhood feeling.

The shifting about from place to place to which Ousley referred was probably due less to "unstable habits of mind" than to grim economic need. When a tenant farmer was wiped out financially and owed more money than he could ever reasonably expect to repay in one locale, he had little real choice but to move on somewhere else and start over. But Ousley's other observations concerning the differences between farm society in Texas and Europe were almost certainly valid. They constitute yet another reason why the 1913 Texas credit union law was never workable.

It is easier to explain why the law failed than it is to explain the 16-year delay between the time the law was enacted in 1913 and the time it was finally superseded by practical credit union legislation in 1929. But one may guess, from the scattered available records of that period, that once the legal machinery for establishing credit unions appeared to have broken down at the state level—as evidenced by the experience in Texas and several other states—the emphasis shifted to the national level. An indication of this shift is found in an article published in the *New York Times* of June 1, 1919, under a headline which read: "Conference Decides to Ask Congress to Make Credit Unions National Institutions." The article read in part:

> "The National Committee on People's Banks was formed yesterday at a meeting at the City Club, of citizens from various parts of the country. George E. Roberts, formerly Director of the Mint, and at present President of the National City Bank was chosen chairman, with Edward A. Filene, of Boston, vice chairman.

The object of the organization is to urge legislation on Congress to make the various people's banks national, instead of state institutions, and to continue in the establishment of additional banks.

"The People's Banks, or Credit Unions, as they are known in some states, it was explained at the meeting, have as their object the extension of credit to salaried workers, small business men and farmers who cannot obtain credit at the ordinary banks without collateral. The organizations are mutual: that is, one must own stock to become a member. Each shareholder has one vote regardless of the number of shares he owns. Loans are made from $200 to $1,000 each, the interest varying slightly with the individual bank, and whatever profits are earned are paid to the members in dividends. The shares are generally sold at $5 or $10 each.

"In making loans to members the banks aim to promote thrift and to abolish the necessity for loan sharks, and professional money lenders. The banks also receive deposits in small amounts.

"In Massachusetts there are sixty credit unions and in North Carolina nineteen. There are said to be 5,000 in France, Italy, Germany, Austria, Russia and Great Britain, doing a business of $7 billion annually.

"There are similar institutions in New York State, Rhode Island, New Hampshire, Wisconsin, California and Texas, but they are of limited number, size, and strength. The aim of the National Committee is to consolidate their interests in a national organization. As typical of benefits derived from credit unions, the following paragraph from a manual of the Massachusetts Credit Union Association was pointed out:

" 'The Credit Union is democratic in its control. Each member has equal vote. The bigger policies are determined by the members, who also elect the officers . . . The simple but effective methods of bookkeeping guide and record their transactions. There is no attempt to deal in matters of high finance, nor in complicated problems in banking, but the fundamentals of banking are faced and mastered. The wage earner, the clerk, the man of hard common sense but little schooling come to appreciate the meaning and operations of our financial system.' "

The article is interesting for a number of reasons. First, it shows the shift in credit union philosophy from state to national scope, which would culminate, some 15 years later, in the passage of the first Federal Credit

26

Union Act with the help of Texas Senator Morris Sheppard and Texas Congressman Wright Patman. Second, it clearly reveals that the credit union movement's main thrust was already shifting away from strictly rural organizations toward those with a base in urbanized commerce and industry. The salaried worker, the small businessman and the wage earner receive more prominent mention than the farmer. To a student of the movement at that time, it was becoming increasingly evident that the successful early credit unions were concentrated in urban, not rural, areas. Most of the sixty functioning credit unions in Massachusetts, for instance, were concentrated around Boston and made up of office and factory workers.

Another interesting aspect of the article is its reference to the existence of "similar institutions" in Texas. As nearly as can be determined, there was, in fact, only one credit union in Texas at the time, but there is no way to be certain that others did not spring up briefly from time to time. There was certainly continuing interest in the movement in Texas, despite the absence of a usable law to facilitate it. Toward the end of the *Times* article, former Texas Banking Commissioner W.W. Collier was identified as one of the members of the National Committee on People's Banks who was unable to attend the New York meeting. It was Collier, a former Texas Ranger, who was believed to have written the 1913 banking laws of the State of Texas, of which the credit union legislation was a part. What effect his attendance at this faraway meeting in Manhattan might have had in speeding revision of the existing Texas law can only be speculated upon at this point. At any rate, another full decade was to pass before such revision took place.

Of all those that may have been briefly attempted and quickly liquidated, including the Santa Fe employees' organization in Galveston, only one Texas credit union organized between 1913 and 1929 is known to have survived for any appreciable length of time. It was the First Credit Union of Texas, which operated for several years as an unincorporated—and, therefore, technically illegal—entity in Houston.

Among existing references to the First Credit Union of Texas is the following paragraph from a 1923 book entitled *Cooperative Banking,* written by Filene's close associate, Roy F. Bergengren, who would become a guiding force behind the formation of the Credit Union National Association (CUNA):

> "The greatest discouragement thus far resulting from the experimental period of the development of cooperative banking in the United States is contained in the fact that the Oregon Credit Union Law (enacted in 1915) and the Nebraska law to provide for Cooperative Credit Associations, effective April 19, 1919, have both thus far proved to be completely ineffective. Until recently, the same could be said of the Texas law (enacted 1913). Recently, however, the First Credit Union of Texas has been organized by Kenneth Krahl of Houston and there is considerable present credit union activity in the state. From this experience will come the knowledge requisite for an intelligent amendment of the law to make it conform with good credit union practice. Enough has been accomplished in recent months in Texas to indicate that there will be credit union development in the state, which will, however, be greatly expedited if the law can be amended as above indicated. An attempt to amend the law will be made at the next session of the Texas legislature."

In his time frame, Bergengren was, of course, overly optimistic. The Texas law was, indeed, amended, but not until six years later. He was also possibly too charitable in finding the 1913 Texas law to be more workable than the subsequent laws enacted in Nebraska and Oregon. Other sources indicate that the First Credit Union of Texas actually operated *in spite of* the Texas law, rather than because of it. One of these is a publication of the Co-op League in the U.S.A., which contained the following report in August 1924:

> "Texas has a Credit Union Law which is so cumbersome that it is practically useless, and the workers and farmers of the state have dodged it ever since it was enacted eleven years ago.

"However, this fact does not deter one group of co-operators from operating a Credit Union. The First Credit Union of Texas (unincorporated) of Houston, presents the following financial statement as of July 1, 1924:"

In the breakdown of assets and liabilities listed for the credit union, capital stock was valued at $1,025. Deposits of $106.36 were shown; $115.50 in loans were in effect, and the amount of cash on hand was $52.79. Obviously, the First Credit Union of Texas was something less than a financial giant. As the article in the Co-op League publication concluded:

"These people might incorporate and thus secure a much larger membership, for the liability of members would be limited to twice the amount of stock. But the charter they would receive would so hamper them that they prefer to operate without one until the law has been brought up to date."

After 16 years of lost opportunities, that updating finally came to pass as the "Roaring Twenties" drew to a close and the nation enjoyed its last few months of "borrowed" prosperity before the "Black Thursday" stock market collapse that plunged it into the Great Depression.

Texas Tries Again

Life for the average Texan had changed dramatically in the years between 1913 and 1929. The automobile had replaced the horse as the principal mode of transportation, and 1,376,000 motor vehicles now crowded Texas streets and roads. The state's population had swelled by nearly 2,000,000 persons in just twenty years, and more than 40 percent of Texas' 5,800,000 residents now lived in urban areas. Dallas was a city of a quarter-million people, but, even so, it had been surpassed in population by Houston, which now claimed the title of the state's largest metropolis. San Antonio was a strong third with nearly 230,000 residents.

Industrialization had made tremendous strides, especially in petroleum and related fields. By 1929, Texas was producing more than 296 million barrels of oil annually, and oilfields dotted the state from the Gulf Coast to the Panhandle (although the discovery of the biggest oil bonanza the world had ever known—the vast East Texas Field—was still a year away).

Women had won the right to vote, and had been instrumental in bringing Prohibition to Texas and the rest of the country. In 1925, the statewide female vote had also helped elect the only woman governor in Texas history, Mrs. Miriam A. "Ma" Ferguson, whose husband, former Governor James E. Ferguson, had been impeached and barred from seeking re-election.

Farming remained an important part of the economy, with Texas producing a third of all the cotton grown in the United States. But it is significant that 1929 was the first year in which oil income surpassed cotton revenues in Texas. At the same time, farming itself was undergoing far-reaching changes. Increased mechanization meant that fewer human hands were needed to plant, cultivate, and harvest the state's agricultural bounty. Mechanization also favored the large "factory-farm" operations and placed an added economic squeeze on the small farmer, prompting many in his ranks to turn their attention toward the cities and such industrial jobs as those offered by the big Ford auto assembly plant in Dallas.

The vast, once-empty expanses of the state, meanwhile, were being drawn closer together by modern transportation. Dallas' Love Field was already one of the busiest airports in the country with service by seven commercial carriers. Airplanes, carrying mail, freight, and passengers, zoomed through the skies above the rolling fields, and the fields themselves were now crisscrossed by some 18,000 miles of state highways.

Like the rest of the nation, Texas began the year of 1929 on a note of high optimism. Business had never been better. Jobs, money and goods had never seemed more plentiful. And to most observers, there was no end in sight for the period of prosperity that had followed World War I and now appeared to stretch out into infinity.

It was with this upbeat spirit, no doubt, that the 41st Texas Legislature convened in Austin on January 8, 1929, with one of its first items of business a set of amendments to existing credit union statutes that would, it was hoped, erase the miscalculations and inequities of the past 16 years. Even at this late date, however, this was to prove easier said than done.

Early in the session, a set of seven amendments, designated as Senate Bill No. 172, were submitted to the lawmakers. On January 24, they passed the Senate handily by a 27-0 vote. A few days later, on February 1, the Senate concurred in a House-sponsored amendment to the legislation by a vote of 30-0, after the amended bill had been approved in the House by a voice vote on January 31. Final approval came on February 11, with the amended law to become effective ninety days later.

From the viewpoint of would-be credit union organizers, the most important change in the law was the amendment to Article 2461, which read: "The words 'Credit Union' shall mean a co-operative association formed for the purpose of promoting thrift among its members, and to enable them, when in need, to obtain for productive and provident purposes moderate loans of money for short periods and at reasonable rates of interest. The capital stock of credit unions organized under the provisions of this Title shall be divided into shares of *five dollars*. Intrance fees (sic) of credit unions may be fixed by the Board of Directors at such an amount as may be prescribed by the bylaws."

When compared to the wording of the 1913 law, the impact of the amendment becomes obvious. For one thing, the term "rural" was omitted from the definition of credit unions in Article 2461 (although it was retained in the title of the overall bill). But most importantly, the cost of a share was reduced from $25 to just $5, and this was the key that finally opened credit union membership to the people for whom it had always been intended.

But before the law was completely straightened out, it was necessary for the Legislature, in a special called session during the summer of 1929, to add three further amendments. In these amendments, styled Senate Bill No. 185, credit unions became simply credit unions, with no "rural" designation involved. The main purpose of the last three amendments, however, was to provide necessary funds to enable the state's banking commissioner and his agents to examine, regulate, and police the credit unions organized under the act. S.B. No. 185 was approved July 3, 1929, by a 31-0 vote in the Senate and a majority voice vote in the House.

The final section of the final amendment in the bill provides an interesting footnote on the lawmakers' feelings about the need for the law. It reads: "The crowded condition of the calendar, and the inadequacy of the present law in failing to provide the necessary funds for the discharge of the duty imposed upon the officers under the law, to facilitate the actual carrying out of its terms, creates an emergency and an imperative public necessity that the constitutional rule requiring bills to be read on three separate days be suspended, and that this act take effect and be in force from and after its passage, and it is so enacted."

Undoubtedly, many Texans helped in the effort to obtain revisions in the old law, but Judge D.M. Alexander of Fort Worth is generally credited as the leader of the statewide campaign in support of the amendments. The January 1929 edition of *The Bridge*, official publication of the Credit Union National Extension Bureau (CUNEB), a forerunner of CUNA, offered these observations on the Texas campaign:

"The Texas credit union law has been long on the statute books but there have been no credit unions organized in Texas because of defects in the law. A bill has been filed to amend the law in such fashion as to bring it into conformity with good practice. It is Senate Bill 172. The Texas campaign is in charge of D.M. Alexander, Esq., 702 Fort Worth National Bank Bldg., Fort Worth, Texas. At this writing the bill has been reported out favorably by the Senate Committee on Banks. If you live in Texas, contact . . . the members of the Legislature from your district urging them to vote for Senate Bill 172."

Texas was one of 15 states where feverish legislative activity on credit unions was taking place early in 1929. Utah and Oregon also were attempting to amend existing laws to render them usable. Connecticut, Maryland, Ohio, Kansas, Arkansas, Arizona, Idaho, Montana, Washington, and Florida were working to enact new credit union laws, and Wisconsin and New Jersey were considering minor but significant changes in laws already on the books. The Credit Union National Extension Bureau was actively assisting credit union leaders in all these states. CUNEB was the brainchild of Edward Filene, but it was Roy F. Bergengren, a Massachusetts lawyer whom Filene had hired to serve as the organization's managing director, who had extended its influence across the nation. Within four years after taking over as CUNEB's head man in 1921, Bergengren's organizational ability had helped to more than double the number of credit unions in the U.S. from 199 to 419. But Bergengren knew that this was only the beginning, and he was counting on states like Texas to send the credit union movement snowballing. Thus, it was hardly coincidence that Bergengren decided to come to Texas that summer of 1929 to lend his personal assistance in the drive to launch new credit unions under the amended law.

33

Meanwhile, that spring, Judge Alexander (whom Bergengren himself praised for "conducting the Texas campaign so effectively") was joined in his efforts by T.K. Hale, also of Fort Worth, and C.T. Bergeron of Dallas. When Bergengren arrived in Texas in June, he and these three Texas leaders immediately began organizing credit unions under the amended law, which had gone into effect only a few weeks earlier. Apparently, they enjoyed a high degree of success.

"Mr. Bergengren organized seven (other accounts said eight) credit unions while in Texas in June," *The Bridge* reported. "One of them involved an interesting, if slightly sultry, trip on a Sunday from Fort Worth to Wichita Falls, a credit union meeting and return by bus, arriving at Fort Worth in mid-evening. The meeting was very worthwhile, indeed, largely due to the credit union enthusiasm of Mr. (J.W.) Vandigriff, who had made the arrangements." Vandigriff was one of the organizers of the Wichita Falls Postal Employees' Credit Union, and subsequently served as its first secretary-manager.

Writing in *The Bridge* some eighteen months later, Bergengren had these recollections of the Wichita Falls trip: "I had promised J.W. Vandigriff of the Wichita Falls Post Office that I would make the trip to Wichita Falls by bus (which would take most of the forenoon) if he would have his group together for a meeting on my arrival. It grew hotter as the day advanced and as we neared Wichita Falls it did not seem possible that there would be anyone waiting (a)round for a credit union meeting at noontime on a red hot Sunday. That is where I figured without Mr. Vandigriff, for he was there and he had his gang with him and we held a meeting. Now the point of this story is that all the credit union instruction this group ever received was during the hour or two devoted to the meeting this warm Sunday noontime."

Bergengren referred to a letter from Vandigriff, dated January 11, 1931, in which he told of a delay in obtaining a charter for the Wichita Falls Postal Credit

Union, which postponed its official opening for business until October 1, 1929. At the time, it had fourteen members, each with a single share worth $5, for a total capital stock of $70. (According to information provided by Dot Wood, president of the Wichita Falls Postal Credit Union at the time of its fiftieth anniversary in 1979, those fourteen original members included A.B. Sparks, Earl G. Davidson, R. Looyengood, George C. Shankle, C.K. Johnson, B.J. McHam, A.A. House, John T. Ryan, C.O. Froman, H.G. Birdwell, J.W. Vandigriff, M.E. Riley, L.R. Scott, and T.P. Norwood. House, Froman, and Ryan were still members of the credit union when it observed its golden anniversary.)

By the time of Vandigriff's letter, the Wichita Falls credit union had grown to 74 members and had assets of $4,441, an amount which Vandigriff figured would have been "well-nigh impossible to have raised in this office at the time of Mr. Bergengren's visit."

Bergengren also visited Dallas and came away deeply impressed with the organizational work done there by Bergeron, of whom he wrote: "Mr. C.T. Bergeron had long been interested in the possible organization of a credit union to serve employees of the Dallas office of the Western Union Telegraph Company and had arranged another fine meeting. Mr. Bergeron is going to assist the Bureau to organize additional credit unions in Dallas. He is a man of very broad experience, a fine war record and of the sort we are proud to have represent the credit union development." (Bergengren's observations were amply borne out some years later, when Bergeron became the first managing director, on a part-time basis, of the newly formed Texas Credit Union League.)

Bergengren and his Texas colleagues apparently were able to organize a total of eight credit unions during his visit. The Bridge listed these as: Fort Worth (B. of R.C.) Credit Union, Fort Worth Postal Employees Credit Union, Montgomery Ward (Fort Worth) Employees Credit Union, Dallas Western Union Employees Credit

Union, Wichita Falls Postal Employees Credit Union, Fort Worth (R.I.L.) Credit Union, Fort Worth Municipal Employees Credit Union, and Houston Postal Employees Credit Union. It is worth noting that five of the eight were concentrated in Fort Worth, which was unquestionably the "credit union capital" of Texas at the time, primarily because of the work done there by Alexander and Hale. Under a small headline which read, "We Start in Texas," *The Bridge* expressed appreciation for the two Texans' "splendid cooperation" and for the "many things (they did) to make Mr. Bergengren's stay in Texas pleasant and profitable."

The first Texas credit unions were not chartered by the state, however, in the same order in which they were organized. The very first one to receive a charter under the new law was the Kingsville Credit Union at Kingsville, which officially became a state-recognized entity on August 2, 1929. How a small, rather isolated South Texas town, whose major previous distinction was its role as headquarters for the vast King Ranch, happened to beat out the major cities in the race for the first credit union charter is not clear. But congratulations were in order for Kingsville, and *The Bridge* happily extended them: "We were glad to get a report recently from the Kingsville Credit Union of Kingsville, Texas, the first credit union in the Lone Star State to receive a . . . charter under the amended law. It already has assets of $1,080 with outstanding loans of $823—twenty-eight members and fourteen borrowers. This is a fine showing."

Following the Kingsville Credit Union on the very same day—August 2—was the American Legion Corpus Christi Credit Union. And before the month was out, on August 29, the charter was granted for the Montgomery Ward Fort Worth Credit Union. Others chartered by the end of the year included: Wichita Falls Postal Credit Union, September 16; R.I.L. Credit Union of Fort Worth, September 25; Houston Postal Credit Union, October 1; Fort Worth City Employees Credit Union, October 5;

Fort Worth Postal Credit Union, October 22; Texas & Pacific Railway Employee Credit Union of Dallas, November 14, and Public Service (Western Union) Employees Credit Union of Dallas, November 14.

It is interesting—and certainly significant—that, of the eleven credit unions organized in Texas during that momentous year of 1929, ten were in the state's larger cities and none was rural in character or had the slightest connection with agriculture. But even more significant is the fact that today, neary 55 years later, five of those eleven original Texas credit unions are still operational—Montgomery Ward Fort Worth (now the state's oldest), Wichita Falls Postal, Houston Postal, Fort Worth City, and Fort Worth Postal.

This time it was no false start. At long last, the ideal of credit union membership was a reality for the ordinary citizens of Texas. The credit union concept was no longer limited, either legally or in the public mind, to rural areas. Both the ideal and the concept were here to stay, but the credit union movement had little relation to the financial giant it has become today.

As Mrs. Josephine Weiler, one of the original eleven employees who put up $5 apiece to form the Montgomery Ward Fort Worth Credit Union, recalled on the occasion of the organization's fiftieth anniversary in 1979: "Members only had to put in 25 cents to join the credit union when it first started, but in those days a quarter wasn't all that easy to come by. It gave our employees who couldn't afford bank accounts an easy way to save 50 or 75 cents a week and to obtain loans. Getting those first five-dollar contributions (from directors) was no easy matter, but we were sold on the credit union concept and we knew what it could do for the employees. I numbered the directors from '100' to '111' and gave myself the last number, so I knew that when '112' showed up, we had our first customer. I'm glad to have had a part in the beginning of a great service organization. To think that it has come from that first $55 to its present position (2,250 members with more than $2.5 million in assets) is miraculous . . . "

It was, indeed, "miraculous." There is no other word for it. But the miracle of Texas credit unions was to be repeated hundreds of times over the ensuing decades.

Times Turn Tough

Outwardly, as we have noted, the nation was still riding the crest of a wave of prosperity during that summer of 1929. It was a wave that had begun soon after the Armistice had been signed in Europe and the "doughboys" had returned home, having presumably made the world "safe for democracy" for all time to come. Although it had ebbed from time to time, this wave had been the dominant influence on American lifestyles for the better part of a decade, and it seemed capable of rushing on indefinitely. Few, if any, Texans could foresee that the wave would suddenly crash onto the rocks of the Great Depression within a few short months—and in so doing make credit unions even more desperately needed than before.

But even in those relatively prosperous years that preceded the collapse of the stock market and the ensuing panic on Wall Street, the financial situation of the average industrial wage-earner or salaried white-collar employee was far from secure. Per capita income in Texas in 1929 was only $478 per year, and while this was the highest figure of any state in the South, it was still well below the national average of $617 and only a little more than one-third of New York State's $1,159.

While the wealthy were able to indulge themselves in hitherto unheard-of luxuries, and such new middle-class diversions as vaudeville, radio, and talking movies helped keep the public's mind off the daily grind, life was much more of a struggle to make ends meet than it is even in the economically volatile America of the 1980s.

Credit buying, although still frowned upon in many circles, was becoming more and more commonplace as consumers responded to the growing lure of mass advertising and took advantage of "installment plans" on major purchases, which they otherwise could not have afforded. (If today's new car prices seem high, for example, consider that a typical new low-priced automobile in 1929 cost almost the equivalent of an average worker's pay for a full twelve months.) Thus, like many of the nation's banks and major investors, the ordinary consumer was becoming dangerously over-extended and falling deeper in debt. At the same time, few working Americans were adequately protected by insurance, and few were able to save any money. Slowly but surely, the purchasing power of the customers who kept American industry humming was declining, making them easy prey for loan sharks. And all of this, remember, was happening in what could have been described as "the best of times," at least within the frame of reference of most Americans then living. When the "worst of times" suddenly descended in the fall of 1929, the proverbial "wolf" came scratching and snarling at millions of doors. President Herbert Hoover declared that a return to prosperity was "just around the corner." But for untold numbers of families, it was disaster that awaited, instead.

After the stock market crash that October, times turned incredibly tougher. A lean Christmas season and a bitter winter found tens of thousand of Texans without jobs in the cities and thousands of others taking pay cuts in order to remain employed. Many clung to a desperate hope that 1930 would bring better days, but as time wore on, the situation turned still darker. If nothing else, however, 1930 was to prove a good year for credit unions.

On February 25, 1930, the Alamo Postal Credit Union of San Antonio became the twelfth Texas credit union to be chartered under the amended law. Here and there around the state, others would follow during the year, but expansion of the number of Texas credit unions was perhaps less impressive than the growth in membership and financial strength of these first dozen credit unions during their initial year of operation.

Random reports reaching CUNEB headquarters vividly described such growth. A few examples follow:

"At the end of business, March 31, 1930, we had 116 members, owning 407 shares amounting to $2,035, and at the same time we had 32 loans amounting to $2,059.06," wrote D.L. Lewis, president of the Fort Worth Municipal Credit Union. "We are very proud of the growth that the union has made in its short period of existence, and have found that it has been a great assistance to city employees."

Added Granville W. Elder, treasurer of the Houston Postal Credit Union: "We began a year ago with a five-dollar bill and our assets are now in excess of $4,400, with a total membership of 155." As of November 1930, Elder was confidently looking forward to a membership of 300 and assets of $10,000 "before long."

In April, meanwhile, the Public Service Employees Credit Union of Dallas, which served Western Union employees, reported through its treasurer, W.M. Vick, that it had already signed up sixty members and had assets of $2,770.

The Kingsville Credit Union, oldest in the state, was also growing. After starting in business with just $305 in August 1929, its assets had reached $4,572 by the end of May 1930. And one of the newest Texas credit unions, the Port Arthur Federal Credit Union, reported late in the year, in a note to CUNEB from Treasurer J.K. Wilson Jr., that it had enrolled 31 members, made loans to fifteen borrowers, had paid-in capital of $625.25, and outstanding loans of approximately that amount.

50th Anniversary Credit Unions

Credit Union	Year Organized
Fort Worth City CU	1929
Fort Worth Postal CU	1929
Houston Postal CU	1929
Montgomery Ward Fort Worth CU	1929
Wichita Falls Postal CU	1929
Abilene Postal Employees CU	1930
Concho Valley Govt Employees CU (San Angelo)	1930
Dallas Postal CU	1930
Government Service CU (Port Arthur)	1930
Postal CU of Galveston	1930
T&FS Employees CU (Port Arthur)	1930
Western Union Employees CU (Houston)	1930
Amarillo Postal Employees CU	1931
C&IR Employees CU (Pampa)	1931
Dallas Teachers CU	1931
Government Employees CU (Austin)	1931
Postal Employees CU (Corpus)	1931
Postal Employees CU (Waco)	1931
Southeast Affiliated Fed Emp CU (Beaumont)	1931
Federal Employees CU (Texarkana)	1932
Govt Employees CU of El Paso	1932
San Antonio Teachers CU	1932
United CU (Tyler)	1932
Galveston Government Employees CU	1933
St Joseph's CU (San Antonio)	1933
U.S. Employees CU (Houston)	1933
Conoco Employees WF CU	1934
Educational Employees CU of Fort Worth	1934
Employees CU Swift & Co (San Antonio)	1934
Entex CU (Houston)	1934
Exxon Houston CU	1934
Houston Area Teachers CU	1934
Kraft Employees CU (Garland)	1934
Morris Sheppard Texarkana FCU	1934
Pollock Employees CU (Dallas)	1934
Valley Postal CU (Harlingen)	1934

In terms of today's inflated dollars, these amounts may sound almost piddling, but in an era in which the average wage earner probably brought home in a year less than many of his modern counterparts bring home in a week, they assume a good bit more significance. By current standards, hard cash was unbelievably scarce in 1930. As William H. Gilmartin, a retired Fort Worth municipal judge and charter member of the Fort Worth Municipal Credit Union, recalls: "Butter was fifteen cents a pound; bread was six loaves for a quarter, and eggs were a dime a dozen. There was lots of bartering in those days. I used to get gasoline for my car in exchange for legal advice. Leonard's Department Store put out wooden money—called 'Leonard's script'—which they gave out in change when you bought something, until the government made them stop. That was how scarce money was. It was very hard to come by. So were jobs. But commodities were dirt-cheap. It's strange that now the situation seems to be just the reverse."

Gilmartin and other longtime members of Fort Worth Municipal, incidentally, give major credit for the organization of that credit union and for its early success to H.C. Michael, who was city auditor of Fort Worth at the time. According to Lee G. Larson, another charter member, Michael's chief concern was the number of city employees who were obtaining money from loan sharks and paying as much as 40 to 50 percent in interest charges. "We wanted to save the city employees— especially the lower paid ones—from having to deal with the loan sharks," Larson said. "That was our main reason for wanting the credit union."

Judge Gilmartin, who did the legal work and filled out the charter application for Fort Worth Municipal, also remembers Michael as the prime force behind the credit union. "Mr. Michael was a very personable man and very interested in people," Gilmartin explained. "He signed all city employees' paychecks in his capacity as commissioner of accounts, and when somebody ran short of money before payday, they would come around and see Mike and he would advance them a few dollars to tide them over. Those were pretty tough times, and he knew that a lot of the employees were having a struggle. As the financial center of the city, you might say, he had an opportunity to know their situations pretty well."

R.C. Morgan, one of four Texans to serve as president of CUNA, also has vivid memories of life in Fort Worth during those deep Depression days of the early 1930s—and of how an early credit union proved to be a lifesaver for him and his growing family.

"I went to work as a farm boy newly arrived in the big city for Armour and Company in 1929," Morgan recalled in an interview many years later. "Claude Orchard (Armour's personnel director who later served as the first director of The Bureau of Federal Credit Unions) visited the Armour plant in Fort Worth (a year or two after Morgan arrived) and assisted in organizing an employee credit union. So I joined that credit union when my first child came along, and I very desperately needed about $50 to pay the doctor. That was my first involvement."

The need for a fast $50—no small sum in those days—would ultimately lead Morgan to a level of leadership in the Texas and national credit union movements that has been shared by only a small handful of individuals. Morgan's service to credit unions has spanned more than half a century, but like most other Texans of the early 1930s, he was originally attracted to them because of the bright symbol of hope they held out in a dark and troubled world.

At the same time, the credit union concept was winning favorable attention from the Texas media. As the *Dallas Morning News* noted in a December 6, 1930, editorial: "The credit union would solve the problem of the man without banking credit and in need of a small emergency loan if it were generally in use. Every financial institution in the country except the loan shark would be glad to see it filling the field whose need it serves. The system merits wider extensions and study by small wage groups."

Yet the extreme scarcity of money during those bleak years certainly hindered and delayed the organization of many credit unions. Those that managed to get started under these conditions quickly proved their merit, but only a tiny fraction of the wage earners in Texas had access to them, and bringing more credit unions into being was slow, tedious work.

By the summer of 1931, however, a total of 42 credit unions had been chartered across the state. Although there was no statewide organization of credit unions in existence at the time, this figure was published in a new publication called the *Texas Credit Union News*, the July 1931 issue of which also contained reports from 29 of the 42 Texas credit unions. The report showed the 29 to have a combined membership of 2,670 and assets of $108,127. C.T. Bergeron was credited as the inspiration behind the new publication and for using it as a tool to stir up interest in organizing more credit unions. A few weeks after the publication appeared, *The Bridge* took note of it, saying: "These reports show splendid progress on the part of these pioneering Texas groups. Texas will be very shortly ready for a credit union league."

Movements were under way in a number of states by this time to establish statewide credit union organizations, and Texas was also moving in that direction. In its larger cities, some of its credit unions were beginning to move out of the nickle-and-dime category and report healthy increases in their assets. By December 1931, the Houston Postal Credit Union had amassed assets of $23,263. And between the spring of 1931 and the fall of 1932, assets of the Dallas Postal Employees Credit Union almost quadrupled, growing from about $10,000 to more than $38,000. During this time, Bergeron continued to publish his *Texas Credit Union News* from time to time, and although it did not appear on a regular schedule, it gave Texas credit unions their first real opportunity to communicate with each other and to spread the word about their accomplishments to those interested in joining the movement. Little by little, the stage was being set for an organization to do in Texas what CUNEB had done across the United States.

A Pivotal Year

In all of credit union history, there has never been a more important year than 1934. During the space of that twelve-month period, the credit union movement, both nationally and in Texas, made notable strides toward becoming the great financial force it is today. Before 1934, even with as much progress as they had made, credit unions were still struggling for a foothold in the American socio-economic structure and a spot of their own in the lives of the general public. After 1934, there was no longer any doubt that they would attain both.

As Edward Filene himself told credit unionists in Dallas in January 1934 during an historic trip to Texas: "These are thrilling times . . . There is so much to talk about—so many different approaches to the discussion of the credit union movement—that I hardly know where to begin or where to stop."

Filene's Texas trip was part of a nationwide tour in which he consulted with educators, businessmen, labor leaders and government officials at all levels in an all-out effort to whip up support for the movement which he had helped to originate in America. In Dallas, Filene met with such leaders as C.J. Crampton, secretary of the Dallas Chamber of Commerce; Professor John O. Beaty, head of the English Department at Southern Methodist University; R.L. Thornton, president of Mercantile National Bank and president of the Dallas Chamber; Tom Doig, field representative of CUNEB; N.L. Brainard, a special credit union organizer; Eli

Sanger, president of Sanger Brothers Department Store; and, of course, Bergeron, who was described as the "key credit union man in Texas."

From Dallas, Filene also made a major stop in Houston, meeting with Gus A. Wortham, president of the Houston Chamber of Commerce; Tobias Sakowitz, president of Sakowitz Brothers Department Store; Beverly D. Harris, president of Houston's Second National Bank, and Houston Mayor Oscar Holcombe, among others.

Filene knew that the stage was set for a series of events which would catapult credit unions to the forefront of national attention, and his trip served to raise the curtain on a pivotal year.

Three events with far-reaching implications took place in 1934. For the purposes of this history, the founding of the Texas Credit Union League was, of course, of paramount importance. But the passage of the first federal credit union legislation in Washington—a law spearheaded through Congress by two Texas leaders, one in each house—also occurred in 1934. This legislation would have a direct impact on the lives of millions of Texans, many of them then unborn. And, finally, the creation of the Credit Union National Association as the successor to CUNEB came in the spring of 1934, giving credit unions in all corners of the nation a strong and self-sustaining service organization to promote their ideals and to work with the state credit union leagues which were rapidly being formed.

There was a new President in the White House, one who had taken over the reins of government the year before at one of the bleakest hours in American history by assuring his fellow countrymen that "the only thing we have to fear is fear itself." Franklin D. Roosevelt had pledged a "New Deal" for the American people, and part of it was individual financial security and freedom from the type of catastrophe that had wiped out the savings and hopes of millions of families since 1929.

Edward A. Filene and Roy F. Bergengren, the founding fathers of CUNA

Sen. Morris Sheppard, author of the Federal Credit Union Act of 1934

Rep. Wright Patman of Texarkana (left), a key friend in Congress

C. T. Bergeron of Dallas (right), an early force in the Texas movement and the TCUL's first managing director

Carl Bodine of Fort Worth (left), a member of the original Board of Directors

James A. Dacus, recording secretary for the League's 1934 organizational meeting in Fort Worth

President Roosevelt was no stranger to credit unions. As a legislator in New York State, he had introduced that state's first credit union bill, and he came into the nation's highest office with a commitment to give the ordinary citizen freer access to credit, safer methods of saving money, and a greater measure of control over his fiscal destiny. Clearly, the nation's banks—some 5,000 of which had failed as part of the terrible toll of the Depression—had not provided these. Something further was needed. Along with such historic measures as the creation of Social Security and the establishment of an agency to insure bank deposits, Roosevelt was also keenly interested in enacting a federal law that would make credit unions equally accessible to people in all the states. But it fell to a pair of native Texans—two of the most colorful in the history of politics in the Lone Star State—to steer the Federal Credit Union Act through Congress.

Although they were both products of the same "piney woods" region of East Texas, both life-long Democrats and both staunch "drys" in the national debate over Prohibition, Senator Morris Sheppard and Congressman Wright Patman were also something of a study in contrasts. The distinguished, silver-haired Sheppard, himself the son of U.S. Representative John Levi Sheppard, whom he had been elected to succeed on his father's death in 1902, was the dean of the U.S. Congress with more than a third of a century of service in the House and Senate. An 1895 graduate of the University of Texas, Sheppard was a Phi Beta Kappa with a master's degree from Yale and an honorary doctor of laws from Southern Methodist University. He was chairman of the powerful Senate Military Affairs Committee and an outspoken supporter of military preparedness at a time when most other senators were more concerned with domestic considerations. He was also a noted Shakespearean scholar who had written (but not published) an exhaustive 35-volume index to the bard's selected comments on more than 4,000 subjects.

But the senior senator from Texas was best known nationally as the author of the bill that became the 18th Amendment to the U.S. Constitution. When it became official law of the land on January 16, 1920, the amendment introduced by Sheppard ushered in nearly fourteen years of nationwide Prohibition. Later, Sheppard also assisted in writing the notorious Volstead Act, the law under which the federal government attempted to enforce Prohibition on a resistant public. And even though the "noble experiment," as it was known, had earned the disdain of many Americans and Texans alike—and its repeal had been one of President Roosevelt's top priorities on taking office—Sheppard remained its most steadfast national proponent. In the months before the 18th Amendment died a much-applauded death on December 5, 1933, he stumped his native state at his own expense to argue against repeal. The fact that his thirsty constituents voted against him on this issue, however, did not keep them from re-electing him handily to his Senate seat in 1936.

John William Wright Patman, on the other hand, was among the most junior members of Congress, having been elected to his first term in 1928 at the age of 35. But in his relatively short tenure on Capitol Hill, the round-faced congressman from Texarkana had already firmly established himself as a vociferous maverick. His first congressional speech had been a demand that the government make immediate cash payments of $2 billion to World War I veterans as compensation for paid-up life insurance benefits granted them earlier. He had pressed for the impeachment of President Hoover's Treasury secretary, Andrew Mellon, accusing him of using his official influence to negotiate concessions for an oil company. He had lashed out repeatedly—as he would continue to do on the floor of Congress for more than half a century—at the trusts, the big bankers and the "wolves of Wall Street," and to champion the cause of the "little man."

Of a decidedly more liberal persuasion than Sheppard, Patman had come by his populist, anti-big money, never-take-no-for-an-answer philosophy naturally and early in life. Born in 1893 in a three-room log cabin on his parents' Cass County cotton farm, he had, as one appreciative Patman-watcher put it, "learned his three R's in such rare intervals as the boll weevil gave him leisure." He had ridden a mule six miles to the nearest school at Hughes Springs, had not managed to finish high school until he was 19, had studied law on his own, and raised cotton to pay his way to college at Cumberland University in Tennessee. Soon after he was admitted to the Texas bar in 1916, the country found itself embroiled in a war in Europe. Patman was rejected for officer training school because of a heart condition, but enlisted in the Army as a private and rose to the rank of first lieutenant. Back home after the war, he was elected to the Texas House of Representatives and then as district attorney of Cass and Bowie Counties. When he decided to run for Congress in 1928, he stunned fellow East Texans by denouncing the Ku Klux Klan, which was then still a powerful political force in the state.

As different as they may have been in style and approach, Sheppard and Patman were in wholehearted agreement on the need for the expansion of credit unions as a benefit to the working people of the United States and as a tool to combat the dire effects of the Depression and the concentration of too much wealth in too few hands. As early as 1915, Sheppard had become interested in rural personal credit, and in February of that year had introduced a resolution in the Senate calling for an investigation of a system of rural credits. As a well-established friend of both labor and small business, he seemed a natural choice to sponsor the Federal Credit Union Act of 1934 in the Senate.

In writing the act and pushing for its passage, Sheppard described it as "a heavy blow at the private loan shark system, which diverts from normal channels of trade billions of dollars through exorbitant interest charges running as high as 42 percent and even higher." Later, Sheppard proudly pointed out that the Federal Credit Union Act was the only New Deal legislation to originate on Capitol Hill during the 1934 congressional session. All the rest of it was part of the flood of anti-Depression bills emanating from the White House.

Sheppard urged his Senate colleagues to support the bill by emphasizing that the measure sought "to solve a great national problem in the only way it can be solved—by making available to people of small means credit for provident purposes through a national system of cooperative credit.

"Through self-sustaining cooperative methods, members of these unions become systematic savers and can obtain loans in comparatively small amounts from a fund established by their own contributions for necessary and provident purposes, at low rates of interest," he explained. "The general use of the credit union by the American people will mean an increased purchasing power of two or three billion dollars a year through relief from the enormous interest rates charged for small loans by loan shark organizations."

In agreeing to sponsor the bill in the House, Patman, too, was convinced of the inestimable potential value of credit unions. In a letter to all members of the House Banking Committee, he urged that the bill "be enacted without delay," adding: "It will serve a useful purpose all over the nation and especially in communities not served by small banks. I am sold on this legislation one hundred percent."

The fight to win final approval of the bill caused a sharp but temporary schism in the highest ranks of the national credit union movement. Bergengren backed the Sheppard bill wholeheartedly, but Filene favored a stronger approach. Filene had become convinced that if enough credit unions were organized quickly enough, the Depression could be ended, and he wanted the federal government to take a direct hand in financing them. Bergengren and Sheppard also felt that credit unions could play an important part in combatting the Depression, but they did not support direct federal aid. They favored only a comprehensive bill that would allow credit unions to be organized in all states and territories under a national law, and in the end they prevailed.

In the July 1934 edition of *The Bridge,* Bergengren gave an intriguing behind-the-scenes account of the frenzied manner in which the bill was rushed through to final passage by a weary Congress which almost adjourned before it got around to the credit union legislation. With the bill on the House calendar and backed by a favorable committee report, there was still no certainty that it would be brought to a vote as the last week of the session wound down, and even Bergengren confessed that he was beginning to "lose courage." Friday passed without action, and so did Saturday. Evening came, and the hopes of the credit union leadership were ebbing lower and lower.

"The sun went down," Bergengren wrote. "Golly—it was a tough day."

Then, with the speed that seemingly occurs in the national legislative process only in last-minute situations, the wheels began to turn in Congress. As Bergengren's narrative continued:

"At 7:15 p.m. Congressman Steagall sauntered into the House and was recognized by Speaker Rainey; he immediately brought up our bill. Debate was limited to thirty minutes . . . In addition to Congressman Steagall, Congressman Luce of Waltham, Massachusetts (a fine friend of the bill from the beginning), Congressman Golsborough of Maryland and Congressman Wright Patman of Texas all spoke in favor. No one spoke against, and in the entire Congress but two votes were cast against the bill.

"Then began a battle against time. Congressman Connery . . . helped us get the bill through the enrollment office. Senator Sheppard got it at about 8:30 p.m. It was still then thought that Congress would adjourn that night; a show had started in the House side and the Capitol was thronged with people. Senator Sheppard at about 10 p.m. interrupted a speaker who was addressing the Senate on air mail contracts, and as a matter of personal privilege got a vote on our bill. It had to be unanimous, and was. The bill was then hustled to the Senate enrolling clerk, and then, along about midnight, to the House side for the Speaker's signature . . . "

Bergengren hailed Sheppard as "the father of federal cooperative banking legislation" and as "the architect of the national (credit union) structure" for his role as author of Senate Bill 1639, which became the Federal Credit Union Act of 1934.

A few months later, in September 1934, Senator Sheppard expressed his own sentiments about credit unions and the historic bill he had written when he said:

"I have never heard the value of the credit union questioned, and if there be any issue against the Federal Credit Union Act, it has to do only with the need for federal legislation.

"Banking has long been considered a matter of national as well as of state concern, and the enactment of this bill will in no wise affect credit unions operating under state laws; its operating practice follows the state laws closely. It does recognize that this matter of stopping wastes of mass buying power is of national concern, and it seeks to make possible credit union development nationally at a time of great national need. Its enactment will make it possible for working people to organize credit unions in states which have no credit union laws, and there are ten of these. It will also simplify organization in states where existing state credit union laws are

53

oppressive or have become so hopelessly defective as to be practically inoperative ... (Apparently, Texas had not been the only state to be shackled with such a law.)

"This bill is simply a permissive bill, giving the right to groups wherever located to ask for the privilege to organize credit unions under proper federal supervision. It comes at a time when we are all concerned with national rehabilitation and when we are doing many things to hasten national recovery. It seeks to eliminate usurious money lending in the only way it can be done, namely by enabling the average man to combine with his fellows to the end that, working together, they may solve their own short-term credit problems at normal rates. The worker who is spending a substantial part of his earnings on interest overcharges cannot spend that amount for the things he needs to buy. On the increased purchasing power of the masses of the people recovery mainly depends."

Before the end of the year, federal credit unions were being organized throughout the country. The very first such organization to receive its charter under the new act, however, was given an especially fitting name. Founded on October 1, 1934, by city and county employees in Texarkana, Texas—the city that both Sheppard and Patman called home—the new organization was called the Morris Sheppard Federal Credit Union. Within the next two years, more than 1,400 similar institutions had been founded under the law and their combined funds totalled more than $1 million.

Sheppard, whose portrait hangs today in an honored spot at CUNA's national headquarters in Madison, Wisconsin, continued to be an active supporter of the credit union movement and its principles until his death on April 9, 1941. When some federal credit unions were threatened with eviction from federal buildings, he introduced and worked for legislation to permit them to keep their quarters and appealed directly to President Roosevelt and the Post Office Department in their behalf. He also authored a consolidated Credit Union Act, which contained a number of needed amendments to the original law, including provisions for inter-lending between credit unions, investing funds in federal savings and loan associations, and conducting research into various credit union needs and possibilities.

In commenting on the passage of the Federal Credit Union Act of 1934, the *St. Louis Post Dispatch* observed that "the New Deal has indeed done something for the little fellow." And the *Dallas Morning News*, in an editorial published a few weeks before Congress passed the act, had this to say: "Senator Sheppard's sponsorship of the federal credit union bill may serve in the long run to perpetuate the memory of his public service longer than will his advocacy and unyielding defense of prohibition. For the uniform success of the small groups aided by Edward Filene has established this type of credit source available to the small wage earner and the federal assistance offered will widen the scope of this service."

As for Patman, he would render even greater and longer-lasting contributions to credit unions and all they stand for during the next four decades. As their most constant and unshakeable ally in Congress, he would see the movement grow within his lifetime to a network of more than 23,000 credit unions nationwide, with assets of approximately $32 billion. By the time of his death in 1976, more than two million Texans would hold credit union membership. And Patman, who was fond of saying that "next to the church" credit unions were the greatest instrument ever created for the public good, took justifiable pride in that growth.

As he noted in 1975 in a keynote address to the annual meeting of the Texas Credit Union League and its Affiliates in Fort Worth, more than forty years after his historic 1934 role: "Senator Sheppard and I believed the federal credit unions would be a success when we sponsored the credit union act back then, but I don't think either one of us realized just how far you would come and how successful you would make this program."

Birth of the TCUL

By the time the Federal Credit Union Act was approved, there were already some 3,000 credit unions operating under state charters in 38 states and the District of Columbia, and claiming a total membership in excess of 500,000. Obviously, Bergengren's pilgrimages around the country had paid rich dividends, since there had been only 199 credit unions in the entire nation when he had begun his organizational crusade in 1921. Because of this growth, Bergengren felt it was now time to pursue another long-range goal for the national credit union movement—the creation of a national association.

To this purpose, Bergengren invited credit union leaders from all over the United States to attend a meeting in August of 1934 at Estes Park, Colorado, and 52 delegates from 21 states—including C.T. Bergeron and R.H. Pitts of Texas—responded. The result was the formation of the Credit Union National Association (CUNA) to replace the old Credit Union National Extension Bureau. The job of extending the credit union concept into a nationwide ideal had been admirably done, and now the emphasis of the national organization was to be shifted to serve, while the task of organizing new credit unions was to be transferred to new credit union leagues at the state level.

This meant that a great deal of further organization was necessary within the various states in order for CUNA to be effective. Until state leagues were established and affiliated with CUNA in every state, the national organization would be little more than a paper entity, Bergengren reasoned. At the time, only five states—Massachusetts, New York, Illinois, Minnesota, and Missouri—could claim fully functional leagues. A few other states had the semblances of leagues, but without any full-time staffs. Texas had no statewide organization at all.

Thus, the stage was set for what must be considered the single most important event in the history of the credit union movement in Texas, and the climactic high point of a climactic year—the formation of the Texas Credit Union League.

The organizational meeting was held at the Texas Hotel in Fort Worth on October 6, 1934, with Bergengren's longtime friend and cohort, C.T. Bergeron, presiding, primarily because of his previous role as a state representative to CUNEB. Thomas Doig, representing the new CUNA, also was present, as was Deputy State Banking Commissioner R.F. Siddons. James A. Dacus was elected temporary secretary to record minutes of the meeting in the first official action taken by the delegates. The exact number of delegates is not known, but according to the earliest records of the League, there were 63 credit unions operating in Texas at the time, and of these more than half sent at least one representative. A total of 33 persons signed the original Constitution and Bylaws which were adopted that day. (See Appendix.)

Dacus, a young man of 22 at the time, recalled being recruited to serve as secretary at the meeting in an interview nearly half a century later. "I got the job," he said jokingly, "because I think I was the only one there who knew how to type."

After graduating from Texas Christian University, Dacus stayed only briefly in Texas, but was caught up in the zeal of the pioneer credit union movement. He helped organize more than 160 credit unions including the Morris Sheppard Federal Credit Union in Texarkana, but most of them were in the Northeast, rather than in Texas. A personal acquaintance of both Filene and Bergengren, Dacus said he "just couldn't escape their enthusiasm" for credit unions. Of the TCUL organizational meeting, he said: "We didn't know where we were going, only that it was very, very important to go." Dacus ultimately returned to Texas and now lives in retirement in Fort Worth, where he remains as vitally interested in credit unions as he was on that October day in 1934.

One surviving account of the meeting reads in part:

"The meeting was opened with prayer, after which Mr. Bergeron introduced Mr. Doig, who outlined in brief the history of the credit union movement, both in continental Europe and in the United States . . . Mr. Doig further explained that it was through the philanthropic works of Mr. Edward A. Filene, a very wealthy Boston merchant, that credit unions had developed in the United States. There are now three thousand credit unions operating in the United States with in excess of seventy-five millions of dollars in assets and somewhat more than five hundred thousand members. Many of these . . . have been organized in the past three or four years, and practically all have been made possible by Mr. Filene's Credit Union National Extension Bureau, which he subsidized as a disinterested public service . . .

"Mr. Doig stated that at a meeting at Estes Park, Colorado . . . it was decided that the time was now ripe to get the Credit Union National Association started. It was also decided at this convention that when ten state credit union leagues had ratified the proposed by-laws and constitution, which were drawn up at the Estes Park conference, the Credit Union National Association would begin operation . . . Mr. Doig then proceeded to read the proposed by-laws and constitution. Open discussion was held. Then Mr. Doig explained how dues in such national association were to be collected. He stated that one-half of one percent of the assets of a credit union yearly were to be paid, one-half of such sum payable in January, and the other half in June. There was a general discussion of this feature. For example, the Houston Postal Credit Union with assets of $70,000.00 would pay yearly dues of $350.00 . . ."

A cooperative spirit seems to have hung over the meeting; with little apparent debate or dissention among the delegates. The Constitution and Bylaws for the new League were adopted by a unanimous vote, and the delegates also voted unanimously to establish "nine geographical centers of the State of Texas," with representatives of credit unions within each of these districts to meet in caucus to select a nominee to serve as the district's member of the TCUL Board of Directors.

With this taken care of, Bergeron was elected as a director-at-large, bringing the total board membership to ten. But at this point, the first lengthy discussion of the meeting took place. As a result, the delegates enacted the first of many amendments to the bylaws, changing the number of members of the Board of Directors and the geographic regions represented on it to twelve instead of nine. In the final action of the day, the following directors from the following districts were named to the League's first Board: J.E. Meador, Texarkana; C.H. Bodine, Wichita Falls; A.S. Anderson, San Antonio; G.W. Elder, Houston; W.O. Freeman, Fort Worth; R.H. Pitts, Dallas; B.S. Wallace, Waco; C.W. Thomas, Tyler; A.T. Earles, El Paso; W.E. Suddarth, Amarillo; T.J. Ford, Beaumont; and C.T. Bergeron, Dallas. (The surviving records of the meeting indicate that Bergeron was to serve as a director-at-large, but that there were to be twelve "geographic centers" represented on the Board. Why only eleven such centers are included in the list above is not clear.)

The League also voted to affiliate with CUNA, and Deputy Banking Commissioner Siddons spoke briefly on the need for the League to appoint a committee to work with the State Banking Commission on a plan whereby credit unions could be more carefully and thoroughly examined. Recalling the session on the occasion of the League's silver anniversary in 1959, W.O. Freeman, the director from Fort Worth, who was also elected as the TCUL's first vice president that day, said: "We discussed general plans of organization and the possibility of small annual dues. The purpose of the organization (was) to bring the credit unions of the state together and solve their common problems." At the time, Freeman was manager-treasurer of the Armour Employees Credit Union of Fort Worth.

Unfortunately, no complete list remains today of those present at this historic gathering. But one member of each credit union represented was asked to sign the newly adopted Constitution and Bylaws of the League. Besides those delegates already mentioned above as directors, those who signed included: W. Hughes Knight, Dallas Municipal Employees; L. Roy Prescott, Houston Farm Credit Administration; James C. Ely, Amarillo Postal Employees; W.M. Vick, Dallas Public Service (Western Union) Employees; Preston Lockhart, Dallas Postal Employees; J.H. Hines, Fort Worth Conoco Employees; A.L. Hoopingarner, Fort Worth Poultry and Egg Company; W.C. Deaton, Beaumont Postal Employees; J.G. Thach, Dallas Armstrong Packing Company; F.S. Reed, Fort Worth Rock Island Lines Railway; Joe Quinn, Dallas Pollock Paper Company; S.J. Smith, Fort Worth Postal Employees; Thomas Vannerson, Dallas La France (Morton Milling Company); J.S. Henry, Dallas Public School Teachers; Frank J. Matula, Houston Swift & Company; Adolph Geue, Austin Postal Employees; H.C. Michael, Fort Worth Municipal Employees, F.E. Record, Wichita Falls Conoco Employees; W.H. Wehman, San Antonio Swift & Company; J. Fred Hoffman, Texarkana Morris Sheppard No. 1; W.M. Crawford, Fort Worth Denver Railway Clerks; Paul H. Scott, Abilene Postal Employees; G.E. Sisk, Houston Railway Postal; and D.W. McKee, Houston Armour and Co.

Subsequently, at the first Board of Directors meeting immediately after the organizational meeting of the

League, the following officers were elected: Pitts, president; Freeman, vice president; Thomas, treasurer; Elder, secretary; and Bergeron, managing director and national director.

As this book went to press, C.H. Bodine, who was elected to the League's first Board of Directors on that eventful day in Fort Worth, was the last of the TCUL's original founders still active in the Texas credit union movement fifty years later. In April 1984, at the age of 83, Bodine attended the TCUL's annual meeting in Houston. Although he has been in retirement since 1965, he remains a member of both the Fort Worth Postal Credit Union and the PTS (Postal Transportation Service) Federal Credit Union of Fort Worth.

Bodine, who represented the Wichita Falls Postal Credit Union on the original TCUL Board and who served two terms as a director from Wichita Falls, moved to Fort Worth in 1944. At the time of the 1934 organizational meeting, he was secretary of Wichita Falls Postal, having succeeded J.W. Vandigriff in that position.

Although his recollections of the Fort Worth gathering have been dimmed somewhat by time, Bodine still remembers signing the original TCUL bylaws and other events relating to the meeting. "R.W. Thomas, another member of Wichita Falls Postal, went to Fort Worth with me," Bodine recalled in a 1984 interview. "There were fifty or sixty people there, and all of them were deeply interested in credit unions. I know that I believed in them strongly. Times were tough, and people with college degrees were walking the streets looking for work. Money was hard to come by, and credit unions came to a lot of people's rescue. I still have a loan on the books at the PTS Credit Union, for my granddaughter's car."

At the time of the landmark meeting in Fort Worth, credit union expansion in Texas was in a somewhat dormant period, probably because the attentions of

Bergengren and other national leaders had been focused so completely on the process of bringing CUNA into existence. At any rate, not a single new credit union had been chartered in Texas during the six months just prior to the TCUL's organization. But the birth of the League was to lead to dramatic developments in the months and years ahead. Between the organizational meeting in Fort Worth in early October and the end of December 1934, eight new credit unions were chartered and added to the TCUL's ranks.

Among the major concerns of Texas credit unions at the time—and one of the matters to which the TCUL was to turn its earliest attention—was the prospect of a state franchise tax, then hanging over all state-chartered credit unions and soon to be faced by federal credit unions as well. The League would play a prominent role in settling the franchise tax issue to the satisfaction of its member credit unions. And although the matter was to be brought before the Legislature on a recurring basis over the years, the League was able to work effectively to keep credit unions exempt from franchise taxes.

Staving off the franchise tax advocates provided the first major test of resolve for the new League, and the fledgling organization might not have been able to handle the task if it had not been for the personal help offered by CUNA and Bergengren, who came back to Texas to help in the fight. Like the leagues in most other states, the TCUL depended entirely on the efforts of unpaid volunteers to carry on its work. It had no paid staff, no permanent headquarters, and very little money. It had no clout with the Legislature to speak of, or with other political powers in Austin, and it was opposed by some of the wealthiest and best-organized interests in the state.

All in all, trying times of crisis and turmoil still lay ahead. But it was clearly apparent by 1936, the year Texans temporarily laid aside the woes of the Depression to celebrate the 100th anniversary of their state's hard-won independence from Mexico, that Texas credit unions and their new League were at least off and running. Their own struggle for independence was far from over, but they had served notice that they would fight for it. They might stumble over the many obstacles in their path, but they would not fall.

Taking a "Breather"

Following the frantic activity of 1934, the credit union people of Texas and their new League seemed ready to take some time to relax and contemplate both the progress they had made and the route they should take in the future. The year 1935 was apparently as quiet as the preceding twelve months had been eventful. To be sure, a number of new credit unions were organized, but there was a notable lull at the statewide level. As nearly as can be determined, there was not even an annual meeting as such in 1935. If there was, no minutes have been located, and there were definitely no officer elections held by the League that year. In fact, the League's first slate of officers, headed by R.H. Pitts, would continue to serve until January 1937, except for Bergeron, who left his post as the League's first managing director in December 1936 and was succeeded by G.W. Elder, who had been serving as secretary since the founding of the TCUL.

On the national level, however, 1935 was a year of tremendous significance, because in May of that year the CUNA Mutual Insurance Society was formed to protect the families of credit union borrowers who died or were disabled before their loans were repaid. The catalyst behind the birth of CUNA Mutual, which was destined to grow into a giant of the U.S. insurance industry within a few years, was an incident in which a power company lineman borrowed $250 from his credit union then was killed in an on-the-job accident two days later. Two of the lineman's fellow workers had co-signed on the loan and managed to pay it off out of their own savings, but the directors of the credit union were disturbed by the chain of events and felt that their borrowers needed a better system of protection.

CUNA Mutual was the answer. Declaring that "the debt shall die with the debtor," it developed a loan protection insurance policy that would automatically repay the loan of a credit union borrower who fell victim to a fatal or disabling accident. A program of share life insurance soon followed, providing for specified compensation to beneficiaries of deceased or disabled credit union members.

CUNA Mutual came into being with the help of a $2,500 loan from Filene and had receipts of only $145 during its first month of operation. Three months later, when it was faced with its first claim of $40, the society had to borrow money to pay it. But that situation soon changed dramatically, and today CUNA Mutual is the leading insurance company in North America in terms of credit life insurance coverage in force and ranks among the top twenty companies in total coverage. Its importance to Texas was to extend far beyond the protection it provided to credit unions and their members in the state, since it would also serve as an example when leaders of the TCUL launched their own insurance operation, Members Mutual, some seventeen years later.

Nevertheless, insofar as the mid-1930s were concerned, the TCUL kept an extremely low profile. One of the men who remembered the period vividly was Joseph Collerain, who had been associated with the very first credit union ever organized in Texas, the brief experiment among Santa Fe Railway employees in Galveston shortly after the original Texas law was passed in 1913. Following the liquidation of the Santa Fe credit union, Collerain had no further contact with the credit union movement until 1934 when organizational activity began on the Humble Employees Federal Credit Union in Houston. Not only did he help found this credit union, but also served as its first manager and as a member of its Board of Directors for more than a quarter of a century.

Collerain's re-emergence and his effective efforts in obtaining state charter No. 96 for the Humble credit union in January 1935 and in signing up 272 dues-paying charter members quickly propelled him to a position of statewide leadership. Consequently, Collerain found himself attending the very first state convention of the League in the winter of 1936 at the Blackstone Hotel in Fort Worth. As he recalled it many years later, the convention bore little similarity to the massive League gatherings of the 1980s. There were, he said, "not more than ten or twelve" persons in attendance, and the meeting lasted only a few hours. What Collerain remembered most graphically about the convention was the weather. "Boy, was it snowing in Fort Worth that day!" he exclaimed.

Plenty of people apparently remembered Joe Collerain, though, since he was elected the second president of the TCUL for the year 1937, succeeding Pitts. It was to a large extent Collerain's influence, too, which caused the main focal point of the League—as well as its unofficial headquarters—to shift away from its traditional base in North Texas for the next few years to Houston and the Gulf Coast area.

Having thus taken note of one of the smallest meetings conducted in Texas during 1936, it now seems only appropriate to devote a fleeting glance to one of the largest gatherings of that year or any other in the Lone Star State—the great Centennial Exposition in Dallas. It was an event that commemorated the past but also pointed toward the Texas of the future, a Texas in which credit unions and their members would play an increasingly large role.

The Centennial

Despite the hardship and poverty that gripped innumerable Texas families at the time, the state has never witnessed a more gala or glorious occasion than the six-month Texas Centennial celebration which drew millions of visitors during the period between June and November of 1936. Although Centennial activities took place all across the state, the main focal point of the celebration of 100 years of Texas independence was the Centennial Exposition in Dallas, featuring $15 million worth of new exhibit halls and entertainment facilities at the city's State Fair Park. It was a genuine, officially sanctioned World's Fair—the first one Texas had ever had—and people came from every corner of the country to join the festivities. For most of them, it was a welcome respite from the rigors of daily life and a chance to forget their troubles for a while.

In collaboration with Bergeron, Bergengren put together a special feature article for *The Bridge* on the Texas Centennial Exposition, in which he noted that Dallas was "a thriving city with a population of 309,658" and the "financial heart of Texas." It was also, he added, one of the leading insurance centers in the entire United States, and one of the educational centers of the South. And yet, as Dallas was enjoying one of its finest hours, the article also pointed out that it was running well behind its neighbor and rival to the west in the organization of credit unions. Dallas had only 21 credit unions at that juncture, compared to 35 in Fort Worth and 28 in Houston. There were also others scattered among 42 other cities and towns across the Lone Star State, and Bergengren was obviously elated by this fact. "The credit union visitor to the Centennial will not have much difficulty locating someone to give him the local history and to talk a bit of shop when he feels so inclined," he wrote.

He also had more laudatory words for Bergeron: "The credit union veteran is C.T. Bergeron of 806 Martinique Street, Dallas. He has been organizing credit unions in the state for years, first for the Credit Union National Extension Bureau and more recently as a member of the credit union section of the Farm Credit

66

Administration. He is one of the high line, outstanding credit union organizers in the United States. After a thrilling service in the World War, fighting overseas with one of the most hazardous branches of the service, Mr. Bergeron, after the war, was identified for many years with the Western Union Telegraph Company at Dallas from which organization he came into the credit union work. He has long been an outstanding national director of the Credit Union National Association. Mr. Paul Mills, 1037 8th Street, Port Arthur, Texas, is also associated in organization work with the credit union section."

There were even some words of praise for the TCUL: "There is a fine Texas Credit Union League of relatively recent origin. Its president is R.H. Pitts of the credit union at the United States Post Office in Dallas. W.O. Freeman of the Armour Credit Union at Fort Worth is vice president and C.W. Thomas of the credit union at the Tyler Post Office is treasurer. G.W. Elder, also of a credit union of postal employees at Houston is secretary and Mr. Bergeron is managing director."

The article in *The Bridge's* issue of May 1936 made it clear that, while the TCUL had not been making a great deal of noise over the previous year and a half, its leadership had not been idle. There were now more than 150 credit unions in Texas, compared to only about 70 in late 1934. And membership in individual credit unions was also soaring at a phenomenal rate as more and more workers took advantage of membership in those that were available to them. By March 1936, Armour and Company employee credit unions, including the ones in Fort Worth and Dallas, boasted more than 22,000 members nationwide, with $1.25 million in assets and outstanding loans totalling nearly $7 million.

By this time, most major corporations had embraced the credit union concept as an important fringe benefit for their workers, and even the employees of the U.S. Senate had their own credit union, with Senator Sheppard as a member of its supervisory committee. Although the movement had still failed to gain any great momentum in rural farming areas, there was, by the end of 1936, scarcely any aspect of urban economic, social, or political life in America that had not been touched by it in some way.

One of the chief problems confronting CUNA at this time, however, was finding a way to make the various state credit union leagues self-supporting. Toward this end, CUNA Supply was formed by the national association in 1936 for the purpose of supplying many types of needed forms and other materials to the state leagues and their member credit unions. During that year of the Centennial, Texas ranked fourth among the states in total number of credit unions. Only Wisconsin, Pennsylvania, and Ohio had more. This made Texas a key target area in CUNA's strategy to strengthen the movement at the state level. And it made Bergengren's article more than a promotional "puff piece" on the Texas Centennial when he concluded by saying:

"In *The Bridge* it is our hope to get credit union members (the whole bloomin' million of them) not only acquainted with each other, but also with this great, grand, and glorious country which is our common heritage. It has been my lot to roam about the United States for fifteen years, visiting all parts of it, poking my nose in here,there and everywhere, and the more I see of it—the better I like it. It's the grandest country in the world. Visit Texas and prove to your own satisfaction one of the outstanding reasons I have for that conclusion."

As the color and splendor of the Centennial celebration faded into the past, the story of Texas credit unions and their impact on the average citizen of the state was about to enter a new phase of expansion and challenge.

PART II:

Gains and Growing Pains (1937-1959)

Beating the Bushes

By early 1937, many of the most familiar names in the Texas credit union movement up until that time began to disappear from prominence and to be replaced by new names and faces from the state's fast-growing credit union community. As we have noted, Bergeron departed as managing director of the TCUL in December 1936 and seems to have dropped quickly into obscurity. Little is heard of him after that time or of his fellow Dallasite, R.H. Pitts, who served as the League's first president.

The last official mention of Bergeron is in the minutes of the December 1936 board meeting, which merely take note of his absence from that meeting. But Phil Davis, one of the premier organizers of credit unions in Texas and now treasurer of the National Credit Union Management Association (NCUMA), sheds some light on Bergeron's role in the TCUL. "Bergeron was with the Farm Credit Administration of the U.S. Department of Agriculture, which at that time had the responsibility for conducting examinations of federal credit unions, and he got into credit union work through his job as an examiner."

Davis adds that the Dallas Western Union Credit Union which Bergeron organized was liquidated in the early 1940s after "somebody absconded with all the funds." Some years later, Davis himself reorganized the Western Union Credit Union and it is currently going strong, he points out.

As to what happened to Bergeron after his term as TCUL managing director, Davis is not sure. "I remember being introduced to him by Mr. (H.B.) Yates in about 1941, but he wasn't active in credit union work at that time as far as I know. Actually, he just kind of disappeared, although he continued to live in Dallas. At least he disappeared as far as credit unions were concerned."

Others of the "founding fathers" of the League continued to play major roles in its activities, but during the last three years of the decade of the 1930s, a definite changing of the guard was taking place in the leadership of the TCUL.

Collerain served as League president in 1937 as Pitts' successor, even though he was a relative newcomer to the League's inner circle, and he found his hands full with sudden problems relating to the recurrent bugaboo of the franchise tax. As Collerain himself explained: "During my term of office a bomb shell hit us squarely in the face. The Texas attorney general ruled that all credit unions in this state were subject to the Texas franchise tax. Bing! Consternation ran wild in the credit union movement, and we prevailed on Roy Bergengren to come down and help.

"We then prepared a bill to exempt us from the tax and had it sponsored in the House by Jeff Stinson of Dallas and in the Senate by (A.M.) Aiken of Paris, with the help of U.S. Senator Morris Sheppard. After much work far into the nights and with educational material placed on the desks of each senator and representative, the bills were passed on emergency reading during a special session. In the House, the passage was by a vote of 120-1 and this lone fellow told us afterward that he was for the bill but pushed the wrong button on the voting machine."

(While in Austin working on the bill, incidentally, Collerain and other credit union leaders had an unforgettable scare—one they were able to joke about in later years, but which was far from funny at the time. While

70

the bill was pending before the Legislature, a certain credit union in Houston announced a 12 percent dividend at a time when credit unions had been cautioned against declaring dividends in excess of 6 percent, and the event was reported in the Houston newspapers. "We thought our goose was cooked," Collerain said. "So we went out and bought up all the Houston papers we could find in Austin and had a nice fire on the Capitol grounds—and no one attempted to stop us. It isn't possible to (repeat) what I told the officers of that credit union when I got back to Houston.")

Collerain also mentioned that most of those who went to Austin to work for passage of the tax exemption legislation paid their own expenses for the trip because no League funds were available. The League was, in fact, extremely short of operating funds at the time—a condition that may be traced in part to the extreme difficulty it was encountering in signing up credit unions as dues-paying members. Part of the problem was simply communication. Texas credit unions were by now scattered from the Panhandle to the Rio Grande and from El Paso to Texarkana, and were separated from each other, and from the Texas Credit Union League, by thousands of miles of highway and telephone lines. There was no money for long-distance phone calls and no personnel available for the endless travel necessary to achieve face-to-face contact. Consequently, many of these credit unions had no real understanding of the League's functions or its needs. A large percentage of them opted not to join the League at all, and many of those who did join were slow in paying their dues. As matters stood, about the only pressure the League was capable of exerting on the non-joiners and non-payers was in the form of an occasional letter pleading for support.

By the end of 1937, there were some 230 credit unions operating in 58 Texas cities and towns. But when the League attempted to survey them to ascertain their memberships and assets, only 120 replied (showing a combined membership of 24,686 and total assets of $1,778,949.15). From all indications, it is doubtful that more than about one-third of the 230 actually held paid-up memberships in the League at the time.

One that did was the Kingsville Community Federal Credit Union (then known as the Missouri-Pacific Federal Credit Union of Kingsville), which was chartered that year. One of the Kingsville credit union's charter members and its first treasurer was Harry W. Hamilton, who later won statewide recognition for attending the greatest number of consecutive annual TCUL conventions of any single individual. Hamilton, who is still active as treasurer of his credit union, has not missed an annual meeting during a 44-year period stretching from 1940 through 1984.

As the League entered the fourth year of its existence, one of its biggest obstacles was its inability to hire a full-time managing director and support personnel and to afford a permanent office setup. By the beginning of 1938, the League's directors were feeling a growing sense of urgency to do something about this and to improve their means of communicating with dozens of credit unions that had not yet responded to their message.

On January 29 of that year, the TCUL board met at the Adolphus Hotel in Dallas with outgoing President Collerain presiding and elected the following new slate of officers: V.S. Judson of Dallas, president; Dr. R.L. Conrod of Denton, vice president; C.W. Thomas of Tyler, treasurer; W.J. Edmonston of Dallas, secretary; and G.W. Elder of Houston, managing director. Significantly, of the original "old guard" which had guided the TCUL since its inception, only two—Thomas and Elder—now remained among the top echelon of League officials. All the rest had given way to relative newcomers.

(Dr. Conrod, an economics professor at what was then North Texas State Teachers College, was later castigated as a "pinko" because of his tremendous enthusiasm for credit unions and other cooperatives. H.B. Yates and Jack Mitchell, leaders of the Dallas Teachers Credit Union, both of whom later served in key posts with the League and CUNA, wrote character reference letters to help clear Dr. Conrod's name. Mitchell said of Dr. Conrod: "He was as fine a human being as I have ever known. He was truly, along with Roy Bergengren, one of the great founders of the credit union movement.")

At this point, the office of managing director was still a part-time one, which energetic young Granville Elder, who also served as secretary-treasurer of Houston Postal Credit Union (the largest in the state), attempted to handle from his home at 3920 Coyle Street in Houston. But at the January meeting in Dallas, his fellow board members showed that they recognized the increasing difficulty under which Elder was working and the growing demands of the managing director's post. They appropriated money for the purchase of various supplies and appointed Dr. Conrod to help with the communications responsibilities by editing a new monthly newsletter for the League.

Known as the *Texas Credit Union League News,* the publication was issued monthly and distributed as a supplement to *The Bridge.* Despite the similarity between the name of the new newsletter and Bergeron's earlier *Texas Credit Union News,* there was no direct relationship. The first edition appeared in March 1938 and was devoted in large part to a reprint of a memorial address delivered by Bergengren in Dallas and other cities across the country on the occasion of Edward Filene's death a few weeks earlier. Subsequent issues, however, were almost entirely devoted to news items pertaining directly to Texas credit unions and the TCUL.

In the April 1938 issue, for example, a report by Elder on the managing director's recent activities revealed a great deal about the rapidly expanding scope of that office. "Since February 1," Elder wrote, "202 letters have been written by the managing director in regard to various phases of the League work. Six of these letters were to the Credit Union National Association. Twenty-six of them were in regard to general League affairs; 159 concerned membership in the League. Three concerned proposed legislation; four replied to inquiries about the dues schedule, and four covered information relative to the credit union organization.

"In addition to the routine work of the office, preparation of membership lists, etc., the expense of the office of the managing director from February 1 to date of writing has been $101.29; $41.29 of which was spent for the purchase of a typewriter for use in the office, as voted by the Executive Committee at their meeting in Dallas on March 4; $25 per month salary for the assistant; and $10 for postage and stationery supplies.

"The membership of the League is very gratifying. As of March 14, 46 of the members had paid their dues for the year 1938. We have 266 credit unions in Texas, 112 of which belong to the League. From February 1 to March 14, the League acquired seven new members. I have received reports from the Credit Union National Association indicating that four new credit unions have been organized in Texas since February 1, and these credit unions will be acquainted with the advantages of membership in the League and furnished with applications for membership."

It seems readily apparent that Elder was getting a lot done with very little, and yet it is most revealing that the managing director of the TCUL still had to receive his first word of newly organized Texas credit unions from CUNA headquarters, more than 1,000 miles away in Madison, Wisconsin. Elder's figures on paid-up League memberships also provide dramatic insight into

74

the League's continuing problems in convincing individual credit unions that the TCUL was doing something worth paying for. Of 266 credit unions in the state, fewer than 45 percent had joined the League at all—and fewer than one out of every five had paid its dues.

Clearly, despite Elder's tireless and valiant efforts, something had to be done to improve statewide communications and to beef up the state organization. This fact was made even more painfully obvious to both state and national officials when it was revealed early in 1939 that Texas had dropped from fourth to tenth place among the states in total number of credit unions within the space of just three years. Something had to be done—but what?

Seeking Direction

Putting someone to work traveling the state to establish physical contact with individual credit unions seemed to be a logical first step in improving the TCUL's overall situation. Thus, at the summer board meeting in Houston July 7 and 8, 1939, this matter was high on the list of topics for discussion. The directors' solution was to replace Elder, who had been the overworked part-time managing director, with W.J. Edmonston, the League's secretary, and to give Edmonston the full-time job of "traveling" managing director. By this time, 14 other states already had full-time managing directors, and the advantage this gave them in recruitment and organization were obvious.

Edmonston, who had been a teacher in the Dallas public schools for more than a decade, had prepared himself for such a role the year before, when he traveled to CUNA headquarters in Madison with Elder and familiarized himself with the national organization and the people who ran it. Now, one of his first steps as full-time managing director was to return to Madison to firm up old contacts, establish new ones and discuss the

Texas situation with the national leadership. During his ten-day trip later in July, he also visited the offices of other state leagues in Kansas City, Minneapolis and Chicago, where he conferred with the managing directors of the Missouri, Minnesota and Illinois leagues. He also arranged with CUNA Assistant Managing Director Tom Doig to return the visit with a ten-day trip to Texas that September to speak to a series of chapter meetings throughout the state.

No sooner was Edmonston back home than he set out on a whirlwind tour of Texas, contacting 37 of the state's credit unions and setting up special chapter meetings in Houston, Dallas, San Antonio, Fort Worth, and Beaumont in preparation for Doig's upcoming visit.

By this time, the *Texas Credit Union League News* had ceased to exist and had been replaced by a Texas section in *The Bridge* edited by Dr. Conrod, who took note of Edmonston's frenetic activities by reporting in the September issue:

"Although no direct effort to obtain new League members was made on this trip (by Edmonston), the principal purpose of which was to get acquainted with the leaders, there were at least ten credit unions to promise affiliation in the near future and several asked that Edmonston meet with the board(s).

"Six league directors were contacted during this period, one new credit union organized, and five groups interested in organizing were visited.

"With his first month's work as an example of his value to the Texas League, Edmonston should prove of tremendous assistance in building up the Lone Star State's membership."

Upon Edmonston's resignation as League secretary, in order to take the managing director's post, he was replaced by C.W. Thomas of Tyler, who had served as the TCUL's treasurer since its founding. Thomas now became secretary-treasurer of the League in what proved to be a permanent combination of the two offices. Elder, the outgoing managing director, meanwhile, remained on the board, but not as an officer. In a statement published in *The Bridge* of November 1939, Elder sounded almost relieved to have the weight of the job taken off his shoulders.

"Having served the League as part-time managing director for several years . . . I feel qualified to state that the job of managing director is a really difficult assignment," he said. "This responsibility—credit union development and progress—is divided equally between the managing director and the credit unions. The cooperation he receives from them governs what success he may achieve in his work."

Elder, meanwhile, was performing yeoman service in his own credit union, Houston Postal, where he continued to serve as secretary-treasurer. As of mid-year 1939, the Houston credit union was reputed to be the largest and strongest in the entire state, with a membership of 543 and assets totalling $183,060.41. The leadership of Elder and other officers of Houston Postal, including its president, John Dunlop, and its vice president, Lloyd B. Wyatt, undoubtedly was responsible in large part for this success.

At about the same juncture, the TCUL began to see the first positive results of the forays around the state by Edmonston and the series of appearances in Texas by Doig. During the last half of 1939, the League was able to sign up a total of 31 new members, bringing its total dues-paying membership to 147 for a net increase of 26 over the figure reported in January of that year. Despite this encouraging news, however, the League still represented less than half the existing 304 credit unions in Texas, with only 48.3 percent of them holding League membership. Among the major credit union centers in the state, Dallas had the best percentage of League members—65 percent, or 34 members out of 52 credit unions. Houston, meanwhile, had increased its percentage of League members from 38 to 52 percent during the course of the year, with 29 memberships out of 56 credit unions. In other areas, the story was not so impressive. In such cities as El Paso, Beaumont, Galveston, and Longview, only one-third or fewer of the existing credit unions were TCUL members. (It is interesting to note that, at the time, the small West Texas city of Pampa had the greatest per capita number of credit unions in the state. With a population of only about 16,000, Pampa had seven credit unions—more than Austin (3), Beaumont (6), Galveston (3), San Angelo (3), Corpus Christi (5), or Texarkana (4). Not only that, but Pampa also had the best percentage of TCUL memberships—five out of the seven, or 71 percent—of any locality in the state.)

The important thing, though, was that the League was gradually gaining ground and chipping away at its membership problems. And with each new "chip," it more firmly established itself as an organization which could truly represent the Texas credit union movement as a whole. That movement had grown amazingly in the five years since the formation of the League. At the end of 1939, it claimed 60,000 individual members in 311 credit unions (224 federal and 87 state-chartered), with assets of $6 million. In its first decade of life, the movement had exceeded almost everyone's expectations. As that memorable decade drew to a close, TCUL President Judson summed up the League's position and its posture for the immediate future by saying: "Now that we have passed the experimenting stage, we really intend to get down to business and begin to do some credit union organization in the state of Texas."

Crisis and Change

The dawn of the 1940s found a shrinking world filled with tumult and conflict. For the second time in just over twenty years, war was again raging in Europe and threatening to engulf the rest of the planet. Adolf Hitler's well-oiled Nazi war machine in Germany had

78

already swallowed Czechoslovakia and Poland, and now confronted a hesitant France and Great Britain. And while the United States maintained an officially neutral stance, as it had in the years before entering World War I on the side of the Allies, public sentiment was already hardening against Hitler's Germany, and in Washington the machinery of military mobilization was beginning to grind into action.

It was to be a decade of national turmoil and personal trauma for all Americans. Before the war was over, some 750,000 Texans would see military service, and thousands of them would die on foreign battlefields around the globe. Texas itself would become a principal focal point of the national defense effort with an estimated 1,250,000 members of the various branches of the armed services receiving their training in the state. Beginning in the early 1940s, Texas would also become a center of the defense industry, with the opening of "war plants" for the production of aircraft, tanks, and other equipment speeding the migration of rural Texans into urban areas which had already begun.

Within the short span of a year or two, the Great Depression and its cruel hardships—which had dominated the public's attention from the beginning to the end of the 1930s—were to be pushed into the background and largely forgotten in the face of overriding new concerns. For many, prosperity was finally returning, but with it were coming crushing new fears and problems that made the old ones seem almost tame by comparison. Abruptly, life for Texans was changing again, and it would never be the same as it had been before.

To the average citizen, and the average credit union member, however, it was mercifully impossible to foresee what the new decade of the Forties held in store as the Texas Credit Union League convened for its annual meeting in Beaumont on the afternoon of January 20, 1940. The primary business of that meeting was dealing with the continuing concerns from the year before, but it was conducted by a League leadership that was obviously a good deal more comfortable with its situation than it had been 12 months earlier. As President Judson reported to the delegates: "Progress in the League has shown a decided uptrend not only from the point of added membership but more especially the better understanding of the credit union's place and program in the daily affairs of the thousands who have learned to use its service and who are assuring themselves of such continued service through the support of the League."

Judson gave liberal credit to Edmonston for the improving conditions of the League. "Again, the progress made during the past year is due in large measure to the activities of the managing director and the splendid support of the national association in arranging for Mr. Thomas Doig and Mr. Charles Eickel to conduct a series of educational meetings with leading chapter groups," Judson said. But the vaguest hint that a current of dissatisfaction with Edmonston was even then circulating among League members may be found in the fact that Judson took some pains to temper the compliments he directed toward Edmonston.

"It should not be overlooked, however," he quickly added, "that progress has been made in all the preceding years since the League has been organized and was made possible by the untiring efforts of past Presidents R.H. Pitts and Joseph A. Collerain, part-time Managing Director Granville W. Elder, former officers and directors, and the loyal credit unions whose interest and support have brought the League thus far."

Edmonston himself told the delegates that, including two credit unions which had just voted to come into the League for 1940, the percentage of TCUL members among Texas credit unions had now reached 51 percent. And he predicted far greater things to come in the months ahead. "It is expected that more than 65 percent of the credit unions in Texas will belong to the League by the end of 1940, and within two years we should expect to have more than 80 percent in the League," he said.

If matters had not turned out as they did, it would be easy to dismiss any idea that, under the circumstances, there were some who took issue with the way in which Edmonston was conducting his job, earning his $816 annual salary and justifying his $1,102.95 in travel expenses for 1939. But, again, because of subsequent events, it should be noted that Edmonston included the following plea in his report to the 1940 annual meeting:

". . . those working full time on credit union work can accomplish very little without the wholehearted cooperation of those credit union leaders in the state that are so willing to use their own time freely to aid our cause. We sincerely hope that these fine people will continue to work with us in 1940."

At this writing, more than 43 years after the fact, it is difficult if not impossible to pinpoint the sources of opposition to Edmonston's leadership. But it is also plain that there definitely *was* such opposition. For one thing, there were still some undercurrents of resistance to the idea of a really strong statewide organization, and since Edmonston was the physical embodiment of the organization to most credit union people out in the field, he probably bore the brunt of this resistance. There also appears to have been a great deal of inter-city rivalry between such major credit union centers as Dallas, Houston and Fort Worth, and this, too, may have played a part in Edmonston's falling out of favor. There was also the conviction in certain quarters that he was simply costing the League and its members too much money. Although the amounts involved may sound inconsequential by today's standards, Edmonston was personally accounting for more than one-third of the total League budget through his salary and expenses.

Under Edmonston's direction, the League established another monthly publication, *The Texas Credit*

Union League Bulletin, to replace the earlier newsletter, which had succumbed to a shortage of manpower and finances after a few issues. The *Bulletin* made its first appearance in July 1940 and became a permanent communications medium. It was intended, according to Edmonston, "to keep the credit unions in Texas regularly informed as to the current developments within the movement."

It is safe to say that, as the world at large became increasingly enveloped in crisis and conflict, the League and its leadership found itself embroiled in a deepening crisis of its own—a crisis that would only end with Edmonston's total departure from the picture.

As of August 1940, Edmonston was still talking bravely about the expansion of the League and his role in that expansion. "Give us more members and we will show you greater accomplishments," he pledged in *The Bridge* that month. "Our motto is 'Forward March.' " In that same commentary in the national publication, Edmonston referred to a 1940-41 League budget of $10,500, which had been approved by the board at its annual meeting in August. "We have every reason to believe that this amount will be available," he concluded. Of that amount, $2,250 was earmarked as salary for the managing director and another $1,500 was set aside for travel expenses for him—a total of $3,750. For the period, this was an extremely attractive financial package, and it shortly became apparent that many of the League's leaders did not feel they were getting their money's worth from Edmonston.

Almost certainly, it was a situation that deteriorated steadily and perceptibly over the next six or seven months, but because of the lack of records and surviving eyewitness accounts during this time, it appeared to come to a head with the suddenness of a thunderclap when the TCUL's Board of Directors met at the Lamar Hotel in Houston on the warm Sunday morning of April 20, 1941.

According to the recollections of League Secretary-Treasurer C.E. Burdick in a *Bulletin* article published more than eighteen years after the fact, strong sentiment to "get rid" of Edmonston emerged at the League's annual convention in Waco a short time prior to the Houston board meeting. "Delegates were at the meeting from West, South, North and Central Texas (as well as from Burdick's own East Texas district), all with only one thing in mind—get rid of that managing director," Burdick recalled. "In caucus it was decided that to accomplish our objective it would be necessary that certain League directors be replaced . . . "

No more than six weeks earlier, Edmonston had attended a meeting of the Executive Committee in Dallas without apparent incident. He had read a report from the Legislative Committee covering a recent meeting with the State Banking Commission, which was routinely accepted. But during this session of the Executive Committee, members accepted "with regrets and thanks for his past services" the resignation of W.R. Eddings as a member of the Board of Directors, and quickly replaced him with R.E. "Hack" Miller of the Fort Worth Railway Postal Clerks Credit Union. The minutes of the Executive Committee meeting on March 2, 1941, note that this action was taken "so that the Fort Worth district would have representation at the (next) meeting of the Board of Directors." No mention was made of this fact, but Miller was no friend of Edmonston's, as subsequent events proved.

This may have been the final straw in the slow erosion of support for Edmonston on the board, which by now was a totally different body from the one that had directed the activities of the league just two or three years earlier. Such leaders as Pitts, Judson, Elder, Thomas, and Collerain were no longer around, and the Board of Directors which assembled at 10 a.m. on that fateful April Sunday consisted of the following (all of whom were present): A.S. Anderson, San Antonio; C.E. Burdick, Longview; O.F. Burgdorf, Texarkana; G.V. Carroll, Houston; W.D. Culbreath, Houston; B.F. Dooley, Jr., Port Arthur; Phil Harvey, Wink; R.E. Miller, Fort Worth; H.W. Mecklenburg, Newgulf; H.G. Turner, Houston; W.D. Turbeville, San Antonio; and H.B. Yates, Dallas.

The careful geographic balance of the board, which had occupied the League's founders at its organizational meeting six and one-half years earlier, no longer existed. Membership on the board was now heavily weighted toward the southern half of the state, with three directors, including TCUL President Carroll, coming from Houston. Two were from San Antonio and two others were from the Gulf Coast area. All of West Texas now had only one representative on the board. So did Edmonston's hometown of Dallas. The League's two most powerful elective offices were now filled by Houstonians—Carroll as president and Culbreath, who had just recently succeeded Thomas as secretary-treasurer.

The morning portion of the all-day session was taken up with seemingly routine business. Culbreath read the financial statement and Carroll made a number of committee appointments. Edmonston himself gave a report on his recent activities in Austin, advising that a bill covering supervision of state-chartered credit unions and a bill to increase borrowing limits had both been favorably voted out of committee. He also warned that an omnibus tax bill, House Bill 8, then pending before the Legislature, contained a clause of major concern to state-chartered credit unions. The bill provided for a franchise tax of $1 per $1,000, Edmonston said, but efforts were being made to rewrite the bill so as to continue the exemption credit unions had enjoyed from such taxation since 1937. Edmonston did not realize it at the time, no doubt, but when he finished his report and sat down, he had also concluded his last official act as managing director of the Texas Credit Union League.

Immediately after lunch, the crisis exploded. Carroll reconvened the meeting for its afternoon session at 1:45 p.m., and the tense moment for which everybody had surely been waiting was at hand. The minutes of the session make it clear that the question of Edmonston's future with the League had been under consideration for some time. Those minutes read as follows:

"Carroll stated that the question of appointing a managing director had been postponed until this meeting and asked Mr. Edmonston if he would like to address the board on this subject. Edmonston read a prepared statement giving his qualifications and accomplishments in the credit union field since 1931 and requested that he be reappointed to his present position as managing director. Edmonston excused himself from the room in order that the directors could discuss the position more freely.

"Carroll read a resolution from the Dallas Chapter adopted at their April meeting requesting that Edmonston be retained as managing director, also a letter from the Dairyland Credit Union and the Postal Employees Credit Union, both of Dallas, making the same request. Mr. Miller presented a letter from the Fort Worth Chapter, making a request that the board make a change in directors. The question of retaining Mr. Edmonston was discussed for one and one-half hours and it was finally decided that Edmonston should not be retained as managing director. Mr. Miller made a motion that Mr. Edmonston be no longer designated as managing director of the TCUL, seconded by C.E. Burdick, motion carried. Turner moved that the board offer Mr. Edmonston the position of office manager at a salary of $187.50 but with no expense account, seconded by Mecklenburg. Miller moved that Turner's motion be amended to read that the position be on a temporary basis, seconded by Dooley, and carried."

Thus, the deed was accomplished. Today, more than four decades later, it is impossible to pinpoint all the underlying factors in Edmonston's dismissal. But it is also impossible not to notice that Miller was probably his strongest and most vocal adversary on the board, making both the motion to dismiss him and the motion to make his subsequent position as office manager temporary rather than permanent. The rivalry that was then so acutely felt between Dallas and Fort Worth in general is also obvious from the minutes, with the Dallas Chapter of the League endorsing Edmonston and the Fort Worth Chapter calling for his ouster. On the other hand, the minutes also leave many intriguing questions unanswered: Did Yates, Edmonston's fellow Dallasite and fellow member of the Dallas Teachers Credit Union, rise to Edmonston's defense? What kind of heated exchanges might have taken place between Miller and Yates, a man who was admired for his strong leadership but not his tact, as we shall see later? And just how close was the vote in the final showdown? Today, as we look back, we can only guess.

The move hit CUNA like a punch to the shortribs, and left the national organization shaking its head in confusion. As Charles Eickel. CUNA's southern field representative, observed several months later in *The Bridge:* "At first glance it appeared that Texas had taken a backward step when in April . . . it was decided to dispense with the services of their managing director and to handle all of the League activities through correspondence."

But as Eickel noted later in the same article, the move was "only a temporary measure," a quick sidestep, rather than a step backward. The TCUL had no intention whatsoever of doing away with the position of fulltime managing director, and, in fact, already had a replacement for Edmonston lined up.

In the meantime, in June 1941, the League opened its first real office in Room 515 of the National Standard Building at the corner of Main Street and Walker Avenue in downtown Houston, not far from Foley's

Department Store. A fulltime secretary, Helen Wood, was hired to work in the office by TCUL secretary-treasurer Bill Culbreath, who proudly reported to CUNA that all correspondence received at the office was being answered within 24 hours. "Bill says this service has made many friends for the League and likewise has brought in new credit unions as members of the League," *The Bridge* reported. "Also, many inquiries have been made about credit union organization since the opening of the office."

Miss Wood, the efficient secretary responsible for this, was destined to play as vital a role in the growth of the credit union movement as anyone in Texas over the next three decades, although it would often be as a background force, rather than as a high-profile official. During one critical period during World War II (which will be dealt with in detail later), she would become, in effect, a one-woman headquarters for the League. And later, as the wife of W.S. MacKinnon, TCUL president from 1971 through 1978, she would contribute to the credit union cause for many years.

Ironically, the beginning of Helen Wood's association with the League could almost be classified as a lucky accident, however. She had been working as a secretary for a Houston motor freight line, but decided to quit this job just at the time when TCUL was looking for a secretary. Her father, a close acquaintance of Culbreath's, happened to mention her to Culbreath, who contacted her about coming to work for the League. "I thought it was a good opportunity," she recalled some 38 years later in an interview. "We had a very small office, and I felt very important—until the board meetings came along, and I realized I was just a small cog in the wheel of operations. They relied heavily on me, though, and it was really a very congenial, very nice group. I just did everything there was to do in the office—answered all the telephone inquiries, filled the orders for credit union forms, handled the mail and the banking, everything."

Edmonston, who had accepted the Board of Directors' offer of temporary employment following his explusion as managing director, also worked with Miss Wood in the Houston office for a couple of months. Other TCUL directors who assisted in setting up the new office, besides Culbreath, were Guy Carroll, the League president and a member of the Texaco Houston Federal Credit Union, and Herbert G. Turner of the United Gas Credit Union. As a tragic footnote, Culbreath's role in obtaining the office and the services of Miss Wood was his last major contribution to the TCUL. He died suddenly that July, only a few weeks after the office opened, and was succeeded as the League's secretary-treasurer by Cecil Burdick of Longview.

All in all, the period from early spring to late summer 1941 had seen more crisis and change than any similar period in the League's brief history. By August, when James A. "Jimmie" Parker arrived on the scene to assume duties as its new managing director—amid loud cheers from its leadership—the TCUL was more than ready for a return to normalcy. Unfortunately, however, even more trying, turbulent—and abnormal—times lay just ahead.

"Regulation W"—and War

By September 1941, the United States, although still offically a neutral non-combatant, was preparing frantically for war. The Roosevelt Administration had plunged headlong into an all-out effort to strengthen the nation's military establishment and increase its capabilities for defense production. While the public still clung to hopes of peace, the odds of America being drawn into the holocaust that was engulfing Europe and Asia grew larger by the day. Hitler had already overrrun the European continent and now menaced Great Britain across the English Channel. In the Far East, Japanese troops had knifed deep into China and were now poised to invade the rich French and British colonies of Southeast Asia. Meanwhile, Nazi Panzer divisions, with the conquest of France and Belgium now secure and the British army still reeling from its narrow escape at Dunkirk, roared 300 miles into the heartland of Russia, threatening Moscow itself.

In short, America had suddenly discovered itself an island of uneasy peace in the midst of an entire planet ravaged by bloody conflict. The isolationism and introspection that had characterized the Depression-ridden 1930s was gone, blown away by the winds of war. Washington was feverishly gearing up for the most titanic struggle of all time, and urgently trying to convince the fearful, reluctant "man on the street" to go along. And the burgeoning credit union movement in Texas and the rest of the nation, it soon became apparent, would also be asked to make its share of sacrifices in the name of national defense.

While the public consciousness was largely occupied with such historic measures as the Selective Service Act, under which tens of thousands of young men were being drafted, and the Lend Lease Act, under which the United States was desperately funneling war materials to beleaguered Britain, there were countless other new laws, regulations, and presidential directives emanating from Washington that would have serious consequences for the average citizen. One that affected credit unions and their millions of members in particular was an order issued through the Board of Governors of the Federal Reserve System. It was known as "Regulation W," and its intent was to impose sharp restrictions on consumer credit, just at a time when the return of prosperity had propelled credit buying to an all-time high.

The order came directly from President Roosevelt, and it forced credit unions and other lending institutions to curtail virtually all consumer loans of less than $1,000 which were repayable in two or more installments. There were a few exceptions, such as mortgage and home improvement loans, educational loans and those to cover medical, hospital or funeral expenses. But the loans with which Americans had been buying automobiles, washing machines, refrigerators, and other heavy goods were suddenly made nonexistent by "Regulation W." The order, at least in the administration's view, was consistent with the war effort and was designed to achieve four distinct objectives:

(1) A reduction of consumer demand for such products as automobiles, thus releasing plant facilities for the manufacture of war materials.

(2) Prevention of inflationary price increases in the event that consumer demand continued unchecked after production was decreased.

(3) A buildup of both demand and consumer credit capabilities toward the time when defense needs would be met and factories could be returned to normal production, thereby stabilizing employment (no one could then foresee that this time was four long years away).

(4) A reduction of the average citizen's personal debt, in the event that a future cutback in defense production should trigger a resumption of the Depression that had just abated.

Today, the restrictions of loans under $1,000 would have negligible effect on consumer buying of heavy goods, since the average automobile now costs $8,000 to $10,000 and even refrigerators can easily cost $2,000. But in 1941, $1,000 represented a year's pay for many American wage earners. And after a reasonable down payment, it was a large enough amount to finance the purchase of almost any new or used car, except for the most luxurious models.

"We are really being asked to change seriously our method of living," said CUNA President William Reid, writing in *The Bridge*. "The money which we have previously spent for luxuries and semi-luxuries must now be utilized in a defense effort. We cannot have the number of automobiles we desire and at the same time increase the number of airplanes for defense. Therefore, we are all being asked to use our old automobiles a little longer, and credit unions and other credit agencies are being requested to retard the demand for automobiles and other articles by restricting credit."

Although the curtailment of auto and other consumer loans struck at the very heart of many credit unions' loan programs, both the national organization and the state leagues sought at first to comply gracefully. "It is our duty as citizens to stick to the letter and spirit of the law," *The Bridge* editorialized. But it quickly added: "But it is also our duty as citizens of a democracy to watch the law, see how it works and if it works unjustly, holler about it."

A lot of "hollering" was about to take place.

CUNA dispatched four representatives to Washington to lobby for modifications in the loan restrictions imposed by the order. They were instrumental in winning the exemption for loans covering medical, hospital, dental, and funeral expenses from the original provisions of the regulation, but they also sought other modifications. As CUNA's Tom Doig explained: "We feel that after a loan has been on the books of a credit union for at least six months and one-third of the loan has been repaid, the credit union should have the right to renew this loan for another eighteen months without a statement of necessity (which Regulation W required), provided neither the original loan nor the renewal is being used to finance the purchase of a listed article . . . We also feel that in many cases the requirement that monthly payments be in amounts of five dollars or more (another stipulation of the order) is unjust and works a hardship on those people having the least . . . "

Nevertheless, the urgency of the nation's defense effort was not lost on credit union leaders. Writing in the October 1941 edition of *The Bridge*, Doig took pains to make this clear. "There are many things about the regulation we do not like," he said. "It smacks of class legislation and seems to place the burden of the defense effort on the shoulders of the man least able to pay. We have protested to the government on this score. On the other hand, we are told that democracy itself is at stake and since credit unions could flourish under no other kind of government, it is necessary first to preserve the democracy and second to preserve our credit unions as best we can during the emergency."

Obviously, the severe curtailment of consumer credit could be expected to have an adverse and limiting effect on the credit union movement in general and on the growth of individual credit unions in particular. Small wonder that many credit union leaders across the country viewed "Regulation W" as a threat to their very existence. But in the final analysis, it may have been the over-reaction of these leaders to the order which posed a greater threat than the regulation itself.

By November, *The Bridge* felt compelled to warn against this over-reaction in an editorial aptly entitled "Take your neck out of that noose!" "Regulation W" was not a rope, it pointed out, and there was no need for credit unions to hang themselves with it.

"There are dangerous signs that some credit unions are trying too hard to reduce their volume," the editorial said. "The majority believe that if a defense program is necessary, no effort should be spared in making it effective. There is plenty of logic in this.

"But not long ago the President was saying that the basis of defense is sound civilian morale. Credit unions have done as much to build morale as any agency in the country. We still have a contribution to make, but we can't make it if we use Regulation W as an excuse to cut our throats . . .

Managing Director Jimmie Parker in 1941

Joseph Collerain, one of Texas' earliest credit union pioneers and second president of the League

Managing Director Jim Barry (left) early in a TCUL career that spanned more than 30 years

H. B. Yates (at far right in photo at right) poses with other Texas credit unionists to promote Defense Bond sales during World War II

"The Federal Reserve Board has not placed a stigma on consumer loans. There is nothing shameful or unpatriotic about borrowing. Many of the best purposes for making loans the regulation has hardly touched: Medical, educational, consolidation of debts, home improvements. There are still legitimate ways of financing the purchase of durable goods, and the board has not wished to close them all. We should be unpatriotic if we let a little red tape get us down; we should be unpatriotic if we failed in our duty to our members and drove them back to the high-rate money lenders."

Indeed, upon close examination and further interpretation, it did appear that numerous loopholes existed in the regulation—loopholes that would be used to avoid severe cutbacks in credit union loan programs. Among these were exemptions that allowed: (a) loans to dealers in listed articles, both wholesale and retail, to finance the purchase of such articles for resale; (b) loans of not more than twelve months to bona fide auto salesmen for the purchase of demonstrators; (c) loans for certain types of insurance premiums; (d) loans to farmers for general agricultural purposes, if approved by the Federal Farm Security Administration; (e) loans repaid in one lump sum; (f) loans of more than $1,000 secured by collateral other than a lien on a listed article. Credit union lobbyists had also obtained a revision, effective November 1, under which loans could be renewed if the borrower signed a statement of necessity.

A few weeks later, of course, the entire matter became academic. On December 7, 1941, Japanese planes bombed Pearl Harbor and America was suddenly plunged into the thick of the war for which it had been preparing. For the duration of that war, most of the consumer goods covered by "Regulation W" would be totally unavailable to the people of Texas and the rest of the nation on any condition or at any price. By early 1942, the entire production capability of the greatest industrial power in the history of the world would be shifted to war materials. The American public would have to wait for four long years to purchase its next new cars, refrigerators and washing machines. In the meantime, they and their credit unions would have plenty to think about besides "Regulation W."

Indirectly, however, the hotly disputed federal order did claim one very important "casualty," insofar as the Texas Credit Union League was concerned. The League's new managing director, Jimmie Parker, had scarcely gotten settled in his job when the furor over "Regulation W" hit the TCUL. It was the first major crisis to be faced by Parker, a Mississippi native who had come to Texas after serving as managing director of the Louisiana Credit Union League for ten months. Only 32, Parker already had nearly a decade of credit union experience, having first become involved in the movement in 1932, when a credit union was formed at the Federal Land Bank in New Orleans, where he worked.

Parker had impressed officials of the TCUL when they met him at a CUNA convention in Jacksonville, Florida, in the spring of 1941, and when they moved to dispose of Edmonston, they also moved to woo Parker away from their neighboring state to the east as the TCUL's new managing director. Clearly, they were very impressed with their "catch." In introducing Parker to the League's membership, the *Bulletin* praised him for his "remarkable record of achievement in the credit union field" and for his "broad experience and background."

Ironically, Parker officially took over as managing director on September 1, 1941—the same date that "Regulation W" took effect. Among the provisions of the order that concerned Parker and the League most was one requiring credit unions to register with the federal government, the same as any other business institution engaged in selling goods or making loans. As Parker himself recalled the situation in a 1979 interview: "The Federal Reserve Bank was designated to administer this federal regulation and there was a branch of the bank in Houston (the Federal Reserve's district headquarters is in Dallas). In an attempt to bring as much information as possible to the credit unions, I went over to the Houston office and requested a speaker to address the credit unions at the Houston Chapter meeting."

At this dinner meeting, Parker talked at length with the Federal Reserve officials who attended, introduced them to chapter members and generally developed a friendly relationship with them. Not long after that, he made a point of going by their office to thank them personally for their help. By this time, the war had started and many observers foresaw extremely difficult times ahead for the credit union movement and for the TCUL. In passing, Parker voiced his concern about the situation, and received a surprising response from the Federal Reserve officials. As he remembers it:

"I happened to comment during our conversation that if the war got any worse I might be looking for a job. I said that more out of fear that it might actually happen than out of any feeling of reality. Shortly after that, they called me and said they wanted to talk to me about something, and they offered me a position. I told them I wasn't interested in giving up my work unless I had to and I had had no notice that the credit unions were in such dire straits. But they mentioned that it was just for the duration anyway, and sometime later, in talking with the president (of the TCUL), who was then H.B. Yates, he told me it might not be a bad idea. He was sure the Board of Directors would give me a leave of absence."

Parker was, indeed, granted a one-year leave of absence to work for the Federal Reserve System. At the end of that time, in December 1942, Parker informed officials at the bank that he was returning to the League, but it simply was not to be. "They offered me a permanent position," he explained, "and it was somewhat attractive in terms of pensions and long-range opportunities, (so) I accepted the position and came to Dallas."

Parker's departure from the League—again leaving it temporarily without a managing director—became official on January 1, 1943. But his contribution to the credit union movement was far from over. He would later serve as president of the TCUL's Dallas chapter and would establish himself as an important friend of credit unions within the federal structure over a period of many years. He ultimately became a vice president of the Dallas Federal Reserve Bank and served in that capacity until his retirement in 1974.

The loss of Parker was keenly felt by the League, but when he first took his leave of absence a few weeks after Pearl Harbor everyone assumed he would return as managing director when times improved. Those were days when events seemed to move with dizzying speed and when all business crises were totally overshadowed by the trauma of seeing sons, husbands, and fathers leaving for military service, by rationing and shortages on the home front and by the disastrous war news pouring out of Europe and the Pacific.

Like everyone else, Texas credit unions and their members were stunned by the war and all its dread implications, and they were determined to do their part. In a year that had been crammed with important events from start to finish—including passage of a bill by the Texas Legislature to provide the first systematic auditing of credit union books by the State Banking Commission, lowering of the TCUL's dues schedule from 4 percent to 3 percent of gross income, the ouster of Edmonston, the hiring of Parker, and, of course, "Regulation W"—the war was by far the most important of all.

A major accomplishment of the year was the qualification of credit unions as agents for the sale of U.S. Defense Bonds, which were soon being sold by the thousands by credit unions across Texas. The League and its various chapters also presented a series of meetings on "Credit Unions and Defense" to help prepare members for the many implications of the war effort and the pressures of wartime. From the very outset, there was never any doubt that the defense of the nation came first with the credit union people in Texas. As TCUL President Carroll stressed in his year-end message to League members amid the tumult and terror of those early days of the war:

"With dictators reaching out for more and more territory, the very foundations of our democratic way of life are threatened. To successfully combat these demons of selfishness, jealousy, envy, and intolerance, we must present a united front; we must present a nation working in complete harmony and cooperation. The millions of credit union members working in this country of ours will be found in the front lines of defense with their dollars, their labor and their lives.

"They will never forget to REMEMBER PEARL HARBOR."

The Defense Effort

In many respects, the war years were to be a time of limbo and stagnation for the Texas credit union movement. Amid the emotional strains and pressures of global conflict, it was simply impossible to carry on business as usual. Not only was there a shrinking demand for loans and other credit union services, there was also a sudden shortage of credit union members, as tens of thousands of Texans marched off to war. But there were also a few bright spots during those trying and troubled times, and one of the brightest of these was the manner in which credit unions and their members rallied to the support of the national defense effort through the sale and purchase of Defense Bonds.

During the first weeks and months of World War II, patriotic fervor was at an all-time high. Stunned and angered by Japan's surprise attack, the civilian public saw Defense Bonds as one of the few ways it could actively fight back, and sales boomed. By January 1,

1942, at least 75 Texas credit unions were acting as agents of the U.S. Treasury Department in the sale of Defense Bonds and Stamps, and the state's larger credit unions were reporting impressive figures. The Humble Employees Federal Credit Union of Houston, for example, showed more than $18,000 worth of bonds and stamps sold during the final month of 1941. Houston Sinclair Employees Federal Credit Union, meanwhile, erected a "Bond Sale Barometer Board" to show off its bond and stamp sales, which passed $16,000 by early January.

The zeal with which Texas credit unions approached the Defense Bond campaign is exemplified by the following letter to the TCUL membership from Granville W. Elder, treasurer of the Houston Postal Credit Union and former treasurer and managing director of the League, in which he set forth a plan for credit unions everywhere to follow.

"I beg to submit a plan which I hope may be given nationwide attention to increase the sale of Defense Stamps and Bonds throughout the country," he wrote. "If accepted as a national project by all credit unions in the U.S., it will mean a minimum of one million dollars each month will be deposited into the U.S. Treasury toward our national security. A minimum figure is used for the reason that every wage earner, no matter how small his salary, can pledge to purchase a 25-cent Defense Stamp each month from credit union treasurers. Doubtless much more than this sum will be purchased to help our country at war.

"Here is the plan. Each credit union (is) to purchase a supply of U.S. Defense Stamps and on each pay period when payments or deposits are made into the credit union the treasurer of same will ask each member to pledge, along with his payments each month, a minimum of 25 cents monthly or more . . ."

As long as a member kept up his monthly pledge, Elder continued, he would be given a Credit Union

Victory Button to wear. These red, white, and blue buttons were being made available by CUNA for a small charge to participating credit unions, and so many members were soon wearing them that those who were not became exceptionally noticeable. Elder predicted that his plan would result in 10,000 credit unions with 3.25 million members joining the defense effort.

"We placed this plan into operation in the Houston Postal Credit Union on January 16," he concluded, "and to date (about two weeks later) we are proud to say the membership has cooperated 100 percent. We have every reason to feel the pledge will be kept 'for the duration.' We hope we have started something."

Just how much of Elder's projections were actually realized can only be guessed today, but his plan was published in the TCUL *Bulletin* for January-February 1942 under the heading "All Out for Victory!" and was approved by both CUNA and the Federal Credit Union Section. It was adopted by a number of Texas credit unions and probably by many others outside the state, although there are no records to indicate just how widespread adoption of the plan actually was.

Elder's fellow Houstonians provided some of the most impressive responses to such pleas. Besides the two Houston credit unions mentioned above, several others also compiled outstanding Defense Bond sales records. In a letter to Managing Director Parker, W.Q. Rothwell, assistant secretary-treasurer of the Houston Fire Fighters Federal Credit Union, proudly noted bond and stamp sales totalling nearly $9,400 as of early January. In addition, the credit union itself had purchased $13,000 worth of Defense Bonds from its surplus, Rothwell said.

"The job you are doing in participating in the sale of Defense Bonds and Stamps is commendable and places your credit union with those that are out in front in this program," Parker responded in a letter dated January 28, 1942.

Although the defense effort was certainly foremost on everyone's mind, there was other important League business to attend to as 1942 got under way. The Board of Directors met in March to re-elect G.V. Carroll as League president. And at an earlier Executive Committee meeting in Fort Worth on January 25, several key items of business were transacted in a session described by the *Bulletin* as "one of the most important . . . in League history."

At that meeting, the committee—composed of Carroll, H.B. Yates, C.E. Burdick, H.G. Turner, and R.E. Miller—approved a new districting plan for the state, which was to be submitted to the delegates at the annual TCUL convention in Fort Worth in March. The plan, which was authored by Yates, called for dividing Texas into ten geographical subdivisions, each of which would have at least one representative on the board of directors. Under the "Y Plan," as it was dubbed, the total number of directors would remain at twelve, since the two districts with the largest number of credit unions would be entitled to two members each on the board. Four of the ten districts designated consisted of single counties—Harris, Dallas, Bexar, and Tarrant. The other six were multi-county districts which could be generally described as conforming to the following geographic sections of the state: The Panhandle, West Texas, South Texas, East Texas, Central Texas, and a narrow strip of North Texas along the Red River.

The plan was an attempt to circumvent the inter-city rivalries that had led to repeated crises among the League's leadership. As the *Bulletin* explained it: "The effect of such a plan has not only the result of providing for a more equitable distribution of representation, but . . . will remove the election of the directorate completely from any element of partisanship or politics. Only those credit unions within a given district may make nominations for the director or directors to represent that district. Each district may have its own caucus and present to the convention in session the name or names of its choice for formal election to the board by the assembly. In the event more names are placed in nomination than the district is eligible for, the assembly in convention will decide by ballot who shall be elected.

These changes were also reflected in an amendment to the bylaws of the League, one of a dozen amendments enacted by delegates at the March 27-28 annual state convention. Other amendments dealt with such matters as the obligations of league membership, the manner in which resignations, suspensions and expulsions of League members should be handled, an increase in the number of League vice presidents from one to three, and the establishment of a new minimum and maximum schedule of dues (10 cents to 35 cents for each individual credit union member per year).

For the first time, the League joyously reported a surplus in its operating budget for 1941-42 of some $718. At the time, of the 408 credit unions in Texas, 261 held membership in the League—64 percent of the total.

Even before Parker took his leave of absence to work for the Federal Reserve System, the activities of the Houston office were focused primarily on maintaining an active network of TCUL chapters across the state (by early 1942, there were 11 such chapters, located in Corpus Christi, Dallas, Fort Worth, Houston, Galveston, Longview, Port Arthur, Edinburg, San Antonio, Waco, and Wichita Falls), and organizing new credit unions. A shortage of staff made it extremely difficult to devote attention to building up the dues-paying membership of the League.

Parker, who spent much of his time as managing director traveling the state in a 1941 Chevrolet, found such wartime measures as gasoline rationing and the shortage of tires and other automotive equipment severely limited his movements. Since a minimum of 100 people was required for a credit union charter in those days, Parker recalled, effective face-to-face communication meant hopping from one major Texas city to another, "all the way from the lower Rio Grande Valley to Amarillo." It was "quite expensive and time-consuming," according to Parker.

Once Parker took his leave, a major portion of the burden of keeping the lines of communication open fell to the League's elected officials, especially H.B. Yates, who soon succeeded Carroll as TCUL president. According to all who remember him—including some who did not like him at all—Yates was a tireless, dynamic, "let's-get-it-done" individual, and one who did not flinch from the prospect of rubbing some people the wrong way. Over the next decade and a half, he was to make a great deal of history, and more than a few enemies, in both the state and national credit union movements. He also was to change the overall course of the Texas Credit Union League by almost singlehandedly uprooting the Houston office and moving it permanently to Dallas.

Altering Course

Yates was a man who left deep and lasting impressions on almost everyone with whom he dealt. One of the people who knew him best was Jack A. Mitchell, former TCUL president, first president of the Credit Union Executive Society (CUES) in 1962-1964 and former president and general manager of the Dallas Teachers Credit Union, where Yates was also a member. Mitchell, in a 1983 interview, revealed a great deal about Yates' leadership during the turbulent war years of the 1940s, and about why he eventually moved the TCUL's headquarters to Dallas.

"In 1942," Mitchell recalled, "I moved from Ennis to Dallas to teach school and met Yates at old Forest Avenue High School, where he and I were both on the faculty. I taught business and he taught social studies, and we had the same off-period, so we spent a lot of time together. I watched him, day after day, dictating letters and taking care of all kinds of League business. After Parker left, Yates was trying to fill the post of managing director as well as League president. He simply *was* the League at that time.

"During those years, I know that every Friday he got on that Southern Pacific train at 5 or 5:30 in the afternoon and went to Houston, where he spent all weekend tending to League business. Helen Wood was the only person in the Houston office, and there was just too much for one employee to handle. He did this week after week until I don't see how he kept going."

Yates took over the reins of the TCUL as its president after Carroll was transferred for business reasons to Joliet, Illinois, only a few weeks after his March re-election to the League's top post. When the Board of Directors met on June 7, 1942, Carroll was absent and the meeting was presided over by First Vice President Turner, who announced Carroll's transfer out of the state and read a letter from Carroll tendering his resignation as president. No formal action to replace him was taken at the time, however.

It was not until an Executive Committee meeting on September 13, 1942, at the Baker Hotel in Dallas that pressure from the League's chapters in Dallas and Fort Worth spurred action on naming a new League president. Carroll had stressed in his resignation letter that he felt a new president should be elected, since he would be living out of the state indefinitely, and now C.W. Hudson of Dallas and R.E. Miller of Fort Worth presented formal resolutions from their chapters calling for the committee to name a new president.

After the committee voted to accept Carroll's resignation "with regret," Yates nominated Turner as Carroll's successor, but Turner declined, citing business pressures and the fact that his "draft classification had been moved up to 1-A," meaning that he might soon be called into military service. Turner then nominated

Yates for the job, and on a motion by Burdick, seconded by Turner, nominations were declared closed. Turner's name was left in nomination despite his protests, but Yates was elected by a vote of three to one, with Yates himself undoubtedly casting the lone vote for Turner. Yates expressed his appreciation, pledged to do his best to serve the League, and received a vote of confidence in which the Executive Committee "assure(d) him of their complete cooperation."

The election was the culmination of a rapid rise to prominence within the League hierarchy by Yates. Not only had he been serving as a League vice president, but was also co-editor (with fellow Dallasite C.W. Hudson) of the *Bulletin*, chairman of the Legislative Committee, and one of the TCUL's three national directors (Carroll and Turner being the other two).

Those long, regular Friday afternoon train trips to Houston, which began that September, soon left their mark on Yates. Parker was now spending virtually all his time working for the Federal Reserve, although he did continue to attend Board of Directors meetings and serve as recording secretary for the League. But the essential day-to-day business of the TCUL was carried out by Helen Wood, with occasional part-time help, and Yates. And the longer this situation continued, the longer the 240 miles between Dallas and Houston became.

By the time the Board of Directors convened on January 17, 1943, Yates was actively agitating to move the League office to Dallas. At the meeting, he went so far as to mention an opening he had located for Miss Wood in which she could "possibly combine League and school work." Parker, who urged that the Houston office be kept open and functioning, countered that Miss Wood did not want to move to Dallas, although she had expressed willingness to go there temporarily to help someone else learn the office procedures.

After considerable discussion, the board voted to keep the office in Houston and gave Miss Wood a raise. But it also indicated that the matter was far from closed and that the office might still be moved on short notice when directors voted to pay Miss Wood a month's salary in lieu of notice "if it became necessary to terminate her services" because of a change in location.

At least Yates was not required to travel to Houston for the 1943 annual meeting, which was styled a "Credit Union War Conference" and held on March 20 at the Adolphus Hotel in Dallas. Although credit unions were being liquidated right and left as a result of the war, the delegates were still intent on showing their patriotism and support of the war effort. Bergengren himself was on hand to help answer questions during a forum on loans to men in military service. Much of the business was grim in character, however, and it was plain that the League was suffering in many areas. This was reflected in various committee reports, including one from Yates' Legislative Committee, which said bluntly that the committee had "distinguished itself more by what it did not do than by what it did for the past year."

P.W. Harvey, chairman of the Dues and Membership Committee, summed up the situation reasonably well when he said: "We have by no means accepted a defeatist attitude toward constructive work on behalf of the membership, or an effort to bolster credit union service against certain discouraging aspects of the war. The conditions that face the country today, however, are quite beyond our control and have resulted in your board considering at some length a program of war-time economy."

A number of budget-cutting measures were approved, with one of the largest savings coming in the form of the salary no longer being paid to Parker, who was referred to in the minutes for the first time as "former managing director." This reference, which may have come from Parker himself, since he was serving as recording secretary, was not technically correct, as he was still on leave and had not officially resigned. There was, in fact, some discussion about where his salary would come from if his services should be required during the last half of the year.

When the Board of Directors met the following day, March 21, Yates was re-elected president by acclamation, after Turner had again declined Yates' nomination for the presidency. All other offices also were filled by acclamation—Turner, first vice president; Miller, second vice president; H.W. Mecklenburg, third vice president; and Burdick, secretary-treasurer. Yates was now firmly in control as the League's chief executive, but he would be forced to endure another full year of weekend train trips to Houston before that matter was resolved— and even then, the moving controversy almost forced him out of office before the board yielded to his wishes.

During this period, there was considerable sentiment for simply closing the League office completely until the war was over and conditions improved. At a board meeting on March 17, 1944, directors rejected a resolution from the Fort Worth Chapter calling for the office to be closed. At the same meeting, however, the board also accepted a resolution from the Dallas Chapter calling for the employment of a full-time managing director and stipulating that "if it is necessary to close the League office to accomplish this, we recommend that this be done."

CUNA was also applying pressure for the TCUL board to find a new managing director. As early as July 1943, the national organization dispatched two representatives to a Board of Directors meeting in Houston to urge the League to "place a man in the field" immediately. The two, CUNA Regional Vice President Harold Moses and Southern Field Secretary C.F. Eickel, asked the board to take action on the spot. But, although the directors did set $3,000 aside in the 1944 budget for a managing director's salary and expenses, they allowed the position to remain in limbo for the time being. In fact, another full year was to pass before the matter was finally resolved. In the meantime, the League leadership had to decide if it was going to maintain an office and if so, where.

The red-hot issue of relocating TCUL headquarters came to a sudden head at a board meeting following another "War Conference" annual meeting, this time at Houston's Rice Hotel, on March 18, 1944. One major item of business on the directors' agenda was the election of officers, and, as expected, Yates was quickly nominated for re-election as president. But by this juncture, the blunt-spoken Yates made it crystal-clear that he had endured as many weekend train trips between Dallas and Houston as he could stand. He did so by refusing to accept renomination for the presidency, citing the difficulties relating to the fact that the League office "was not in the same city in which the president resides."

Whether Yates was merely fed up to the point that he no longer cared or it was a calculated gamble to win the relocation of the office is open to conjecture. Obviously taken aback by his refusal of the nomination, the board could have turned to someone else, but they did not. Significantly, they moved to appease Yates instead. As the minutes of the meeting note: "Mr. Turner asked Mr. Yates if he would accept the position (of president) if the office was moved to Dallas. Mr. Yates answered that he would."

Yates was quickly re-elected on that basis, but even then, his fellow directors refused to come to grips with the transfer of the office on which his election was predicated. Just how bitterly contested the move really was is illustrated by what happened next.

Director Frank McLain of Amarillo, arguing that a Dallas office would better serve the needs of the League's membership because of its more central location, made a motion that the office be moved there.

There was a great deal of spirited debate before the motion came to a vote, and during the discussion Director W.D. Turbeville of San Antonio argued loudly and at length against the move and the motion. The vote, when it finally came, was by secret ballot, and it ended in a 6-6 deadlock, which meant that the motion failed.

It had been a long day—one with more than its share of frustrations—and the weary directors on both sides of the controversy were still at loggerheads, seemingly no closer to resolving their differences than they had been hours earlier. Dispirited, they decided to adjourn, even though the situation was clearly intolerable.

The sequence of events that followed may have been a well-planned subterfuge by Yates or his supporters, but no one can say for sure. Immediately after adjournment of the regular board meeting, Turbeville, one of the most adamant foes of moving the office to Dallas, left the meeting room. All the other directors remained, milling around in little groups and talking. As they talked, a consensus began to develop that the board should reconvene in a special session to try to iron out its differences over the move. When the special session was called to order, Turbeville could not be located, but since a quorum was present without him, the meeting was nonetheless official. The motion to move the office to Dallas was made again, and this time it was approved. No record of he number of votes for and against the motion was kept in the minutes, but it seemed highly probable that Turbeville's absence made the difference.

(In recounting this dramatic chain of events, Jim Barry, who would shortly be hired as the League's new managing director, emphasizes that no real animosity existed between the Dallas and Houston members of the Board. "The feeling of rivalry between the two cities may have been felt at the grassroots, but these men were all good friends," Barry says. "Turner really felt that it was terrible for Yates to have to come to Houston all the time to conduct League business, and he was solidly in favor of moving the office. Yates, on the other hand, really wanted Turner to take over as president, but Turner was too busy. He much preferred moving the office to Dallas to being president.")

At any rate, the die was cast. The wording of the motion gave Yates the authority to move the office to Dallas "as soon as practicable," but the League president managed to resist the urge to effect the transfer immediately. It was decided to postpone the move until the continuing dilemma over the managing director's post could also be resolved.

That happened on July 16, 1944, at an Executive Committee meeting, also held at the Rice Hotel in Houston. Yates informed other committee members that Parker, who had been referred to as "former managing director" in official documents for more than a year, did, indeed, want to resign the post which he technically still held, in order to remain with the Federal Reserve System. A motion was quickly made and seconded, and the committee accepted Parker's resignation.

This step was a mere formality, since Parker's successor had been present throughout the meeting, and had, in fact, already been questioned as to what monthly salary he would accept as the TCUL's new managing director, even before Parker's resignation was official. His name was James M. Barry, a name that was to become synonymous with the League's top leadership over the next three and one-half decades. Before this historic committee meeting was adjourned, Barry had been elected the TCUL's new managing director, a position he would hold continuously until his retirement in 1975. His beginning salary was set at $275 per month (after he had declined to accept $250) and he was given a travel allowance not to exceed $175 per month. The expenses of his move from Kansas City, Kansas, where he had served as managing director of the Kansas-

Nebraska Regional Credit Union Association, were to be borne by the TCUL.

No sooner was Barry hired, effective September 15, 1944, than the Executive Committee again turned its attention to the projected transfer of the League office to Dallas. Concerned about the legality of the earlier Board of Directors vote, Fort Worth's R.E. Miller asked that the committee formally reaffirm the Board's action. Again, there was a lengthly discussion, and Miller finally made a motion, which seemed more or less to satisfy all concerned, that Yates, Turner, and Barry decide among themselves "when it will be practicable to move the office to Dallas." There was then still further discussion of "all facts and questions pertinent to the efficient operation of the League." What emerged was the "combined opinion," according to recording secretary Helen Wood's minutes, "that the office should be moved to Dallas on or about October 1, 1944."

A new era was about to begin.

Enduring "The Duration"

As 1944 drew to a close, there were numerous reasons to feel a new surge of optimism about the future of the League and the credit union movement in Texas, even though the present situation could best be described as a shambles. Yates had won his point and the decision to relocate TCUL headquarters was now irrevocable. And, at last, the League had a full-time managing director again. Too, the tide of the war had turned dramatically during the year just past. Mile by bloody mile, the Allies had driven the Germans up the Italian peninsula, and in June the most massive military operation in history had culminated in the Normandy invasion and the beginning of the drive to reclaim France from the Nazis. Victory was still far from secure, but for the first time since the dark hours after Pearl

111

Harbor, Americans could catch a glimpse of the proverbial "light at the end of the tunnel."

Still, there was to be no "quick fix" for the catastrophic effects that three years of war had produced for
the League and its member credit unions. From ranking
among the top three or four states in the number of credit
unions during the 1930s, Texas had tumbled to 13th
during the war years and was continuing to lose ground
rather steadily. During 1944, for example, the League
had managed to add 17 new members to its ranks, but it
had simultaneously lost eight member credit unions
through resignations. Not only that, but 31 Texas credit
unions had begun liquidation proceedings.

As Jim Barry remembers it, the attrition in the ranks
of the state's credit unions had been so great that nobody
knew for sure exactly how many were still doing business. "When I came here in 1944," he says, "one of my
first chores was simply to establish the number of
existing credit unions. There never had been any good
records, and there wasn't such a problem with federal
credit unions, but state agencies had been relatively
inactive (during the war). We eventually sorted out
which credit unions were still operating and which ones
were not. As I recall, there were about 340 active ones
left."

Barry plunged into his duties as managing director
while the League office was still in Houston and found
his extensive background in mathematics helpful in
tallying up the survivors. A native of upstate New York,
Barry had been a math teacher and chairman of the
Mathematics Department at Depew High School near
Buffalo during most of the 1930s. It was here that he had
become the unsalaried head of the Depew Teachers
Credit Union, a position that ultimately led him into
fulltime credit union management, and to Kansas,
where he had moved some five years earlier. By the time
he was approached by Yates and Burdick at a CUNA
annual meeting, Barry felt he was ready for the chal-

lenge of a larger league. At the time, there had been another opening in Michigan, which was closer to home for Barry and his wife, Marjorie, but he had taken the Texas job because of the potential he saw in the Lone Star State.

"Texas didn't have any real handicaps to hold back its growth," Barry says. "It was suffering from sheer inertia, that's all."

It became Barry's task to find some kind of quarters for the TCUL's new Dallas headquarters at a time when office space was extremely scarce. When commercial construction had come to a virtual standstill across the country because of the war, Dallas was in the process of completing its tallest office building to date—the 31-story Mercantile Bank Building—but even this large chunk of new space was not nearly enough to alleviate the shortage. According to Barry, "Office space was almost impossible to get during the war, especially in a growing city like Dallas. I got down here and found us a duplex, and there just wasn't any other place to put the office, so I had it in my house."

Barry, his wife, and one child lived in one side of the duplex at 3119 Hester Street, a block north of Knox Street, and utilized the living room and kitchen of the other side as the official headquarters of the League. The move from Houston took place pretty much on schedule in early October, with one notable casualty. Helen Wood, who had served the TCUL so well during the hectic war years as its one-woman staff in the Houston office, elected to remain behind when the move finally came. Joseph Collerain, the former TCUL president who was currently serving again on the Board of Directors, offered Miss Wood a job at Humble Oil Company, where he was manager, and she accepted it. Barry hired a secretary in Dallas as her replacement, but as it turned out, Helen Wood's association with the League was far from over.

Barry immediately took to the highways to begin the arduous task of mending the sagging fences of the credit union movement in Texas, but within a few short months these efforts to regain some of the ground that had been lost over the preceding three years would be brought to an abrupt halt by events totally beyond the control of anyone in Texas.

Ten days before Christmas 1944, in a desperate last-ditch effort to split the Allied armies that were now poised at the very borders of Germany and repeat his stunning triumph of 1940 when he had overrun France and Belgium and almost driven the British Expeditionary Forces into the sea, Hitler launched his last great offensive. Striking suddenly out of the snowy mists, thousands of German tanks tore through the Allied lines in the historic Ardennes Forest, catching the U.S. First Army completely by surprise, and the Battle of the Bulge was under way. Although the courageous American defense of the key road junction of Bastogne helped to turn the tide back in favor of the Allies before New Year's Day 1945, the German offensive threw a temporary scare into the nation's military leaders and caused them to intensify the draft.

When he had tried to volunteer for service two days after Pearl Harbor, after reading in the newspaper that the Army needed mathematicians, Jim Barry had been told he "didn't have enough teeth" to pass the physical. ("I wanted to know what that had to do with math," Barry recalls, "and they said that actually 'We never should have put that in the paper because it wasn't true.' ") But apparently, the Battle of the Bulge changed all that. The Army either lowered its dental qualifications or decided it needed mathematicians, after all. As the fighting raged in the Ardennes, some 5,000 miles from the borders of Texas, Barry received his draft notice, ordering him to report for induction on February 1, 1945.

After a year of struggling mightily to get itself back on an even keel as a fully functional organization, the

114

TCUL suddenly found itself right back where it had started—without the services of a managing director.

As a result, 1945 was destined to go into the record books as the most uneventful year in League history. Barry's last official activities before departing for the Army included attending an Executive Committee meeting in Dallas on January 14. Slightly more than two weeks later, he was gone, and the day-to-day operation of the TCUL office in the duplex on Hester Street became the responsibility of his wife, Marjorie.

At that January meeting, faced not only with the temporary loss of Barry but with a request from the Federal Office of Defense Transportation asking that all nonessential travel be curtailed for the duration of the war, the Executive Committee decided to cancel the 1945 annual meeting. There was, in fact, only one other official gathering of TCUL officials during the entire year, according to surviving minutes in the League's archives. This was a Board of Directors meeting in Dallas on July 1, at which Mrs. Barry served in her husband's stead as recording secretary.

Ironically, although Barry himself attributes his being drafted to the Battle of the Bulge, he was to end up about as far away from the Ardennes Forest as it was possible to get on Planet Earth. He was trained in anti-aircraft before leaving the States, but was then assigned to the headquarters staff of General Douglas MacArthur's Western Pacific Command in the Philippines. "I actually got to the Philippines just as the war ended," Barry remembers. Even so, there was to be no quick return home. Barry was to remain in the Pacific for the better part of a year, not receiving his discharge and returning to his job with the TCUL until mid-1946.

In the meantime, he was assigned to a job with the Philippine Highway Planning Commission, which was sent to the islands by President Harry Truman to evaluate damage caused by the war to roads, bridges, and ports. "They sent a group of officers from all the armed services, nearly all of whom had been state highway department engineers or federal highway engineers," Barry says. "I was assigned with them and my job was to dig out the history of public expenditures by the Philippine government in connection with the civil work. It became quite a job because, of course, Manila was really torn up."

With the unconditional surrender of Japan on August 15, 1945, the most catastrophic conflict of all time was at an end. In cities and towns accross the state, jubilant Texans celebrated "V-J Day" to mark the end of nearly four years of wartime suffering and sacrifice. But the conversion to the post-war era and a return to normalcy and "business as usual" would take many additional months. Factories which had been spewing forth record numbers of warplanes, tanks, guns, bombs, and military vehicles could not make the change-over to eagerly awaited consumer goods overnight. The millions of American men and women who had been scattered around the globe by the demands of the war could not all be rushed home at once.

But the big hurdle was past. Because of the two atomic bombs dropped on Hiroshima and Nagasaki, the war had ended much earlier than most Americans had believed possible even a few weeks beforehand. Peace had come almost as suddenly as the war had come in December 1941, but once the public adjusted to the idea, it was seized with a pervasive sense of optimism and anticipation. Suddenly, people could foresee the end of rationing and the constant shortages of everything from gasoline to light bulbs and from meat to chewing gum. Suddenly, people by the thousands were signing waiting lists for the first new cars and appliances to roll off the post-war assembly lines. Suddenly, there was a new-fangled gadget called television that everybody was talking about and wanting to buy. Suddenly, there was again the prospect of new homes for countless hopeful families.

For the 319 surviving credit unions in Texas, it was the end of one of the darkest periods in the movement's history and the beginning of one of the brightest. Between 70 and 80 Texas credit unions had fallen victim to the disruptions caused by the war, and according to a report by TCUL president Yates, the ratio of losses in Texas ranked "very high" on the national scale. But now, with the nation's economy set for the kind of boom it had not experienced since the "Roaring Twenties," and with the demand for mortgage loans, auto loans, and other forms of consumer credit expected to hit an all-time high, the contagious spirit of optimism now infected the League and its members.

Credit union people around the state eagerly jumped into the process of planning the first League annual meeting in two years, as the 1946 convention in San Antonio took shape for early April. Jack Mitchell, who by then had just begun his 31-year tenure as treasurer — then president of Dallas Teachers Credit Union, remembers going out to the house on Hester Street with a group of other credit union leaders that spring to help Marjorie Barry collate the TCUL's books in preparation for the convention. "Barry was still in the Philippines at the time," Mitchell recalls, "but we managed to do everything that needed doing before we went to San Antonio. There were several of us there that day, including Yates, C.W. Hudson, Jimmie Parker and (NCUA official) Buford Lankford."

Mitchell also remembers the condition that his credit union—then, as now, one of the largest in the state—found itself in at the time. "When I took over in January 1946, we only had about $62,000 in loans," Mitchell says, "and about $45,000 of that was delinquent." The first financial statement signed by Mitchell showed the credit union with shares and deposits totalling less than $300,000 and with a membership of about 1,300. When he retired in the spring of 1977, Dallas Teachers had more than $72 million worth of loans in

117

effect, assets of more than $91 million and a membership of 51,827.

It was this kind of growth that lay just ahead as TCUL delegates made their reservations for the San Antonio convention that spring. The rule was "two to a room" because of the continuing shortage of space, but nobody seemed to mind a bit of overcrowding. "If you have someone you wish to share your room with, please state this in your letter," delegates writing for reservations were instructed.

The convention, held April 6 at San Antonio's Gunter Hotel, was characterized by a cheerful, positive atmosphere and a feeling on the part of those attending that they were standing on the threshold of the most exciting, expansive era their organizations had ever witnessed. In Barry's absence, Marjorie Barry and Helen Wood served as co-recording secretaries for the convention, where a main topic of conversation was the pending return of the managing director. Barry had by now been discharged from the Army, thanks in part to an appeal filed directly with his commanding officer by the TCUL, which had pleaded its own extreme hardship in seeking Barry's early release. Yates told the convention that a cable confirming the discharge had been received on April 4, just two days earlier, but Barry was still in Manila awaiting passage home.

It was with an air of near-jubilation that the delegates voted to give Yates $200 in appreciation of the work he had done in promoting the credit union movement throughout Texas during the period when the League had been without a fulltime managing director. They also passed a resolution commending Mrs. Barry for "diligently and faithfully" serving the Board of Directors and for performing "splendid work" for the League membership.

A few weeks later, Barry was finally home from overseas and ready to resume his interrupted career and the task of revitalizing the credit union movement in

Texas while expanding the membership and influence of the TCUL. When the Executive Committee met in Dallas on June 30, 1945, Barry was back on the job, much to the relief of Yates and everyone else who had tried to fill in during his absence. In preparation for the post-war push ahead, the League completed the process of incorporation that summer.

There had been more than a few casualties along the way, but somehow the League had managed to endure "the duration," and the turmoil of the war years could now be mercifully relegated to the past. At long last, the time for marking time was over. The time had come—literally—to "hit the ground running."

Peace and Progress

The immediate post-war period was to see the most rapid growth in almost every area that the TCUL and its member credit unions had ever experienced. Barry's skilled leadership quickly began to have dramatic impact on the fortunes of the League. By January 1947, the *Bulletin* reported that Texas credit unions had added 3,974 new individual members during the Fourth International Membership Drive conducted between September 1 and December 1, 1946, almost doubling the state's assigned quota of 2,100. The Dallas and Houston districts led in this campaign, enrolling 783 and 764 new members respectively, but the Southwestern Greyhound Employees Credit Union of Fort Worth accounted for the most new members of any single credit union, with 151.

These gains were extremely important if Texas was to regain its position of prominence in the credit union movement nationally. Among the top seven or eight credit union states as of 1940, depending on which measuring statistic was used, Texas had been the only one to lose significant numbers of individual members during the war. While California had been gaining more than 15,000 members and New York more than 31,000 in the space of three years, Texas had lost a net total of 15,795 members. In the meantime, Texas had dropped from a rank of seventh or eighth nationally to a position of thirteenth or fourteenth. But by the summer of 1947, the state had battled its way back into ninth place in the number of operating credit unions.

In addition to the effect of being deprived of its managing director's services during the war, the League had also suffered tremendous losses related to two other factors: (1) the friction and divisiveness that had grown out of the feud between Houston and Dallas factions over where the League headquarters should be located; (2) a generally hostile attitude among Texas officials of the Federal Deposit Insurance Corporation, to whose jurisdiction the Federal Credit Union Section had been transferred from the Farm Credit Administration. The latter factor had led to a rate of liquidations among federal credit unions in Texas which far exceeded the national rate.

Too, statistics from other states showed that when credit unions could be kept as active dues-paying members of a state league, they were better able to survive the lean war years and prepare for the better days that peace would bring. Near the mid-point of the war, the League's membership had dwindled to scarcely more than half of all the credit unions in Texas, and Barry's earliest efforts were directed at improving that percentage—an utter necessity if the League was even to remain solvent. His results were impressive, as the percentage climbed to 64.4 percent by the end of 1946, although the League was still operating at a loss out of reserves.

Another major chore for Barry was trying to put the Texas Federal Credit Union, which had been established in 1937 for the benefit of the state's credit union officers, on a stable financial footing. FDIC hostility, the ravages of war, and the waning influence of the TCUL had exacted a heavy toll on Texas Federal. Almost a

120

third of its loans were delinquent and its assets amounted to only about $7,000. Barry moved the credit union into the TCUL offices in order to keep a close personal watch over it and took over as its treasurer. At the credit union's annual meeting on January 20, 1947, a four percent dividend was declared, and Barry, with the help of former managing director Parker, persuaded the members to try to secure life savings insurance as a means of bolstering savings, explaining how this insurance worked and that it could be obtained through CUNA Mutual with FDIC approval.

At the annual convention of the League that March in Fort Worth, inspired campaigning by C.W. Hudson, president of the Texas Federal Credit Union (later Texas Central Credit Union), and others brought in a flood of new capital for the troubled credit union. An appeal on the floor of the convention produced an incredible 300 percent jump in its assets, from about $7,000 to more than $22,000. Shortly thereafter, the credit union had sufficient income to allow it to hire its own one-member office staff and Barry to resign as its treasurer. Within a few years, its assets had grown to more than $500,000.

As the TCUL launched its big push to reconquer lost ground and add new, it was led by a seasoned corps of veteran statewide officers. Yates, who was now in his fifth year as the League's president, was joined on the Executive Committee by Turner, first vice president; Miller, second vice president; Collerain, third vice president; and Burdick, secretary-treasurer. Other members of the Board of Directors included O.F. Burgdorf of Texarkana, Arvin Eady of Wink, P.W. Harvey of Pampa, C.W. Hudson of Dallas, C.W. McCoy of Port Arthur, G.B. Reed of San Antonio, H.T. Sanderson of Corpus Christi—and the first woman to be elected to the board, Miss Willie Martin of Waco. Reed was editor of the *Bulletin*, which had its own address at 311 Insurance Building, San Antonio, and John L. Quinlan, a trained journalist and member of the Southwestern Bell Credit Union of San Antonio, was assistant editor. Seven chapters remained active across the state, their presidents including Sanderson, Corpus Christi; J.A. Parker, Dallas; H.D. Rockwood, Fort Worth; S.D. Jackman, Houston; A.F. Dalton, Sabine; Charles Dufner, San Antonio; and H.W. Mitchell, Waco.

National directors Yates, Turner, and Harvey now found themselves working with a new managing director of CUNA. Roy F. Bergengren, the architect of the national organization and the man who had headed it since its birth, had retired in 1945 and had been succeeded by Tom Doig. Now, as the post-war era began to burst into full bloom, Bergengren issued a call to the 4,000,000 members of nearly 12,000 credit unions in North America for renewed efforts to carry the ideals of cooperative credit to new plateaus.

"The credit union movement had no sooner weathered the storms of the industrial depression than it was catapulted into the most terrible war in all history," he pointed out. "Now we are in for another period of trial as part of a world trying to adjust to the exhaustion and accumulated passions of war."

What was to be the function of the credit union in this new world? Bergengren asked. "Are we simply one of many factors in the small loans business, operating with a higher morality than some of our competitors? If that is our object we are blind indeed. We have contributed greatly to the solution of the small loan problem and we shall continue an expanding service in that field. (But) *It will become decreasingly our major activity* (Italics Bergengren's). Every credit union treasurer, who watches the widening gulf between his assets and his loans, knows that to be true."

The next ten years, he said, offered "greater challenge" and "greater opportunity" than any time in the past. He foresaw an America with 100,000 credit unions and 100,000,000 individual members. "We are at the beginning, not the end, of the journey," he warned. "If we would be a worthy factor in the difficult days ahead, there is no time for resting."

Based on what was to happen in Texas over the next decade, one may assume that the leadership of the Texas Credit Union League took Bergengren's eloquent words very much to heart. During the ten years of which he spoke—the period from 1947 to 1957—the number of credit unions in Texas jumped from 329 to approximately 1,000, an increase of 300 percent or more. At the same time, membership was soaring by more than 500 percent, from well under 100,000 to 500,000-plus. Assets of Texas credit unions, meanwhile, zoomed upward from about $18 million in 1947 to $215.7 million in 1957, an increase of nearly 1,200 percent, and loans outstanding skyrocketed from $9.4 million in 1947 to $172.6 million in 1957—a staggering 1,800 percent increase.

Beginning in 1948, the full attention of the League was focused on the organization of new credit unions. As the year began, the statewide figure still stood at only 338, meaning that a net gain of just nine credit unions had been registered in 1947. But by the end of 1948 no fewer than 43 newcomers had been added to the state's ranks, and every one of these also became League members. The work of G.B. Reed, who left his post as editor of the *Bulletin* that summer to become the first designated field representative of the TCUL, undoubtedly had a great deal to do with this success. By adding an additional 12 members from the ranks of the state's existing credit unions, the League was able to bring its membership up to 73 percent of all the credit unions in Texas. Its energetic organizational efforts placed Texas fourth among all states in new credit unions formed in 1948, and this was only the first in a string of record-breaking years for Texas and the TCUL.

But along with the golden opportunities of the post-war period, the challenges of which Bergengren had spoken were also very much in evidence. There was, for example, yet another move under way in Congress in 1947 to slap credit unions with a new federal tax. Fortunately, the measure was killed in the House Small Business Committee, chaired by the movement's longtime friend and ally, Congressman Wright Patman of Texas. Patman charged that big-money interests—using a lobbying group known as the National Tax Equality Association—were deliberately misleading the public in order to create favorable sentiment for additional taxation of credit unions and other cooperative organizations. Investigation by Patman's committee, however, disclosed that cooperatives were paying the same taxes as corporations, partnerships, and individuals, and that there was no basis for the charges of favoritism levied by certain special-interest groups.

"I am in favor of credit unions and I want to do what I can to help them," Patman assured the TCUL's Dallas Chapter during the height of the controversy. "I don't want to see them restricted. I do want to see them grow and increase in number." With the East Texas congressman's continuing help in high places, credit unions were allowed to do precisely that.

Closer to home, a tragedy that was keenly felt by all Texans also created a formidable challenge for several of the state's credit unions—a challenge unlike any Texas credit union had ever faced before. On April 16, 1947, a chemical-laden French merchant ship, the S.S. Grandcamp, exploded in the ship channel at the bustling Gulf Coast port of Texas City. It was one of the deadliest and costliest disasters in the state's history. When the raging fires that engulfed the ship channel, several oil tankers anchored there and the adjacent Monsanto Chemical plant were brought under control and the toll in human lives and property finally calculated, more than 570 persons were dead or missing. Some 4,000 others were injured, many critically, and damage estimates ran as high as $70 million.

With matters in a state of total chaos, and the future of at least four credit unions hanging in the balance in the stricken city, Barry hurried to the scene. "We'd never had anything like this happen before," he says, "and the big issue was what was going to happen to these credit unions and all the hundreds of their members who were killed or hurt. CUNA Mutual authorized me to go down and expedite their claims service. I made a lot of settlements right on the spot, and the credit unions came through with flying colors."

As far as can be determined, this was the first time that CUNA Mutual had relaxed its rules on claims to such an extent, but the Texas City disaster was to set the stage for other similar operations by the insurance company in the future. The four most severely affected credit unions—Southport Employees Federal Credit Union, Monsanto Employees Credit Union, Texas City Federal Credit Union and Republic Federal Credit Union—all managed to survive because of quick humanitarian actions by the League, CUNA Mutual and the credit unions concerned.

The *Bulletin* of August 1947 featured a detailed account by Barry of the recovery of the Texas City credit unions. *Bulletin* editor Reed called it a classic illustration of "the magnitude of humanity and brotherhood that a credit union transmits to its members."

The Texas City disaster graphically emphasized the real service that credit unions perform for their members in times of great personal tragedy. And in every catastrophic event that has touched the lives of Texans since then, that service has been emphasized again and again. The Texas City incident prompted Members Mutual's procedure of sending special teams into disaster areas to expedite claims, a practice which has helped tens of thousands of stricken Texas families in the years after this insurance company for credit union members was organized.

Growing Like a Weed

The last years of the 1940s were a time of heady accomplishments and record-shattering growth for the Texas credit union movement. As he reviewed the achievements of 1948, Barry noted proudly that the League's income was sufficient to pay for full-time operations for the first time since 1941—yet only two other states with full-time leagues had a lower dues schedule than Texas. With less than $20,000 in total gross income from all sources during the year, the TCUL had obtained results comparable to leagues spending more than twice that amount.

The addition of fieldman Reed as a full-time staff member and the creation of a corps of "volunteer organizers" had yielded big rewards in the number of new credit unions organized and enrolled for League membership. Meanwhile, a separate campaign to add individual members to the state's credit unions also had proved "highly successful," Barry reported.

But the snowballing growth of the period was not taking place without interference. Some thorny obstacles and formidable resistance still blocked the path of the credit union movement from time to time. While improved relations with the FDIC and then the transfer of credit union supervision to the Department of Health, Education and Welfare (and specifically, the Social Security Administration under HEW) had facilitated the organization of federal credit unions, the State Department of Banking had become increasingly difficult to deal with. As a result, federal credit unions were being formed right and left, but the establishment of new state credit unions was at a virtual standstill. By the late 1940s, federal credit unions outnumbered state-chartered credit unions in Texas by four to one.

In February 1948, Deputy Banking Commissioner H.L. Bengtson had assured the TCUL Executive Committee that his department "was interested in credit unions and wanted to help them prosper," although he admitted that the department had sometimes been rather hostile in the past. "Perhaps in former years, the department had not encouraged the best relations with credit unions, but that was over," official minutes of the February meeting quoted Bengtson as promising. He also pledged that changes would be put into effect to make it easier to charter new state credit unions.

But by the time the Executive Committee met again in July, no such changes were in evidence. If anything, matters seemed to have grown worse, and committee members were angered and alarmed by the fact that only one solitary state credit union charter had been issued since early 1947. A report by Yates soon clarified the situation, however. The report made it clear that, as usual, Yates had lost no time in getting to the heart of the matter in his characteristic style of jaw-to-jaw confrontation.

"Since there has been only one credit union chartered by the State Department of Banking in the past eighteen months, I made a trip to Austin for a conference with the Banking Department on June 17," the report began. "I had a lengthy conference with Commissioner Faulkner and Deputy Commissioner Bengtson.

"Mr. Bengston, the credit union supervisor, made several comments on credit unions, the substance being: that credit unions are only supposed to make small loans for short periods of time and that many credit unions remain small and do not encourage their members to save. He stated that he objected to scattering organization papers over the state, that many sets of papers came into the office not completely filled out and that it was impossible to form a clear idea of the need of a credit union without an investigation. He also stated that credit unions were not carrying their share of the load and that the banks had to take over the credit union examinations for a part of the year because the credit unions did not provide a full year's work."

In return for Yates' promise that the League would be careful to organize only "substantial groups" and see that all papers were properly filled out, he was given a supply of organization forms in order to facilitate the process of applying for charters. Yates also agreed to go along with some increase in the examination fees charged credit unions, but only "if the need was shown." And since the board empowered with approving state credit union charters included not only the banking commissioner but the state's attorney general and treasurer as well, Yates also dropped in on Attorney General Price Daniel during his Austin visit to ask for cooperation. He also called at the office of State Treasurer Jesse James but found him out of town.

Yates had done his work well. Within a few weeks, state charters were again being issued on a reasonably frequent basis and the worst of another crisis was past. It was this willingness to take tough, direct action when called for, and to go straight to the top levels of authority in search of answers that was winning favorable notice for Yates in the highest echelons of the national credit union movement. For Yates, a key leadership post in CUNA was less than a year away.

In the meantime, other, somewhat more subtle steps were being taken to strengthen the financial resources of credit unions. One was a new interlending service between member credit unions initiated at about this time by the TCUL. After some early resistance to the system, based mostly on misunderstandings about how it was to operate, many Texas credit unions began to participate in it. During 1948, hundreds of thousands of dollars were loaned by Texas credit unions to other Texas credit unions at 3 percent interest per annum. Significantly, the new service caused banks in all areas of the state to cut their lending rates to credit unions accordingly.

At the League office, business was booming. Barry reported handling more than 42,000 pieces of mail to and from Texas credit unions during the year. A total of 5,692 letters had been written and mailed out by the office, along with more than 25,000 copies of the *Bulletin* and other informative materials, and 2,089 supply orders. Discounts on supply orders alone accounted for more than 11 percent of the annual dues paid in by member credit unions, and surveys showed that supplies ordered through the League office would have cost members $29,000 more than the League charged if they had been purchased locally.

So brisk was business, in fact, that it became necessary to relocate the office. The duplex on Hester Street had now been outgrown, and since the office "crunch" in Dallas was easing somewhat, League officials began searching for suitable new quarters.

As early as January 1947, Barry had communicated the need for additional space in a letter to the Executive Committee. "You will appreciate the present strain on our present quarters by recalling that we moved from 250 square feet in downtown Houston to 180 square feet in our present location. This legerdemain was possible due to the distribution of various League effects into the household of your managing director. Within the past six months the Texas FCU has been moved in and the highest supply business in our history has necessitated both the expansion of supply department inventory and the employment of a boy after school hours."

Barry then took note of the fact that federal regulatory agencies were still very much a factor in rentals, even though the war had been over for some 17 months. Apparently, the U.S. Office of Price Administration (OPA) would have forced the TCUL to seek another home, even if the space had not been a consideration. "Our lease expires February 15 and we are presently under OPA eviction notice to move by April 4," Barry's letter said. "We need to move, and into more space. Since downtown office space seems still unavailable, probably our best bet will be an office in a converted residence in one of the various neighborhood shopping centers until we are able to find a downtown location."

What was located differed slightly from Barry's expectations, however. From the Hester Street address, the office moved temporarily to an upstairs location at the corner of Knox Street and Cole Avenue a few blocks away. Downstairs was a popular tavern, which is still operating on the site today as the Knox Street Pub. Not long after that, the office moved again, this time to its first downtown location. By October 1948, the League headquarters had found a home at 410 Southland Building Annex on Commerce Street, where it would remain until 1951, when the office moved to another downtown Dallas location at 1319 Young Street.

In one dizzying four-week period in late 1948, an even dozen new credit unions were established in Texas through the efforts of Barry, Yates, Reed and other hardworking volunteer leaders from various chapters around the state. This spurt elevated Texas to second place in a CUNA nationwide organization drive scheduled to run through May 1949. It also set the stage for what may still hold a legitimate claim to the title of the "greatest year" ever experienced by the Texas credit union movement. Although it would be surpassed by other "greatest years" in some categories, 1949 would provide an exhuberant climax to a decade in which the TCUL had truly come into its own.

It was a memorable year in many respects. Some of the key ingredients in its claim to fame included: (1) the first national convention of CUNA and its affiliates ever to be held in the Lone Star State, which convened in Houston in March 1949 two months before the same city hosted the annual meeting of the TCUL; (2) the elevation of Yates, who had served as League president for seven years, longer than anyone in League history, to the vice presidency of CUNA as the first Texan ever to hold this exalted office; (3) the milestone marked by the establishment of the 400th credit union in Texas by mid-year and

This duplex at 3119 Hester Street in Dallas housed the League's offices during World War II and the hectic period just after the war.

The League's second Dallas location was above a bar and grill at Travis and Knox Streets.

Early in 1956, the League moved into its own new building on Ross Avenue in Dallas.

n the 1950s, the League moved into this office uilding in downtown Dallas.

the organization of a record 73 credit unions during the year, the largest number organized in any state in the nation that year.

It was also a year of far-reaching changes in leadership and style for the TCUL. Yates' fellow Dallasite C.W. Hudson, himself a dynamic (if somewhat more tactful) personality, became the new president of the League in May 1949, succeeding Yates. A member of the Dallas Railway Employees Federal Credit Union, Hudson was joined on the Executive Committee by holdover officers Burdick, secretary-treasurer; Miller and Sanderson, vice presidents; and S.D. Jackman, who had succeeded Collerain in the third vice president's post. Yates remained an ex-officio member.

Hudson quickly let it be known that he had no intention of resting on Yates' laurels—or of allowing the League to rest on its, either. During 1949, he personally visited each organized chapter district, traveled some 4,200 miles and contacted more than 500 credit unionists face-to-face. While praising the League staff for its previous efforts, he called for those efforts to be redoubled as a new decade loomed on the horizon. "Hats off to the past; coats off to the future" became his motto. He called for the organization of at least 70 new credit unions in 1950, the addition of a second full-time fieldman to the staff, the hiring of a full-time bookkeeper for the League office, the approval of an unprecedented budget of $44,000 for the year ahead, and the launching of an even more intense campaign by the TCUL's "volunteer organizers" for 1950.

The changes that had taken place in Texas during the decade of the Forties had been little short of incredible. The difference between 1940 and 1949 was like the difference between a "flying jenny" biplane and a supersonic jet. Growth was a major part of the story. The population of Texas was about to pass the 7.7 million mark, and more than six out of every ten Texans were concentrated in urban areas. Houston and Dallas were well on their way to becoming "supercities," with populations of about 590,000 and 430,000 respectively. San Antonio was not far behind with some 400,000. Increasingly, the state was becoming the home of some of the world's largest industrial complexes. Dallas, for example, expanded its industrial base at the rate of 18 new manufacturing plants per month in 1949, and added new businesses of all types at the rate of five each day for the entire year.

As the new decade dawned, the State of Texas was being swept along on a floodtide of prosperity and expansion that seemed virtually limitless. The opportunities for credit unions had never been greater—perhaps would never be greater—than in the years just ahead. Hudson fully sensed this when he addressed the TCUL's Executive Committee in January 1950 at the Hotel Adolphus in Dallas.

"As this committee assembles in this first meeting of 1950, you . . . are facing one of the most vital and challenging situations to confront an Executive Committee during the history of the Texas credit union movement," he said, and pointing to the achievements of the preceding twelve months, he added:

"You will not be an egotist, nor stand in danger of being criticized as a braggart, if you go back to your district and tell the people whom you represent that every officer of the League has worked in complete and almost perfect harmony during the year 1949. The results have been a record of achievement for the good of credit union people far beyond the fondest anticipations of any member of this committee. We are stronger as a League, and in much better position to serve the credit union people of Texas, by reason of the records established last year, than we have ever been before . .

"If our record of progress had closed right here and no other goals had been reached, we would have fulfilled, in a large measure, the primary purpose of the

League, namely, the spreading of the philosophy of the credit union movement to a great number of Texas people . . ."

Hudson complimented the League on wiping out a budget deficit and establishing a surplus, and he lauded the work of the "volunteer organizers," especially those in the San Antonio area (where *Bulletin* editor John L. Quinlan, with seven new credit unions to his credit, was setting a torrid pace for the rest of the volunteers). But Hudson was obviously much more interested in what lay ahead than what lay behind.

"One vital, history-making, inescapable question confronts us," he said. "We challenge you to answer it intelligently: Where do we go from here? Nineteen forty-nine is history. Nineteen fifty is filled with opportunities. This is not a proper time to allow the least semblance of a program of retrenchment to creep into our thinking . . .

"We must realize that the Texas Credit Union League is now a full-grown organization. Our swaddling clothes have been exchanged for full-dress uniforms. We are experiencing growing pains, and our future is as bright as the sun."

With these words of inspiration ringing in their ears, the leaders of the TCUL marched out to confront whatever the "Fabulous Fifties" held in store.

Bigger and Better

No decade in American history had ever held more golden promise or exciting prospects than the 1950s. It was a time of amazing technological developments which brought the elusive "good life" into the reach of more average citizens than ever before, and which promised to make life increasingly better as the decade unfolded. By the early 1950s, Texans were receiving their first full-scale exposure to the wonders of television, as the coaxial cable that had crept west and south from the New York area after the war finally reached the borders of the Lone Star State, bringing network programming with it. Almost overnight, the lives of countless thousands of families were transformed forever by the advent of the irresistible "small screen" in Texas living rooms. And almost every passing month produced some other new consumer sensation—much to the delight of a public that was off on its biggest buying binge ever.

Everything was bigger and better in the early 1950s. Cars were longer and lower, faster and flashier, and at twenty cents or less per gallon, the gasoline they burned was the least of anybody's worries. Houses were also larger and more luxurious than their pre-war counterparts. Such amenities as "family rooms" and second bathrooms were becoming commonplace, as were two-car garages. And outside the back door was no mundane, old-fashioned back porch, but an exotic new patio. Inside, houses now came equipped with such incredible new gadgets as built-in ovens and ranges, washers and dryers, central heat, and sometimes even air conditioning. New products were hitting the market in such numbers that it was practically impossible to keep track of them, and many Texans were having their first giddy encounters with freeways, automatic transmissions, hotrods, drive-in movies, dishwashers, wire recorders, hi-fi's, outdoor barbecue grills, pizza, ballpoint pens, 45-rpm records, bikini bathing suits, chartreuse socks, and Milton Berle.

The TCUL joined right in with the "bigger and better" spirit of the times by adding new impetus to its "volunteer organizers" movement, and planning its most gala annual convention in history, under the direction of Dallasite L.P. "Phil" Davis as its chairman.

The League voted to pay volunteers $5 for each new credit union organized between March 5 and December 31, 1950, plus a $50 cash award to the person who organized the largest number of credit unions during this period. *Bulletin* Editor John Quinlan of San Antonio won the $50 going away.

The TCUL's sixteenth annual meeting at the Adolphus Hotel in Dallas was by far the largest gathering ever staged by the League, with more than 350 delegates and visitors attending. The austere conditions under which most annual meetings had been conducted in the past, especially during the war years and the Depression, were completely missing from this one. Delegates were welcomed to "Big D" by Dallas Mayor Wallace Savage, then treated to a two-day round of festivities including a style show, a banquet, a dinner-dance, a speech by CUNA Managing Director Tom Doig, and a variety of entertainment.

Quinlan took note of the occasion by taking a look back at some darker times in an editorial in the *Bulletin*. He recalled the little group of credit union stalwarts who had gathered in Fort Worth sixteen years earlier, in 1934, to start the TCUL. "Remember 1934?" he asked. "It was far from a banner year. The nation was still in the grip of the most severe depression in history. This editor was pounding the pavement with a shining new college diploma in his nervous hand, enviously eying fellow graduates who were running elevators and working in filling stations. A melancholy year, 1934."

The contrast between 1934 and 1950 could hardly have been more sharply drawn. Of course, even 1950 would have its dark moments. By mid-year, the United States would be drawn into a bloody and inconclusive war in Korea, a three-year conflict that would intensify the Cold War between the United States and the Soviet Union and Communist China. Once again, young Americans would be conscripted for military service and sent abroad to fight and die on foreign battlefields. And, at home, fears of atomic destruction and Communist infiltration of American government and industry would grow and intensify.

But none of this could negate the resounding successes of 1950. The "peace and prosperity" euphoria of the late 1940s was evaporating in the face of new threats and perils, but from a financial standpoint the first year of the "Fabulous Fifties" could hardly have been more fabulous. The average Texas wage earner was making more money and improving his standard of living, and so were his credit unions.

Jim Barry called 1950 the "greatest year" the credit union movement in Texas had yet experienced. The 62 new credit unions established during the year—49 federal and 13 state—did not quite measure up to the record crop of 1949, but other forms of credit union growth more than substantiated Barry's claim. Savings in Texas credit unions increased by 33 percent over 1949 to reach more than $38.8 million. Loans jumped by 49 percent, despite some lingering problems with Regulation W, passing the $35 million mark. And individual membership in Texas credit unions climbed by 21 percent to a total of 181,739. The percentage of credit unions affiliated with the League rose slightly, to 77 percent.

During 1950, an effort was made to beef up the League's field staff, and Paul H. Mullins, a former examiner with the Bureau of Federal Credit Unions, joined the TCUL in August as field representative for the northern and western sections of the state. A native of St. Paul, Minnesota, Mullins had come south in 1919, heading for New Orleans. But, as he puts it, he "went broke in Oklahoma City" and ended up staying there for about 30 years, working for the Federal Employment Security Commission and helping to organize the first credit unions in Oklahoma. In the late 1940s, as an auditor for the newly formed Bureau of Federal Credit Unions, Mullins finally made it to New Orleans when he was transferred there by the Bureau.

But Mullins had had his fill of government work by then, and when leaders of the TCUL approached him about joining the League as a fieldman, he jumped at the opportunity. "One night Barry, Yates, and Hudson called me and asked if I'd be interested in coming to Texas. I said 'when,' because by then I'd been dissatisfied with the Bureau for some time."

The feds' loss was the TCUL's gain. Mullins became a key figure in the League's dynamic expansion of the 1950s and 1960s, serving as assistant managing director from 1952 until his retirement in 1964. Mullins' help to hold the League together during the hectic period when Barry was deeply involved with the formation of Members Mutual and spending most of his time on business relating to the burgeoning new insurance company, which will be discussed in detail later. In his first year in Texas, Mullins recalls "driving 33,000 miles in a bloody old Ford," organizing new credit unions and servicing existing ones. In all, Mullins estimates that he helped "well over 200" credit unions get started, but readily admits that he was not the all-time champion at the organization game. "That honor definitely belongs to Phil Davis," Mullins said in a 1983 interview. "Phil was the undisputed champ. He even organized the prison at Huntsville." (More on Davis later.)

Unfortunately, however, G.B. Reed, the League's first field representative, also resigned during 1950, leaving the southern part of the state without a fieldman. The following year, Ernest C. Moore was hired to fill the vacancy and field representation returned to normal. Inspections of member credit unions and other types of services were now taking a large share of the fieldmen's time and organizational efforts were being passed more and more to dedicated volunteers in various areas of the state.

Hudson was proving an extremely effective president. Not only was he traveling thousands of miles each year to promote the credit union cause, but was utilizing his considerable public relations talents with good results in Austin. According to Mullins, it was Hudson's influence with Governor Allan Shivers that caused the governor to pass the word to State Banking Commissioner J.N. Faulkner to give more favorable attention and better service to credit unions. As Hudson told the Executive Committee at the meeting in San Antonio in January 1951: "Governor Shivers has shown a friendly attitude toward our movement and has been cooperative with us in every way . . . We believe you will see the organization of more state-chartered credit unions in the future."

The League's Board of Directors had also been pressing for appointment of a credit unionist to the powerful State Finance Commission, and Hudson reported at the same meeting that the board was about to be rewarded for its efforts: "We are happy to report to you that our efforts were successful and that Governor Shivers will submit the name of L.E. McMakin of Sinclair Refining Company Federal Credit Union of Houston to the State Senate as the appointee."

By the fall meeting of the Board of Directors on September 22, 1951, in Dallas, it was obvious that the number of new credit unions coming into existence during the year would be well below the total for 1950, and Hudson issued a challenge to League members to organize a minimum of fifty new credit unions before the annual meeting in Fort Worth the following March.

The Korean War, which had erupted in June 1950, was having definite effects on credit union activities, although nothing like the impact of World War II. Hudson noted some of these effects when he told delegates at the annual meeting in San Antonio in March 1951: "We cannot predict the full results of world conditions on credit union operations in 1951. There are some signs, however, which we cannot escape. Government regulations have already materially reduced the loan balance of many credit unions. Unless the international crisis clears up, we have been told that more stringent curbs are on the way. We have also been advised by Congress and by the Executive Branch of Government that more and more and higher and higher taxes are inevitable."

Faced with this, Hudson asked, "What course shall we take? Shall we travel the road of retrenchment, or shall we push forward to even greater achievements?"

By September 1951, it was apparent that the conflict in Korea would not be quickly resolved and that world conditions would not "clear up" anytime soon. But it was equally apparent that no retrenchment was in Hudson's or the TCUL's plans. Hudson called for the employment of a third fieldman, this one to be stationed in the San Antonio area, and he asked the board to consider creating the position of assistant managing director (which would shortly be filled by Mullins) to help absorb "the mass of detail constantly piling up in the office."

"We must remember that our task, in addition to the organization of new credit unions, is to give service to the credit unions already organized," Hudson emphasized. "More and more responsibility will be placed in our hands. We will discharge that responsibility, not by a program of retrenchment, but by constantly and everlastingly expanding our League . . . "

Almost as an aside in his report to the directors that September, Hudson also made what may have been the first official reference to what was taking shape behind the scenes as one of the most far-reaching developments—perhaps the most far-reaching development—since the League was founded.

For several years, some leaders of the Texas credit union movement had been intrigued with the possibilities they saw in establishing an insurance company to operate under the auspices of the TCUL. The great growth by that time of the CUNA Mutual Insurance Society, which had begun with a $2,500 loan from Edward Filene, into a giant operation with more than $5 million in assets and $50 million worth of insurance

140

coverage, provided an arresting example of what could happen with credit union-related insurance. Why couldn't the same kind of insurance company be set up in Texas, specifically to serve the needs of Texas credit union members?

The question had already touched off considerable debate and dissention among the League's leadership, and it was to cause a great deal more in the months and years ahead. But Hudson, for one, seemed totally convinced that a League-affiliated insurance operation was simply too lucrative and too packed with potential benefit to Texas credit unions to pass up.

"Let us concentrate more of our thinking and efforts toward the establishing of our own insurance agency" he urged. "The fact that almost $38,000 per month is now being paid in premiums through our present insurance connection proves that we could well afford to hire a man to take care of just the present business we have. You can imagine what could happen if we had someone who could devote all his time to this important matter."

The first shot in the battle to create Members Mutual had just been fired.

Birth of Members Mutual

Since the very inception of the national credit union movement, insurance of one type or another had occupied the attention of many of the movement's top leaders around the country. As noted earlier, CUNA Mutual had been founded in the mid-1930s, only a year or so after the birth of CUNA itself. What the national life insurance company did was very important to credit union members. The first major type of coverage available through CUNA Mutual was called borrower's protection insurance, and was paid by member credit unions at no additional cost to the individual borrower. The coverage provided that any time the member died owing money to the credit union, the debt was cancelled. It gave rise to the slogan: "The debt shall die with the debtor."

As Jim Barry describes it, borrower's protection insurance was a "very important social service" to credit union members. "Obviously," he explains, "the people who borrowed small amounts were the people with the greatest need, and this insurance helped credit unions grow tremendously." It was so successful in this regard that, beginning in the late 1930s, CUNA Mutual instituted another form of coverage known as life savings insurance. This, again, was a great boost for credit unions, since the same people who needed loans were often the same ones who also were short on life insurance. Life savings insurance provided one dollar's worth of life insurance for every $1 placed in a savings account in a participating credit union, up to a maximum of $1,000—again at no cost to the individual member.

But as Ted McGehee, who served as president of Members Mutual from 1968 to 1972, explained, the coverage offered by the new life savings insurance also had a much broader appeal not limited to the under-insured. "It was a super-plus marketing program and better than anyone realized at the time," McGehee recalled.

Within a few years, this type of coverage caught on in Texas and spread like wildfire through the state's credit unions. According to Barry, only two credit unions in the entire state carried life savings policies for their members in the mid-1940s, but within a few years, fully 80 percent of all Texas credit unions had adopted the program. "It helped them grow like the dickens," Barry says. By 1950, Texans were paying more than $172,000 in premiums to CUNA Mutual.

While the insurance programs were bringing vital new services to credit union members and making the cooperative credit concept more attractive to prospective members, they were also making CUNA Mutual an extremely wealthy enterprise. As the insurance company grew into a true financial giant, it also became the source of deep divisions and lingering problems within the national leadership over its relationship to CUNA, which was its parent organization but which was soon dwarfed by the enormous growth of its offspring. With its own separate management and board of directors, CUNA Mutual could not be effectively controlled by CUNA. When CUNA Mutual evolved into a totally separate operation, it cost CUNA the management, personnel and financial resources which the insurance company built up.

Leaders of the TCUL, who had been seriously studying the possibilities of forming their own insurance operation for four or five years, thought they might be able to avoid some of the problems encountered on the national scale by keeping the leadership of both the League and any new insurance company virtually identical in makeup. Also, they decided to concentrate on automobile insurance instead of competing with CUNA Mutual in the life insurance field.

The first major step toward launching a TCUL-affiliated insurance company came when the League set up an Automobile Insurance Committee in 1947. At the time, it had become increasingly difficult for credit unions to obtain insurance on the automobile they financed, and state law required that such insurance be maintained anytime an auto loan was issued for $300 or more.

It had become the task of the Automobile Insurance Committee, headed by R.E. Miller of Fort Worth, to find a way to obtain comprehensive insurance coverage for the thousands of new cars that Texas credit unions were being asked to finance in the frantic wave of buying during the immediate post-war period. As Barry explains: "A lot of insurers were simply refusing to write comprehensive coverage at all because of factors like industrial pollution along the Gulf Coast and sandstorms in far West Texas which were causing widespread damage to automobile paint jobs. But credit unions had to provide comprehensive coverage when making loans, so we had to find an insurer to write it."

Barry became closely involved with the work of the committee. He was able to obtain an arrangement, with the sponsorship of CUNA, under which Employers Insurance of Wausau, a Wisconsin company, would handle auto insurance for all Texas credit unions. Barry believes it was the first such car insurance program for credit unions in the United States, and it also became a huge money-maker for the insurance company. Within two or three years, Texas credit unions were providing approximately 25 percent of the company's national volume in this type of insurance—and, according to Barry, an even higher percentage of profits. As this situation developed, the idea of establishing the League's own insurance company grew more and more popular.

Almost from the moment the Automobile Insurance Committee had been formed, the founding of an insurance company had been considered as one of several options. In the early 1950s, the option was made more attractive when Employers of Wausau pulled out of its arrangement with the committee and refused to write their auto insurance program in Texas. According to McGehee, there were two key reasons for the pullout: the fear of a hurricane hitting the Texas coast and a disagreement over claims resulting from a type of "acid rain" from Texas petrochemical plants that was damaging the finishes on workers' automobiles. At this point, the three-member committee formally recommended to the TCUL Board of Directors that an insurance company be organized.

The board, in turn, submitted the recommendation to the entire League membership at its annual meeting in Fort Worth on March 21-22, 1952. In his official message to delegates, TCUL President Hudson called for the membership to "stand up and be counted" on

144

four major issues: (1) approval of a record annual budget of some $60,000 with no increase in dues; (2) a campaign to bring a minimum of 100 new credit unions into being during 1952; (3) adoption of a militant new stance on state and federal legislation affecting credit unions; and (4) acceptance of the Auto Insurance Committee's recommendation to start a League-affiliated insurance company.

The vote by the assembled delegates was overwhelmingly in favor of the committee's recommendation. There was, in fact, only one dissenting vote among the hundreds cast. Not only that, but all the necessary startup funds for the new company — approximately $250,000 in debentures — were pledged by individual credit union members within a few minutes during the same meeting. (Credit unions themselves were prohibited from buying debentures, but not from issuing loans to allow their members to purchase them.)

Fittingly, Miller, the committee chairman who had worked so long and diligently in the studying and planning phases that had preceded the actual birth of the insurance company, was named the first president of Members Mutual. Almost immediately, it was chartered as a mutual company by the State of Texas, and within a few months Members Mutual was writing its first insurance policies.

Ironically, although it was born at a time when many insurance companies were claiming losses on automobile insurance, Members Mutual was an assured financial success from its first moment of life. Low overhead resulting from its credit union affiliation was one key reason for this, but the fact was that Members Mutual soon outstripped the expectations of even its own architects in the volume of business it did. In his initial report, for instance, Miller noted that the company had written far more policies than anyone had anticipated during its first two months of operation. And the company paid a dividend at the end of its very first year of operation, a feat that was virtually unheard-of among Texas insurance companies prior to that time. Within eighteen months of its founding, the company claimed assets in excess of $1 million.

The birth of Members Mutual was truly a "historic and heart-thrilling occasion," as Hudson eloquently phrased it, and one that was to have almost incalculable impact on the League and its member credit unions in the years ahead. Surely, it answered, once and for all, Hudson's pointed question about whether the League would "travel the road of retrenchment" or "push forward to even greater achievements." As the first major TCUL Affiliate, Members Mutual pointed the way toward an era of greater service, greater strength, greater influence, and greater wealth for the Texas credit union movement.

But as with the birth of any other healthy offspring, Members Mutual's arrival also entailed some problems of management and direction. Having witnessed at reasonably close range some of the difficulties that had arisen between CUNA and CUNA Mutual—difficulties that were, in fact, still very much apparent at the time, even after a seventeen-year partnership—leaders of the TCUL were determined to avoid similar troubles with their new insurance company. The answer, they felt, was to have Members Mutual administered by exactly the same top management and Board of Directors that ran the League. Consequently, all members of the TCUL board were named to serve on the board of the insurance company, and Barry became managing director of Members Mutual as well as managing director of the TCUL. The only departure from this concept of parallel administration came when it was decided that the three members of the Auto Insurance Committee from which the new company had evolved should rightfully be given seats on the Members Mutual board. However, since none of the three were currently board members of the TCUL, a disparity arose. There were now sixteen members on the insurance company board, but only thirteen of these also served concurrently on the TCUL board. Undoubtedly, the disparity seemed inconsequential at the time, but the parallel management concept had been flawed and problems would gradually arise because of this.

Members Mutual President Miller had been serving on the League board at the time he was named to the top post in the insurance company, but had resigned a short time later because he found the demands on his time too heavy. When he left the TCUL board in August 1953 to devote his full attention to Members Mutual, he had been a League director and Executive Committee member for thirteen years, his service dating back to the Edmonston crisis of 1940-41. He had also been a national director of CUNA for six years. A native of Carthage in East Texas, Miller had worked for the railway mail service in Fort Worth since 1923 and was a charter member and first treasurer of the P.T.S. Federal Credit Union there.

As the *Bulletin* noted: "Miller became president of the Members Mutual Insurance Company not by accident, but because of his great interest in a sound automobile insurance program for credit unions. He was on the original Automobile Insurance Committee of the League, which in 1947 studied various plans and recommended the adoption of the Employers Mutual program. His was the first credit union to actually enter such plan."

On the Executive Committee and the Board of Directors of the League, the *Bulletin* pointed out, Miller was well known for "his spirited discussions and frequent espousal of a minority point of view." In recent years, he had "mellowed considerably," the article continued, but "his fiery devotion to the cause of the little man remained his most characteristic trait."

In accepting Miller's resignation from the board, even the eloquent Hudson had difficulty expressing himself: "There is not sufficient words (sic) in my vocabulary to express the deep feeling of gratitude that I am sure all of us have for the many years of long service Bob has rendered to the credit union people of Texas and the nation . . . "

But as amicable as the situation was between the League and its new progeny in the beginning, serious problems lurked not far ahead. For one thing, Miller, the chief elected official of Members Mutual, no longer held a position of authority in the TCUL hierarchy. He had been forced by illness to gradually relinquish his elected responsibilities.

Within the TCUL, certain parties also felt it was inappropriate for the insurance company to have a larger board—sixteen members as opposed to thirteen—than the League itself. In an attempt to balance this disparity, the League board was also increased to sixteen members, but, unfortunately, not all the additional seats were reserved for persons who also served as Members Mutual directors. As a result, instead of resolving the problem, matters grew still further out of hand.

For another thing, there were two conflicting perspectives on Members Mutual's function and purpose which now began to divide the Texas credit union community into two camps. One faction, generally concentrated in Dallas and Fort Worth, felt the company's sole purpose should be to give credit union members a better, low-cost auto policy. A second group, centered on the Gulf Coast, believed that Members Mutual should be obligated to write insurance on any car on which a credit union loan was issued, regardless of the risk.

When the insurance was being handled through Employers of Wausau, the credit unions had been paid a ten percent commission, but the federal regulators ruled that such commissions could not be paid to federal credit unions. Finally, as Phil Davis, the champion credit union organizer who served as treasurer of Members Mutual, explained, "The feds agreed to let Members Mutual pay $5 for the cost of each credit report prepared by a federal credit union on a member applying for insurance, and the Members Mutual Board ruled that it would also pay only $5 to state credit unions, although there was no restriction on them. There was a big difference in the amount of money involved, and it became even bigger as the cost of policies went up. I argued for letting the state credit unions have their ten percent commission, but the rest of the board wouldn't go along. This caused numerous arguments on the floor of annual conventions for years—and I lost them all."

The rift between the credit union factions within the state may have been exacerbated by the gradual trend toward completely separating the boards of the two institutions, although there is some disagreement over this, even today.

As Barry recalls it: "Over a period of time, it became politically feasible to make the boards totally separate. Eventually, there were 32 individuals involved, and not a single one of them was on both boards. There were sixteen people on the League Board and sixteen other people on the Members Mutual Board. It got harder and harder to get any kind of consensus to work with."

Barry found himself in the posture of a man riding Roman-style atop two horses charging in opposite directions. As managing director of both the TCUL and the insurance company, he sometimes found himself being torn in half.

"Barry got very involved with setting up Members Mutual, and I ended up pretty much running the League," Paul Mullins recalled in a 1983 interview. "During 1952 and 1953, Barry and the (TCUL) Board were badly split." Mullins, too, found himself increasingly caught in the middle of a pressure situation that would eventually cause him severe health problems. "At the time, the bylaws contained a rule that said I was supposed to report to the Board, not to Barry," Mullins said. "But I bypassed the rule and it was later amended."

Given this scenario, some viewed the addition of the three members of the former Auto Insurance Committee to the Members Mutual Board as a "shakeup" designed to undermine the TCUL's control over its already-muscular offspring. This attitude added fuel to the fires of separatism which were already blazing.

It would be many years before the Boards of Directors of the League and its insurance company were reunited into a single 32-member body. When that finally happened, Barry viewed the conflict between the two entities as having been "straightened out" once and for all by having gone back to the original concept of having just one governing body for the League and all its Affiliates.

Despite the problems that have sometimes troubled their relationship, the success of Members Mutual has undoubtedly enhanced the success of the League and greatly broadened its influence. Due to the farsighted leadership of the Texans, the two entities have managed to avoid the unhappy experience of CUNA and CUNA Mutual in breaking completely apart. Today, Members Mutual is one of five insurance enterprises operating under the League umbrella, including Members Insurance Company, Members Services Insurance Company, Members Life Company and the Members General Agency, in addition to Members Mutual itself. All told, these companies had more than $100 million in assets in 1983 and served more than 250,000 policyholders.

Undeniably, when it all began on March 22, 1952, there were many trials and tribulations ahead which its founders could not foresee on that "heart-thrilling day." But TCUL President Hudson's words were certainly prophetic when, in reviewing that day just a year later, he said: "After four years or more of long, tedious and detailed study and planning, you launched the Members Mutual Insurance Company, and out of your own

150

Jim Barry (left) and Assistant
Managing Director Paul Mullins
visited Filene House in Madison,
Wisconsin in the early 1950s.

The well-traveled Mullins steps off a
Braniff flight during one of his many trips
to major Texas points.

Jim Barry's demanding dual role
as managing director of both the
TCUL and Members Mutual was
lightheartedly illustrated in this
picture of a "two-headed" Barry.

As the top leadership of
the Texas credit union
movement looks on,
Members Mutual
President Bob Miller signs
the charter for the newly
formed insurance
company during an
historic meeting in 1952.

savings provided the money to start the company on its way . . . I have no doubt of the success of the company, for with your help and with the continued hard work and cooperation of the directors of both organizations, we cannot fail."

Feud, those directors sometimes did. Fail, they did not.

Organizers Deluxe

The drive to organize new credit unions in Texas, which had sputtered along for nearly two decades until it began to show substantial results in the late 1940s, hit its full stride during the first half of the 1950s. During this period, the magical barrier of 100 new credit unions per year—a barrier that had never been crossed before—was breached again and again. And, since the vast majority of the new credit unions also became active members of the League, the percentage of Texas credit unions holding TCUL membership also increased markedly. It was a kind of "golden age" for credit union organization, and in terms of sheer numbers of new credit unions it probably will never be repeated again. At the time, though, it must have seemed—literally—that only the wide Texas sky was the limit for the League's dedicated and determined corps of professional and volunteer organizers.

Paul Mullins, with his role as assistant managing director greatly magnified by Barry's occupation with Members Mutual, is given most of the credit for coordinating the massive statewide organizational effort that led to the addition of hundreds of new credit unions to League ranks between 1951 and 1955. Mullins was assisted by a growing staff of TCUL field representatives and dozens of volunteer organizers.

For the first time in the movement's history in Texas, more than 100 new credit unions were established in 1952. The final count was 102, a figure that prompted a glowing report from Hudson: "Your Board of Directors points with pardonable pride to the rapid and almost unbelievable growth of the League. From an humble and small organization . . . with a managing director as the only employee, we now have six men and five women devoting their wholehearted energies to the organization and servicing of credit unions. Reports from all corners of the state give us a thrill because of the work of our field representatives. Our heartiest thanks go to Ernie Moore, Jim Vest, T.R. Thomas and Carl Blomquist for a job well done."

So intense was the organizational effort that it resulted in a serious casualty just as it was getting started. The hard-driving Mullins, who had pursued a gruelling schedule of nearly constant work and travel since joining the League in 1950, accompanied Barry to CUNA headquarters in Madison, Wisconsin, in December 1951 for a special orientation course. The trip was part of the groundwork being laid for the all-out organizational blitz scheduled for 1952. It came at the end of a year of twelve-hour days and seven-day weeks for Mullins, and it proved to be the proverbial "straw that broke the camel's back." In fact, it came very close to proving fatal for the League's key organizer.

After several days at Filene House in Madison, Mullins headed home to Texas by way of Chicago, where he planned a stopover and visits with local credit union associates. But when he reached Chicago on December 15, Mullins collapsed and was rushed to Holy Cross Hospital with severe abdominal hemmorhaging. Doctors diagnosed Mullins' ailment as a perforated ulcer in a far advanced and critical stage, aggravated no doubt by the rigorous routine of the previous months. Immediate surgery was performed, in which a large portion of Mullins' stomach was removed. His wife and son were flown to Chicago and for a while his survival hung in the balance. Even after the danger was past and Mullins was removed from the critical list, months of convalescence were required before he could return to work. A lesser man might have called it quits and found a less demanding job, but Paul Mullins' best efforts in behalf of the League and the credit union movement in general were still very much ahead of him. He was back in action by the spring of 1952, in time to play a vital role in the TCUL's biggest year up until that time.

At the League's annual meeting in Galveston in February 1953, Hudson paid special tribute to Mullins and his phenomenal comeback. "To our Assistant Managing Director Paul Mullins," he aid, "we owe a debt of gratitude for spearheading, among many other duties, the organization of new credit unions. When Paul returned to active duty shortly after the (1952) annual meeting at Fort Worth, I asked him to give us at least 100 new credit unions in 1952. Through his unrelenting efforts and dogged determination, and with the help of the voluntary organizers, 102 new credit unions were brought into being."

As outstanding as it was, though, the organizational record set in 1952 was not destined to stand for very long. Mullins and the League field staff surpassed it the very next year, organizing 134 Texas credit unions—a high-water mark that has never been surpassed to this day. They followed up on this effort with 121 new credit unions in 1954 and 97 in 1955. These fantastic strides during the first half of the decade led to a call by Hudson for a total of 1,000 credit unions in Texas by 1955. Although this goal was not quite reached, Texas could count a total of 933 operating credit unions, or well over twice the number in existence at the beginning of the Fifties. From 1950 through 1955, the TCUL's "organizers deluxe" had helped put 579 new credit unions in business, and if it had not been for mergers and liquidations, Hudson would have attained his goal of 1,000 by a comfortable margin. In the meantime, the percentage of credit unions maintaining membership in the League

154

was also growing steadily, passing the 90 percent plateau by 1955.

Of equal importance, however, were the other areas of dramatic growth being registered by the credit unions of Texas. By the end of 1953, total individual membership had climbed well above the 300,000 mark, a net increase of around 60 percent in three years. At the same time, the savings held by these members had ballooned to some $84 million, up from just $38 million in 1950. Far from stagnating or lying dormant, the existing credit unions in Texas were growing at a pace that could be considered even more amazing than the rate at which new ones were being formed.

And as their numbers grew and multiplied, so did the meaning and importance of these credit unions to their individual members. Granville Elder, a pioneer TCUL managing director and long-time treasurer of the Houston Postal Credit Union (who left that job to become Houston's postmaster in 1947), helped drive this point home in a June 1953 article in the *Bulletin*. Noting that his own credit union had more than doubled in size in the past six years, Elder said:

"If we could but read the human glory back of every savings and credit union passbook; if we could see the home, the work, the business trials and the hopes each passbook represents; if we could clearly visualize the problems of each depositor . . . if we could really evaluate the significant role we play in the economic advancement of our members, I believe we would approach our daily work tomorrow with a new sense of its great importance. No other responsibility in our business life transcends it."

It was such a firm belief in the inherent good of which credit unions are capable that intensified the efforts of the League's volunteer organizers. Certainly, there was some prestige involved, as well as a $50 cash award to the top organizer at the end of each year and $5 in cash for each credit union organized, but without

155

their belief in their cause, few if any would have been willing to commit the time and energy it took to get the job done.

Champion organizer Phil Davis was a good example of the evangelical zeal that infected many of these people. As Davis himself put it in a 1979 interview: "I thought that more people ought to be involved in credit unions because I could see that it was a do-gooder organization that saved people money on their loans. The people who could least afford it were having to pay the biggest interest, and a credit union was a place where they could get out of that. So I took it upon myself to be kind of a missionary, I guess you'd call it, and I started organizing credit unions."

Davis, a native of Chicago who had come to Dallas as a boy and become manager of the City Employees Credit Union there in 1942, began smashing records as a credit union organizer—not merely state records, but national and international records as well—in 1954. He repeated the feat annually all through the middle years of the decade, and was credited by the *Bulletin* in May 1955 for organizing "more credit unions than anyone else in the Western Hemisphere." His organizational efforts during that period culminated in 1958 in his being selected from 12,500,000 individual credit union members as winner of the International Brother's Keeper Award given by the National Conference of Christians and Jews. Davis was chosen as a representative of CUNA for his "unselfish and outstanding volunteer credit union service."

Interviewed by a reporter for the *Dallas Morning News* shortly after the award was announced, Davis himself summed up his career as an organizer with characteristic modesty and classic understatement. "I like people and I believe in credit unions," he said in reply to a question about why he had spent so much time as a volunteer organizer.

ung journalist John Quinlan, shown here at work 1950, became editor of the League *Bulletin* and rved in that capacity for many years.

H. T. "Sandy" Sanderson of Corpus Christi served the League well in many capacities, including its presidency.

C. W. Hudson provided many years of leadership as president of the TCUL during the eventful years of the 1950s.

H. B. Yates was renowned for his taciturn manner, but could also enjoy a lighter moment, as he demonstrates here with CUNA's Orrin Shipe.

TCUL Field Representative Ernie Moore could not say enough good things about the volunteers of the period, but he tried. "The ones that I work with in a charter meeting are beaming with enthusiasm, similar to that of a proud father over the new baby. Not so much for the intrinsic value of the reward, but that they have given a little of their time to brighten the lives of others," Moore wrote in the *Bulletin*.

While Davis undoubtedly won more widespread recognition for his organizational work than any other volunteer, there were many others who performed similar services. As mentioned earlier, John Quinlan of San Antonio was also an outstanding organizer, as were C.E. Burdick of Longview, H.A. Davis of Houston, Mrs. Adele Whitt of San Angelo, O.L. Cannon of Wichita Falls, President Hudson himself, and any number of others.

The contributions of all of them were a vital part of the energy that was flowing through the Texas credit union movement in the "Fabulous Fifties." As Moore very correctly concluded: "Their fortitude and persistent interest in others have paved the way that working people may enjoy the fruits of their labors and have financial independence. They have (been) . . . in the right place at the right time with the credit union message."

Reaching Maturity

As the League observed its twentieth birthday in 1954, it was becoming apparent to friend and foe alike that the credit union movement in Texas wasn't a baby anymore. Signs of the League's growing strength and impending maturity were everywhere. Not only had it fathered an insurance company that was on its way to becoming one of the largest in the state, but the League itself was prospering. With a proposed annual budget for 1955 of more than $137,000, it had—in striking contrast to the conditions into which it had been created—a healthy surplus of funds, a well-organized staff capable of serving the needs of credit unions in all parts of Texas, and even plans to build and occupy a new headquarters building of its very own in the near future. In national credit union circles, the influence of Texas and its League had never been stronger. Native son and pioneer League leader H.B. Yates had taken over as President of CUNA in 1953, been handily re-elected in 1954, and then moved over into a perhaps even more influential role as CUNA's managing director in 1955 (see following chapter), giving the state a more powerful voice than it had ever had before. Meanwhile, with some $111 million in savings and $105 million worth of loans, as of the spring of 1955, Texas credit unions had become a genuine force to be reckoned with in the economic structure of the state.

Thus, by the time of the TCUL's 21st annual meeting in Houston on March 25, 1955, there were plenty of reasons to celebrate a series of successes that had made the first half of the Fifties even more fabulous than even the most optimistic credit unionists had dared to predict a few years earlier. To join the celebration, a record throng of 1,200 persons converged on the glittering Crystal Ballroom of the Rice Hotel to hear an opening address by Houston Police Chief Jack Heard, a member of the supervisory committee of the Houston Police Federal Credit Union.

In a report delivered with his usual flair, Hudson joined the celebration of the League's tremendous accomplishments. "As we assemble in Houston after six years of action," he said, "the number of our organizations has increased almost two and one-half times. There are now 861 credit unions doing business in 143 (Texas) towns and villages . . . favorably affecting the economic life of more than 350,000 people . . . The five (TCUL) employees of 1949 have multiplied over eight times, giving us a total of 42 now on the payroll. Your

Board of Directors has recommended that you adopt a budget . . . four and one-half times greater than the one you adopted six years ago. Plans are almost complete for the erection of our own building. By the time we meet next year, we hope to be installed therein. Truly, yesterday's dreams are becoming today's realities . . . our horizons have been extended and the challenge for service rings loud and clear."

But Hudson also sounded a grim warning. Its growth and vigor were bringing the credit union movement "a tremendous amount of recognition," he warned, "both from those who favor our activity as well as those who oppose our philosophy. In recent months the forces who oppose us have become more voluble and vociferous in their attacks. We can be assured that as our credit unions grow in importance in the economic life of the nation, the tempo of the attacks will be increased. Most of you are already aware of the ferocity of these attacks. Without a doubt, we are at a crucial hour in the history of the League and of the national association."

In his own report to the delegates, Barry elaborated on the rising tide of credit union opposition and the sources of it. "We are for the first time, I believe, experiencing the more serious problems that are beginning to appear as the credit union movement begins to mature," he said. "Since our last meeting, the activities of the National Tax Equality Association in its attacks on the tax status of savings banks, mutual insurance companies, savings and loan associations, credit unions, and cooperatives have grown in intensity as the new Congress started.

"The American Banking Association has obtained wide publicity in its action in appointing a committee to study credit union legislation. This seems to have been brought to a head by the introduction in the Congress of the Regional Federal Credit Union Bill and also as a reaction to the rapid growth of credit unions in recent years. Recently, it has been revealed that the American Banking Association has been urged into this action by the small loan industry."

Barry also noted that in a recent message to Congress, President Dwight Eisenhower had urged a study of some form of federal insurance program to cover credit union deposits, a measure that had long been opposed by credit unionists.

"These various signs indicate," Barry concluded, "that the public relations of the credit union movement must be pursued with a vigor and a know-how far beyond the extremely modest efforts which have characterized our history to date. As we all know, we have a clean history and a wonderful story, but our reputation can suffer severely in a short time under the skilled attacks and well-financed efforts of those who, for whatever reason, wish the credit union movement to be deterred, if not destroyed . . . Behind these various attacks, if we search deeply enough, we will find the high-rate money lending interests of the country."

First as a struggling infant, then as a toddler testing its wobbly legs, then as a strapping youngster flexing its muscles, the credit union movement had depended upon the inherent rightness of its cause to extend its influence among those who could benefit from its services. By and large, the story of credit unionism had been spread by word of mouth, by hard-working organizers—most of them volunteers—traveling long and lonely highways, and by inward-looking publications within the movement whose aim was more to convince the needy that help was at hand, rather than to "sell" the credit union concept to the world at large. Now, however, with "the youth of the credit union movement . . . in the past," as Barry phrased it, it was time to take a different and much wider-ranging approach. Increasingly, over the next quarter-century, it would become essential for the movement to counteract its foes through well-orchestrated programs of public relations and public education, to penetrate the mass media with the credit union message, to take advantage of the limitless possibilities offered by modern advertising and promotion techniques.

Beginning in the latter half of the 1950s, such promotional efforts would become one of the overriding concerns of the League, of CUNA and of individual credit unions. Promotion, they would find, was a job that refused to stay done, a task that had to be done over and over again. As J. Orrin Shipe, manager of CUNA's Advertising and Promotion Service, explained in a *Bulletin* article in May 1955: "Advertising is like farming. You've got to do it steadily and with a plan in mind. You cannot jump in and out. You cannot expect to plant one ad and reap a harvest, any more than you can plant one turnip and make a million. Advertising is a process of cultivation . . .

"The problem in advertising, therefore, is not so much to tell people something as to remind them of it. So you use letters, bulletins, postcards, pay envelope stuffers, posters, counter displays, lapel buttons, book matches, pocket calendars, imprinted pencils, publicity stories, banners, contests, leaflets, pamphlets, newspaper and house organ advertisements, possibly even radio and television—just to remind them."

Slowly, credit unionists were learning that the best way to sell the concept was to concentrate on the practical advantages it offered for the ordinary person, rather than on the deep underlying philosophy of cooperative credit. It was far easier to convince someone to join a credit union by explaining to him that he could save ten percent on his next new car purchase than by telling him he would be gaining more control over his finances, Shipe emphasized.

Consequently, Texas credit unionists began a concerned education-public relations effort in the mid-1950s. At the 1955 annual meeting, Hudson exhorted every member of every credit union in the League to give "a portion of your time, talent and money to continue to propagate the philosophy of credit unions to every nook and corner in Texas." Their response took many forms, from the establishment of a booth at the State Fair of Texas to distribute public information about credit unions to a noticeable new militancy in the pages of the *Bulletin*. And the voices of individual Texans were raised far and wide in wholehearted support of credit unions.

"To a lot of people in this country, a credit union is next in importance to the church," Texas Congressman Wright Patman, co-sponsor of the Federal Credit Union Act of 1934, told the annual meeting of the District of Columbia Credit Union League. "It is my belief that you are continuing to carry on the crusade which our Savior commenced when he drove the money changers out of the temple . . . You are doing great work. You are helping poor people . . . You are doing a tremendous lot of good; you are making our country stronger by helping the people who built our country . . . I am proud of the credit unions."

And former TCUL President Joseph Collerain drew headlines in far-away Ireland when he met with Irish President Eamon DeValera and spoke in behalf of credit unions over the Eire Radio Network. " 'There is no reason why a savings co-operative system like the American Credit Unions should not work here,' Mr. Joseph A. Collerain of Houston, Texas, said in Dublin yesterday," reported the Dublin *Sunday Press* of July 24, 1955. The "courtly, dignified elder statesman of Texas credit unionism," as he was dubbed by the *Bulletin* in reprinting the story, also met with the Irish National Co-operative Council while visiting in the homeland of his forebears.

One gratifying result of the new "higher profile" posture being taken by the Texas and national credit union movements was the widespread public support accorded them by various labor organizations. In an article headlined "Bankers Seek New Curbs On Fast Growing Credit Unions," *The Railroad Clerk,* a newsletter of the International Brotherhood of Railway Clerks, leveled the following broadside at the big banking interests:

"The bankers opposed the insurance of savings accounts, predicted that Social Security would destroy the incentive to save, missed the boat on automobile financing, and now are again showing their ability to keep behind the times by trying to make it tough for credit unions to continue to serve their seven million members. More honestly, the bankers are jealous of that business, so turning it down when it was offered they now find it suits their purpose to destroy their competition through legislation.

"Many of our own Brotherhood lodges operate very successful credit unions, and there are many others on railroad properties which serve employees. It is the same throughout most industries, and if the bankers believe credit unions are now a threat, then why didn't they believe in the business ability of the people who formed and operate successful credit unions?

"Credit unions will continue to grow in strength and numbers because they serve their members well, and very little sympathy need be wasted on the bankers . . ."

Even more significantly, George Meany, president of the powerful American Federation of Labor (AFL), pledged organized labor's support for the aims and principles of the credit union movement and praised its "high standards of service." Said Meany: "Trade unions and their members are among the staunchest supporters of credit unions. Increasingly, unions are discovering that organization of these people's banks provides a practical democratic way for workers to invest their savings at a good return and to borrow funds when needed at reasonable interest rates. The American Federation of Labor is in fundamental sympathy with the aims and principles of the credit union movement and will continue to give it every possible support."

Meany's remarks were sent to CUNA in connection with the observance of International Credit Union Day

164

on October 21, 1955, along with a similar message of support from Walter P. Ruether, president of the Congress of Industrial Organizations (CIO), who characterized credit unions as "truly the friend of every American worker."

Beginning as an annual observance commemorating the establishment of the first credit union in Germany, Credit Union Day was first celebrated in 1948. The event officially marked the 100th anniversary of the movement (although many historians say the first credit union was not actually started until 1849, which would have made the anniversary observance a year premature). It was not until the early and middle years of the 1950s, however, that Credit Union Day came into full flower as a nationwide promotional tool for movement. As a national event of the third Thursday in October, it prompted outpourings of congratulatory messages from dignitaries ranging up to the President of the United States. The message sent to CUNA Managing Director Tom Doig in 1953 by native Texan Dwight Eisenhower, then in his first year in the White House, said in part: "The thousands of credit unions now operating in this country exemplify eloquently the American ideals of individual enterprise and free initiative."

But "CU Day" was also an excellent vehicle for public relations at the grassroots. Virtually every TCUL chapter held its own local observance on the occasion, and each provided a golden opportunity to extoll the virtues—and the growing impact—of credit unions in the local press. When Wright Patman rose to address the North Texas Chapter in Texarkana on the "wonderful service" its members were rendering, his words were certain to make Page One of the *Texarkana Gazette* the next day. Elsewhere, the occasion would cause the *San Angelo Standard Times* to take note of the fact that there were now "3,428 credit union members in San Angelo (as of October 1954)" and that "total assets held by the 13 credit unions here is $763,758.09."

In a larger sense, of course, "CU Day" was also a time of true thanksgiving, a time to pay solemn homage to names like Raiffeisen, Desjardins and Filene. But it was also a time for credit unionists to reap handsome dividends in printer's ink.

During this period, credit unions also became interested in specialized training and educational programs for their employees. To meet this need, the League established a Credit Union Employee Training Service, under the direction of Art Woolard, and provided on-the-job training for new credit union employees with limited experience in the field. In 1954, both CUNA and the TCUL set up special university-based schools for credit union personnel. CUNA's was held at the University of Wisconsin in Madison, while the Dallas and Fort Worth Chapters of the League conducted an eight-week program of evening classes on the campus of Southern Methodist University.

Meanwhile, the TCUL field staff was rapidly becoming a well-oiled machine for servicing existing credit unions and establishing new ones. During the mid-1950s, a number of fieldmen were on-board, some of whom were to see long and distinguished service with the League. They included Anthony Gehring, who served the Waco district; John Stanton, San Antonio district; Robert Bennett, Dallas district; Ray Ersland, West Texas district; and Carl Blomquist, who worked in both West Texas and Houston.

Church-oriented credit unions had always been an important part of the overall movement—in fact, the very first credit union in the United States had been formed by a church group—but parish credit unions really began to come into their own during the 1940s. One key reason for this was the tireless work of John L. Quinlan, veteran editor of the *Bulletin* and third vice president of the League, who stumped the state as an organizer specializing in parish credit unions. Altogether, Quinlan organized approximately 40 parish credit unions, most of them in San Antonio, where Quinlan worked as a manager for Southwestern Bell Telephone Company. This was not only a record for such organizations in Texas, but in the entire nation, and his handiwork stretched as far away as California, where, as he jokingly recalled many years later, he organized one credit union "by remote control."

When it came to public relations, Quinlan was one of the movement's strongest voices. In a quarter-century association with the *Bulletin,* including 23 years as editor, he was best known for his work with the printed word, but he was also an accomplished speaker who filled scores of speaking engagements around the state. He was a founder of Members Mutual, later serving as the company's treasurer and as a director for seventeen years. "I didn't have much spare time in those days," Quinlan said in a classic understatement.

A native of Iowa, Quinlan came to San Antonio in 1930 to attend St. Mary's University, where he majored in English and journalism. He found a job with Southwestern Bell in the rock-bottom Depression year of 1934—the same year the Federal Credit Union Act was passed—and encountered his first credit union soon after. "When I first heard about credit unions, I thought the idea was kind of ridiculous, really," he recalled. "As a college graduate, I thought financial matters should be handled by pros, but a credit union was being formed at Southwestern Bell, so I joined. As I went along and saw how the credit union operated, I realized the good it could do for people and I began to see how really valuable it was. Most of the people at the San Antonio telephone company were relatively well paid and steadily employed, but many of them still didn't know how to save money. The credit union showed them how. I was impressed by that, and I did so much talking about it that the next thing I knew I was elected a director (in 1938) and became president of the credit union in 1941."

The lesson learned by Quinlan back in the Thirties was one that credit unions were still finding it necessary to teach over and over again two decades later in the 1950s. And Quinlan and other dedicated Texas credit unionists were busily applying themselves to that task.

But there were still innumerable people who believed, as Quinlan once had, that financial matters should be "handled by the pros." Certainly, the professional bankers and other big-money interests believed this, and as the 1950s wore on they gave every indication that they would do everything in their power to make the public—and especially the state and federal governments—believe likewise. The attacks to which Barry had referred would intensify to fever-pitch before the "pros" were through.

Since the passage of the first workable credit union law in Texas, the chartering process for state credit unions had been under the auspices of the State Banking Department, and there is no way to calculate the extent to which this arrangement may have retarded the growth of credit unionism over the years. But as the attacks of the banking interests mounted in these pivotal mid-1950s, it began to dawn on some prominent credit unionists that this arrangement, in effect for nearly thirty years, desperately needed changing. By early 1956, TCUL Director R.C. Morgan, chairman of the Legislative-State Committee, was telling the League Board that the law on this matter demanded attention. Morgan reported that the committee was in favor, "right now anyway," of removing credit unions from the supervision of the Banking Department and putting them under a supervisory authority "that would be friendly toward us."

It would be thirteen long, arduous years before the creation of the State Credit Union Department with its own independent commissioner was finally completed. But the first tentative moves in that direction were being made. They were yet another indication that the credit union movement was mature enough to recognize its own best interests—and tough enough to fight for them.

Yates—Sinner or Saint?

While there were many important contributors to the credit union cause during the 1950s, it seems indisputable that the one individual with the greatest impact was Texas' own H.B. Yates. During the middle years of the decade, his influence extended far beyond the boundaries of his home state, and he became the most powerful credit union figure in the entire nation. First elected president of CUNA in 1953, Yates easily won a second term in 1954, and the following year he took over the managing directorship of the national organization, a position in which his influence became even greater.

It was during this time that what Yates' old friend Jack Mitchell terms the "big bang" in the national organization took place. Deep-rooted problems had developed within CUNA, many of which were related to the increasingly bitter conflicts between CUNA and its giant offspring, CUNA Mutual. Too, the departure of Bergengren as the guiding force in the national organization in the early Fifties had led to other problems. Some felt that Bergengren's successor, Tom Doig, had betrayed his old boss while trying to gain the post of CUNA managing director for himself. Then, when Doig himself became ill and developed what was described by some as a "severe drinking problem," pressure mounted for his removal, as well as for the removal of various other key CUNA staff members who had been appointed by Doig and whose loyalty to him appeared to be undermining the national organization.

"Yates found himself squarely in the middle of all this," explains Mitchell, who had known Yates intimately for many years as a fellow teacher, fellow member of the Dallas Teachers Credit Union and a fellow leader of the Texas credit union movement. "His role was to clean

169

up the mess that had developed, and that's what he did. He was strictly honest and honorable, but he didn't know the meaning of the word 'tact.' People respected him, but he also made a lot of political enemies. He fired a lot of people at CUNA as managing director. It was a clash of personalities and an all-out power struggle."

Like Mitchell, most Texas credit unionists held Yates in the highest possible esteem. True, he had his differences with some of them, especially in the hectic days when he was fighting to move the League's headquarters from Houston to Dallas, but his dedication to credit union philosophy, his devotion to duty and his capacity for hard work were widely recognized across the state. The feelings of many of his fellow Texans were summed up in an editorial in the *Bulletin* on the occasion of his election to the presidency of CUNA in 1953:

> "Honor and glory have come to Texas through the election of a native son to the presidency of the Credit Union National Association. Natural pride rises in the hearts of Texans when they realize that such a man as H.B. Yates is a product of Texas. To become outstanding in the credit union movement, Texans have applied themselves diligently and their efforts have been successful through the guidance of leaders like Yates . . .

> "Great though this victory may be for Texas, greater still is it for the credit union movement as a whole. Often it has been said that the only danger we face is from within . . . that this philosophy of the brotherhood of man that we subscribe to may be weakened by selfishness and greed. Under the leadership of H.B. Yates, we may be assured that these temptations will be warded off. Yates has long been a man of firm conviction and a zealous proponent of credit union philosophy. In the face of opposition, he has steadfastly defended his beliefs. At the risk of personal degradation, he has promoted the welfare of the credit union members.

> "All of us in this movement can be certain that with H.B. Yates as our president . . . the thinking of our leadership will be clear, that our leader will be militant, that the bulwarks of this movement will be strengthened, that our philosophy will be protected, so that we may continue to improve our service to our fellow man."

Congressman Wright Patman thought so highly of the sentiments expressed in the editorial that he had it inserted in its entirety in the *Congressional Record,* saying: "Having known Mr. Yates for many years, my opinion is that no better selection of one to fill the presidency of the Credit Union National Association could have been made. By his past work in connection with the credit union movement, he has gained the complete confidence of the members of the association; and under this leadership, this movement will be advanced and the service steadily improved."

A sparkling personality was not, however, generally regarded as one of Yates' strong points. He had little tendency toward mirth or joviality, and he smiled infrequently. "Somber" and "taciturn" were adjectives that were often applied to his demeanor. Students at old Forest Avenue High School in Dallas, where Yates taught economics, civics and history for some 35 years—and also served a stint as a track coach—remember him as a strict disciplinarian. And associates in the Dallas Teachers Credit Union, where Yates continued to serve as president, even while heading CUNA, recall that when he made a decision to turn down a loan request, his decision was final and irrevocable.

Yates pulled no punches in condemning or castigating those he considered dishonest and unscrupulous. As a CUNA vice president in 1950, Yates struck out in a *Bulletin* article at the "dozens of parasitic money-raising organizations preying on the ignorance of corporation executives and businessmen of the country." A good example of Yates' biting rhetoric includes the following blast: "Probably the most notorious and well-heeled is the Committee for Constitutional Government, conceived by Frank Gannett and headed by ex-jailbird Edward A. Rumley. These organizations mine the sucker lists annually for untold millions of dollars that are charged to business expenses or public relations, which allow the promoters to live on the largess of the rich men of America."

Yates did, on the other hand, have his lighter moments, and those who knew him intimately during his long period of leadership recall that beneath his granite-like exterior lay a keen wit and an active sense of humor. As R.C. Morgan recalls: "I saw him convulse many an audience, of two or three or 1,000 with a single pithy, to-the-point sentence."

One example of Yates' dry wit carrying the day came during a heated debate on a proposal to increase fees paid to credit unions by a young, struggling Members Mutual. Yates took the floor, according to Morgan's recollection, and laconically compared the fledgling insurance company to a newborn calf "staggering around, trying to find its legs, with 400 credit unions trying to milk it." The comparison drew cheers and howls of laughter from TCUL delegates, and the proposal to increase fees was resoundlingly defeated.

Yates' blunt outspokenness was appreciated by most Texans, and by the time he took over the administrative reins of CUNA as its managing director, he was virtually being defied in certain quarters. *Bulletin* Editor John Quinlan summed up this attitude eloquently as he reflected in print on the 22nd annual meeting of the TCUL in 1956.

"As we looked at individuals, separate from the throng (at the meeting), we wondered what motivated them," he wrote. "Love of fellowman . . . the carnival conviviality of a convention . . . the hope of personal advancement . . . election to a high office?

"Of one man we had no doubt. Standing head and shoulders above the throng was the taciturn, somber, slender, revered H.B. Yates. Tested in the crucible of the years, of the experiences, of the knowledge, his principles are unquestioned.

"As Filene, Bergengren and Doig were appointed as founders and pioneers of the movement, we wonder if this humble man, H.B. Yates, was not appointed as the savior of this movement. As we stand at a crossroads in a titanic struggle, is this man the one pointed to by the finger of God to lead us in the right direction?

"In this period of clouded issues, when many confuse themselves by thinking they as persons are big in scope, when actually the credit union movement, dedicated to service to fellowman, is where the greatness lies, do we not need firm, gentle guidance? To preserve the principles, ideals and philosophy of the credit union movement during this time of turbulent eruption, is the calm assurance, the executive ability, the experience, the proven qualities of H.B. Yates needed?

"Of the answer we are positive."

There were plenty of others, however, who were not so positive about Yates' qualifications as a "savior." His appointment as CUNA managing director in 1955 came at a time when factionalism—much of it based on fierce interstate rivalries—was running rampant in the national movement. The states with the strongest credit union leagues were vying for control of CUNA and CUNA Mutual, and some leaders from other states saw Yates as a distinct threat. Illinois, in particular, produced an abundance of Yates critics, some of whom advocated withdrawing their state league from CUNA affiliation because of Yates.

Marion F. Gregory of Illinois, who served as CUNA president when Yates was secretary of the national organization and who later served under Yates as public relations director when the Texan was CUNA's managing director, had few kind words for Yates in his 1981 book, *Memoirs, A Credit Union Career.*

"Yates had expressed dissatisfaction with Tom Doig and staff and came into the presidency with the intent of removing him," Gregory wrote. "He was also determined to curb the influence of CUNA Mutual, accusing the Society (the tail) of wagging the dog (CUNA). This was the start of a conflict that split the movement down the middle from 1955 to 1971.

"Yates was named managing director of CUNA in November 1955, when Doig was on his death bed. This put him in a better position to tear down staff of CUNA and to oppose CUNA Mutual. Within a year, most of the top staff of CUNA resigned and took positions in CUNA Mutual."

Gregory accused Yates of attempting to get Doig fired during his term as CUNA president, but said the Executive Committee of CUNA refused to go along. As managing director, however, Yates quickly got rid of Assistant Managing Director Charles F. Eickel, the man whom many had hoped to see succeed Doig. With characteristic bluntness, Yates announced to the Executive Committee that he had appointed J. Orrin Shipe as "my assistant," thereby replacing Eickel with no advance warning.

While he "credited" Yates with splitting the national credit union movement, Gregory was highly critical of Yates' abilities as a manager. "He might have had a greater effect had he the managerial ability and experience," Gregory wrote. "He proved inept in trying to implement the management consultant's report while he had no authority to do so."

Of Yates, Gregory concluded flatly: "He obviously did not like me and did not try to hide his feelings. We had a mutual dislike for each other."

Joe DeRamus, who was managing director of the Illinois Credit Union League at the time, also had sharp differences with Yates. At first, he supported the Texan and persuaded the Illinois delegation to vote for Yates in his bid for the presidency of CUNA, in which he was opposed in 1953 by Ohioan Paul Deaton. But DeRamus soon became one of Yates' most vehement critics, accusing Yates of betraying and sabotaging the national credit union movement.

But not all out-of-state credit unionists were as harsh toward the tall Texan. In June 1957, shortly after he stepped down as CUNA managing director, Yates was honored with a special resolution by the Minnesota League of Credit Unions. The resolution read in part:

"Whereas: H.B. Yates has contributed a great many years of volunteer service to the movement on the credit union, chapter, league and national levels; and

"Whereas: H.B. Yates perceived a pronounced need for basic reforms in the manner in which certain paid professionals at the national level were performing their duties; and

"Whereas: When a clear and imminent need arose for an interim CUNA managing director to begin to effect these reforms H.B. Yates consented to carry the load in spite of the definite inadvisability of his doing so because of his health; and

"Whereas: H.B. Yates has clearly demonstrated that there is no personal sacrifice too great for him to make to further the movement; and

"Whereas: H.B. Yates rendered a highly commendable service while he was CUNA managing director. Therefore, be it

"Resolved, that the Board of Directors of the Minnesota League of Credit Unions expresses its deepest gratitude to and profoundest respect for H.B. Yates for his many valuable and untiring contributions to the movement."

It is safe to say that the vast majority of Texas credit unionists held similar feelings for Yates. To a person, all of the surviving TCUL leaders who knew Yates and worked with him over the years are unstinting in their praise of him. As the League's former Assistant Managing Director Paul Mullins expressed it many years later in summing up the leadership of the 1950s: "Yates and (C.W.) Hudson were real leaders. The rest of us were just people."

And much more important than the controversy that swirled around him was the precedent set by Yates for those Texans who would follow him into positions of national leadership. By the time he resigned as managing director, the chain of succeeding Texas leaders at the national level was already established with C.E. Burdick of Longview serving in the CUNA vice president's post once occupied by Yates. By that same time, R.C. Morgan of El Paso was serving in Yates' old job as TCUL president, and would, within a few years, follow Yates into the presidency of CUNA.

The Fifties firmly established Texas as one of the keystones in the nationwide credit union movement. And whether he was sinner or saint, H.B. Yates was the man most responsible. Jim Barry may have summed it up best when he said: "No credit union son of Texas has carried her banner abroad into the credit union world with such honor and glory."

A New Home, A New Era

On July 15, 1955, a long-standing dream became a reality for the Texas Credit Union League as groundbreaking ceremonies were held for the League's new home on property at 4533 Ross Avenue in Dallas, which had been acquired by the TCUL the preceding spring. With President Hudson, Members Mutual President Miller, Director John Quinlan and L.P. Davis, chairman of the Building and Property Committee, turning the first spades of dirt, the ceremonies marked the beginning of construction of a 12,000-square-foot, one-story brick structure designed to house all League and Members Mutual operations.

It was the culmination of many months of work by Davis and his committee, which included H.T. Sanderson of Corpus Christi, Quinlan of San Antonio, Dave Hackley of Dallas and Ray W. Roberts of Houston. A classic example of the low-slung modernistic look of the period, the building was designed by eminent Dallas architect George L. Dahl, and the general contract for its construction was awarded to Baeco, Inc. Overall cost of the project was $300,000—a truly staggering sum to those who could vividly remember the time, a dozen years earlier, when the League had the utmost difficulty raising $10,000 a year for its annual operating budget.

After a final inspection by the Building and Property Committee on February 18, 1956, the building was ready for occupancy, and TCUL and Members Mutual personnel began the considerable job of transferring their offices and operations from the old downtown office on February 25. At the time, there was not a more modern facility in Dallas. It included such features as year-round air conditioning, an intercom system with piped-in music throughout the building and a complete underground lawn sprinkler system. Such luxuries seemed a far cry, indeed, from the old duplex on Hester Street.

The new building became the glittering centerpiece of the League's 22nd annual meeting less than a month after the staff moved in, as proud credit unionists from all corners of the state came to see the dream-come-true with their own eyes. Chaired by Dallasite Jack Mitchell, the 1956 convention was easily the largest in League history when it was called to order for its opening session on March 22. In keeping with the spirit of newness that pervaded the convention, it was headquartered in Dallas' newest hotel, the sleek, sophisticated Statler-Hilton.

"When we stop to ponder the unsurpassed and thrilling cooperation of credit union people in Texas," President Hudson said in his report to the delegates, "we are amazed beyond mere words of expression. From an humble beginning of just a handful of men in a meeting in Fort Worth 22 years ago, without money or an office, to a $300,000 building and grounds is nothing short of miraculous."

On March 25, the final day of the convention, formal dedication ceremonies were held at the new building to the theme of "Bless This House, Oh Lord." Numerous out-of-state dignitaries and virtually all the top officials of CUNA and its related enterprises were present for the occasion, including CUNA President Mel Weiderman, CUNA Mutual President Gurdon P. Farr and CUNA Supply President Leonard R. Nixon. "Good Old Jim" Barry, as he was introduced by Master of Ceremonies R.C. Morgan, led the singing of the *Star-Spangled Banner;* talks were made by Hudson and Miller, and a prayer was offered by Dr. Willis M. Tate, president of Southern Methodist University. But the honor of delivering the main dedicatory address was reserved for "Texas' number one credit unionist"— CUNA Managing Director H.B. Yates.

In noting that the conference room in the new building had been formally named the Yates Room, Morgan said: "H.B. Yates has become, throughout the years, so much parcel and part of the credit union movement in Texas and in the nation that I cannot conceive of a program of this kind being truly complete without him . . . We cannot honor this man too highly."

It was an extremely heady time for the League and the credit union movement in Texas, and the end of the period of growth and expansion that had characterized every year of the 1950s was nowhere in sight. In fact, by the time the Board of Directors of the TCUL and Members Mutual met in a joint session in Corpus Christi in October 1956—just six months after the dedication of the new building—it was already apparent that the League and the insurance company were outgrowing their new home. "It seems probable," Barry told the directors, "that a second floor to the present building will have to go into planning in another year or two."

In a sense, however, the opening and dedication of the Ross Avenue headquarters marked the end of an era in the Texas credit union movement and the beginning of another. Within a year of those events, many important leadership changes were to take place within the state and national organizations. In the spring of 1957, after serving as TCUL president for eight years, Hudson made the decision to step down. In his final report,

Joined by Phil Davis (left) and Bob Miller (right), League President C. W. Hudson took the wheel of a heavy earth-moving machine as ground was broken for the new Ross Avenue building.

President R. C. Morgan addresses the League's Silver Anniversary meeting in Houston in 1959.

A large crowd of proud credit unionists attended dedication ceremonies for the League's new home in 1956 (top photo). But a few years later, growth of the League and Members Mutual necessitated the addition of a second story to the building.

submitted to the annual meeting in San Antonio that March, he spelled out his reasons for the decision. "I have not had a vacation since 1950," he said. "In addition, many long, trying hours have been devoted to League activities, while my duties as an employee of Dallas Transit Company have been neglected. There are no regrets, however, as I step down, save that of wishing that I could have been of more service to a movement dear to my heart. May I assure you that the more than 70,000 miles traveled and the 300 addresses delivered were not for selfish motives or ambitions. There is a firm conviction in my soul that God has given every man and woman . . . a duty to discharge, a task to perform, a mission to fulfill . . . There is the sweet consolation as we approach this last long mile that I have meant something to most of you—and helped those in trouble to smile."

As he turned over the reins of the presidency to R.C. Morgan, Hudson could take satisfaction in the realization of one of his most cherished goals. The magic milestone of 1,000 credit unions had finally been reached. When Hudson had assumed the League's top elective post in 1949, there had been only 354 credit unions in Texas; on the day he relinquished it, there were 1,002, of which 896 were League members. And this was only one example. Eight years earlier, the League's staff of five people had been crowded into a one-room office in the Southland Building; today there were 59 "of the finest employees in the world occupying a beautiful and spacious office building."

Morgan, Hudson's successor, had been active in the credit union movement for some 28 years at the time of his elevation to the League presidency, and since 1939 had been a leader of the Government Employees Credit Union in El Paso, where he continues to serve as full-time treasurer-manager and president. His credit union had grown to the second largest in Texas by the late 1950s, with more than 7,000 members and more than $3 million in assets. He had first been elected to the

180

TCUL Board in 1953 and had quickly established himself as a thoughtful and hard-driving leader. A native hill country Texan from Burnet County, Morgan had organized and assisted in organizing numerous new credit unions in the region.

Hudson steadfastly refused to take any personal credit for the advancements made during his presidency, preferring to give credit to other individuals and the organization itself. "Organization," he noted, citing a slogan in the dressing room of the St. Louis Cardinals baseball team, "is the art of getting men to respond like thoroughbreds. When you call on a thoroughbred, he gives you all the speed, heart and sinew in him. When you call on a jackass, he kicks."

By the standards of all concerned, C.W. Hudson was a true thoroughbred.

His was not the only key departure of this time, however. Almost simultaneously, Bob Miller decided to step down as president of Members Mutual after serving continuously in that post since the company's founding in 1952. He was succeeded by Lester P. Shannon, who had served on the Auto Insurance Committee with Miller prior to the formation of Members Mutual. Shannon, president of the Quaker Employees Federal Credit Union of Sherman, took over the insurance company's top post in 1956 as it continued the phenomenal rate of growth that had characterized it from the beginning. By the end of 1956, Members Mutual had more than 20,600 policyholders and had paid more than $2.5 million in claims during its lifetime. In July of 1956, the company added fire insurance on dwellings and household goods up to $25,000 for credit union members and issued more than 100 such policies by the end of the year.

So successful was the Members Mutual experience—the only one of its kind in the national credit union movement—that by 1957 a TCUL committee was studying the possibility of setting up a separate life insurance company as a League affiliate. Although the proposal to establish such a company was at first voted down by League member credit unions, it was one that would resurface very shortly.

The changing of the guard in the leadership circles of the League was further accelerated at the annual meeting in Galveston in March 1958. Morgan was re-elected president at the Board of Directors meeting that followed, and such veteran officers as C.E. Burdick, secretary-treasurer, H.T. Sanderson, first vice president, and John Quinlan, second vice president, also were re-elected. Jack Mitchell became third vice president. But the membership of the Board overall underwent perhaps its greatest shakeup since the League's organization in 1934; as no fewer than seven new members were named to the sixteen-member body. Hudson was succeeded on the board by Burton C. Eubanks of Austin Steel Credit Union, Dallas; S.D. Jackman, Jr. was succeeded by Jim Dodd of Houston Telephone Federal Credit Union; and M.A. Henderson was succeeded by James W. Huggins of Postal Employees Federal Credit Union, Waco. In addition, three directors joined the board from districts newly created by an amendment to the by-laws. They included William L. Fanning of the Texas Employment Commission Credit Union, Austin; Dr. J.K. Lamar of the Medical Branch Credit Union, Galveston; and O.M. Fletcher of the Foremost West Texas Federal Credit Union, Abilene. Only holdover directors re-elected were Sanderson, Mrs. Dyalthia Benson of Hereford and L.E. McMakin of Houston.

One of the new Board's first major actions was approving the addition to the Ross Avenue headquarters that Barry had predicted would be needed soon. At a joint meeting with the Members Mutual Board in September 1958, a contract was approved for adding a second floor that would more than double the building's size, to 26,830 square feet. It was scheduled to be ready for occupancy in March 1959—just in time to celebrate the League's Silver Anniversary.

The Silver Jubilee

What a difference 25 years makes!

Texas credit unionists celebrated that difference in 1959 as they staged a Silver Jubilee in honor of the TCUL's 25th anniversary. Truly, they had a great deal to celebrate. Their ranks had swelled from 8,048 members to more than 700,000 in the quarter-century since 1934 and the number of credit unions in Texas had increased from 38 at the time of the League's formation to more than 1,100 by early 1959. Members' savings and outstanding loans were now measured in the hundreds of millions of dollars, instead of in the "nickel-and-dime" amounts of 1934.

In March of 1959, all roads led to Houston as the focal point for the Jubilee. A total of 1,312 registered visitors and delegates turned out for the League's 25th annual meeting on March 20 and 21 at Houston's Rice Hotel, the product of many months of planning by General Chairman Joseph Murray and co-chairman Sid Jackman. President Morgan told them that, although the credit union movement had reached a plateau in its development, it was still a long way from the peak of its potential.

"I think," he said, "if we have courage and vision and if we dream the dream of service dreamed by Raiffeisen and by the founders of the Texas Credit Union League, that we stand on the threshold of the greatest period of development and growth we have ever known. The world needs credit unions . . ."

Items of major importance reported to the delegates to the convention by Morgan and Jim Barry included the establishment of a permanent Public Relations Department for the League, a step that had been under consideration for a couple of years and which had

183

finally been taken in the fall of 1958. "Our Public Relations Department is a reality," Morgan pointed out. "For the first time, we have in the person of Public Relations Director Glenn Addington someone who is professionally trained and qualified to help us improve our public relations—with the managements of our companies, with legislators, with community leaders, with the general public and, last but not least, with our own members. Our Public Relations Department is not an "apple-polishing' project. In the beginning, our efforts seem small, but as time passes, we will accomplish more and more."

There was a spirited floor fight at the convention over the adoption of a record TCUL budget of $230,000 for the coming year. An amendment to trim it by $30,000 lost at first by a razor-thin margin of 149 to 151. Later, it was resubmitted and voted down by a larger margin. Part of the opposition was based on an increase in the dues schedule for credit unions now paying the maximum annual dues of $1,000. These credit unions were required to pay an additional 10 cents per member to finance the increased League expenditures. Delegates also voted to support a bill pending in the State Legislature (S.B. No. 252) that would increase examination fees for state-chartered credit unions, but decided to drop proposed legislation to create a separate supervisory body apart from the State Banking Department for state credit unions.

The Houston convention also commemorated the seventh anniversary of the founding of Members Mutual. In another sense, however, it was also a time of mourning for the insurance company, since its first president, R.E. Miller, had passed away the preceding August. But the company's current president, L.P. Shannon, urged policyholders to look ahead and work toward the future. "We are justifiably proud of our outstanding progress of yesterday," he said, noting that records had been set in 1958 in premium dollar volume, policyholder reserves and surplus and both in the number of credit unions and number of individual members served, "and with your continued support we look forward to greater service and growth for tomorrow." At the Members Mutual Board of Directors meeting on March 22, T.J. Ford of Port Arthur succeeded Shannon as president. Ford had been one of the League's organizers in 1934 and had served on the first Board of Directors. Shannon was elected vice president along with a slate of officers including Joseph A. Collerain, secretary, and John L. Quinlan, treasurer.

Back at the Dallas headquarters, meanwhile, TCUL and Members Mutual staffers were still celebrating the expansion of the home office building. And all across the state, Texas credit unions were experiencing the greatest building boom in their history during this Silver Anniversary year. No fewer than nine credit unions occupied their own new buildings within a period of approximately twelve months. They included Dallas Teachers, which opened its own $275,000 building on Ross Avenue in Dallas, across the street from TCUL headquarters; Carbide Employees of Texas City, which moved into a new $50,000 home; and Humble Employees of Baytown, whose new building cost $36,000. Others involved in the building boom were Shell Refinery of Deer Park, Cotton Belt of Texarkana, Houston Telephone, San Antonio Telephone, Fort Worth Telephone and Southern Pacific Mechanical Employees of El Paso.

The Jubilee continued in the fall of 1959 with the observance of the actual founding of the League on October 6 and observances of International Credit Union Day on October 15. A special twenty-page edition of the Bulletin, one of the largest ever printed, commemorated the Fort Worth organizational meeting of 1934. The edition honored four Texas credit unionists whose efforts and dedication had been instrumental in building the League to its present size and position—H.B. Yates, C.W. Hudson, L. Phil Davis, and the late R.E.

Miller. The four were cited as being "indicative of the fiber of the leadership that has developed in the past 25 years."

The 25th anniversary of the signing into law of the Federal Credit Union Act of 1934 also came in 1959, of course, and on September 22 of that year, President Eisenhower signed a bill designed to thoroughly modernize that original law. Designated as Public Law 86-354, the new bill incorporated 18 amendments into the Federal Credit Union Act, plus a complete recodification. The President's action followed quick and unanimous passage of the bill in both houses of Congress.

In its final version, the bill accomplished practically everything the organized credit union movement had set out to obtain when it had launched a campaign to secure the legislation more than three years earlier. Major features of the bill included:

(1) Increasing the maximum unsecured loan limit from $400 to $750.

(2) Increasing the loan maturity limit from three to five years.

(3) Permitting the appointment of loan officers to approve up to the maximum unsecured loan limit.

(4) Permitting the selling of negotiable checks and money orders to members, and the cashing of checks and money orders for members for a fee.

(5) Providing for conversion from federal to state charter and vice-versa.

(6) Permitting allocation of space in federal buildings for credit unions having a membership composed of at least 95 percent of persons who are or were federal employees.

(7) Permitting loans to directors and committee members up to their shareholdings in the credit union, plus the total unencumbered and unpledged shareholdings of any co-signer.

(8) Providing for declaration of dividends by the board of directors.

(9) Permitting annual or semi-annual dividends by the board of directors.

(10) Allowing appointment of a supervisory committee by the board of directors, one of whom may be a director other than the treasurer.

(11) Permitting dividend credit for a month on shares which are or will become fully paid up during the first five days of that month.

(12) Prohibiting compensation to any director, committee member or officer other than the treasurer for services rendered as such.

(13) Permitting appointment of an executive committee of not less than three directors to act on the purchase and sale of securities or the making of loans to other credit unions, and to act on membership applications, and permitting appointment of a membership officer to approve applications for membership.

CUNA Director Cecil Burdick of Texas was among a delegation of leading national credit unionists who went to Washington in May 1959 to testify on the proposed amendments to the law before a sub-committee of the House Banking and Currency Committee, chaired by Congressman Wright Patman, the movement's longtime friend and ally.

The signing of the law by President Eisenhower made his proclamation of International Credit Union Day some two weeks later even more meaningful. Some of the nation's largest observances of "CU Day" were in Texas, where the largest banquet audience ever to assemble in Texarkana heard Senate Majority Leader Lyndon Johnson, Congressman Patman and CUNA Managing Director H. Vance Austin pay tribute to the credit union movement.

"Thirty years ago, credit in the United States was largely the exclusive privilege of those who needed it least," Senator Johnson told the group of more than 500 persons. "Today it is one of our biggest businesses and one of the most vital factors in the functioning of our economy." He pledged that Congress "will encourage and strengthen the existence of your credit unions."

TCUL President Morgan presented the senator with a plaque in appreciation of his outstanding service to his fellowman and for his notable statesmanship. In a personal aside, Morgan recalled seeing Johnson campaigning many years before at a small general store in Central Texas during his first congressional race and remarked how impressed he had been with the young LBJ.

Visibly touched, Johnson accepted the plaque, saying: "I pledge anew my faith in you, my confidence in the fiscal soundness of your program and my confidence in your integrity."

The faith and confidence of many other people in the Texas credit union movement was amply evidenced by the strong position enjoyed by that movement as the historic decade of the Fifties passed into the record books. Total savings of Texas credit union members stood at the quarter-billion-dollar mark, with loans not far behind. Members were being added at the rate of nearly 50,000 per year and savings were growing at an annual pace of $27 million. Membership in the TCUL, meanwhile, had grown to an all-time high of 999 credit unions by the end of 1959 (although the percentage of the state's credit unions holding League membership had declined slightly to just over 87 percent). According to CUNA figures, new credit unions were being formed around the country at the rate of four per day during the year, and Texas had recently climbed into third place among all the states in the number of active credit unions, behind Illinois and California. According to financial statements issued by the company at year's end, Members Mutual—which had not even existed when the Fifties began—had amassed assets of more than $3.25 million by the decade's close.

188

TOTAL MEMBERS SAVINGS — 1977 THRU 1983

Year	Savings	% of Savings
1977		
Regular Shares	$3,408,786,753	93.2%
Share Drafts	48,426,207	1.3%
Other Savings	200,821,024	5.5%
Total	$3,658,033,984	100%
1978		
Regular Shares	$3,507,024,897	89.7%
Share Drafts	95,783,696	2.5%
Other Savings	305,725,397	7.8%
Total	$3,908,533,990	100%
1979		
Regular Shares	$3,314,931,210	77.6%
Share Drafts	150,687,423	3.5%
Other Savings	807,703,650	18.9%
Total	$4,273,322,283	100%
1980		
Regular Shares	$3,205,402,841	66.6%
Share Drafts	228,361,579	4.8%
Other Savings	1,376,646,016	28.6%
Total	$4,810,410,436	100%
1981		
Regular Shares	$2,942,969,998	58.2%
Share Drafts	314,204,164	6.2%
Other Savings	1,797,062,207	35.6%
Total	$5,054,236,369	100%
1982		
Regular Shares	$3,328,517,991	58.6%
Share Drafts	421,515,592	7.4%
Other Savings	1,932,287,753	34.0%
Total	$5,682,321,336	100%
1983		
Regular Shares	$4,068,248,440	58.0%
Share Drafts	760,798,036	10.8%
Other Savings	2,189,358,855	31.2%
Total	$7,018,405,331	100%

"All in all, 1959 was an excellent year," concluded Jim Barry. It marked an excellent final chapter in a decade of exceptional accomplishment. But now a new decade was at hand, one in which the League and its member credit unions would not be allowed to rest on their laurels, one in which the maturity of the movement must not be allowed to stagnate into senility, settle comfortably into complacency, or lose its enthusiasm for conquering new frontiers.

As robust as it had grown during the 1950s, close scrutiny still revealed some serious cracks and flaws in the strong facade of the credit union movement. As its own leaders had repeatedly warned, the movement's enemies had also grown stronger, just as it had. And there were also rifts within the movement itself. They were apparent in the continuing friction between CUNA and CUNA Mutual, the latest outburst involving plans to organize a casualty company—plans which the TCUL opposed, incidentally. And at the state level, currents of dissent still rippled under the surface between the League and its own insurance affiliate, Members Mutual.

So, as the Fifties faded away, the need for goodwill, good sense and hard work did not fade with them. The uncharted waters and unknown challenges of the Sixties lay just ahead. It was time to lay the celebration of past accomplishments aside and prepare for the hard realities of a tomorrow that was already here.

PART III:

Reaching for Tomorrow (1960-1984)

The Soaring Sixties

By the dawn of the 1960s, rising economic aspirations had become an ingrained part of the lifestyle of most Americans—and, consequently, so had credit. The ability to buy virtually anything the consumer desired on long-term or short-term credit was no longer a "new toy," but a vital tool in the typical wage-earner's pursuit of the "good life." But the mild recession of the late 1950s had caused widespread public disenchantment. There was again the feeling among the public that the economy could—and should—continue its phenomenal upward spiral indefinitely, and that the "good life" could keep on getting better and better if someone could just "get the country moving again."

Fifteen years of steady postwar economic growth and ever-higher salaries had wiped away the memory of Depression-era poverty and hardship from many minds, and mass-media advertising fueled the public's desire for all the varied ingredients it identified as making up the "good life." Among young wage-earners and their families, there no longer seemed any reason to postpone the major purchases of a lifetime. Automobiles could be bought for little or no money down, and even new homes were available for a total move-in cost of a few hundred dollars. But unfortunately for many, it was much easier to "buy" something than it was to pay for it. As Americans eagerly reached for the moon and the promise of more and more fruitful tomorrows, the high-rate money lenders were reaping a bonanza. The age of "credit card-itis," plastic money, instant financing and "fly now, pay later" was being ushered into tens of thousands of Texas homes. Americans were eager to soar with this soaring new decade. But as they soared, so did their installment debts. So did the number of wage-earner bankruptcies. And so did the number of pleas for help from families who found themselves on a runaway merry-go-round of indebtedness. Countless such families were asking the same plaintive questions: "How can we make ends meet and still meet our financial obligations? How can we ever pull ourselves out of this hole we've spent ourselves into?"

Obviously, it was a time of great opportunity for credit unions and a time of great need for the services they could offer. An actual case history compiled by the Austin Texas Employment Commission Credit Union, based on the experience of one of its own members, and published in the *Bulletin,* graphically illustrated what a difference a credit union loan could make to the debt-ridden. When a member of the credit union obtained a loan from a finance company of $1,059.83, the total note was for $1,680, by the time insurance, interest, service charges and various fees were added on for the 24-month term of the note. In other words, the cost of borrowing $1,059.83 from the finance company came to $620.17, while the credit union could have loaned the same amount and charged just $105.98. The message was clear: "See your credit union first!"

But millions of Texans still had no access to credit union services. Before credit unions could take full advantage of the opportunities of the 1960s and extend their services to those who needed them most, the movement needed to "clean up its own act" and achieve a greater degree of internal unity.

President Morgan addressed some of the inner ills afflicting the credit union movement in his report to delegates at the TCUL's 26th annual meeting in Austin on March 26, 1960. He had harsh words for those engaged in the current squabble over whether CUNA Mutual should organize a casualty insurance company, saying that there were "vastly more important" matters to be discussed at top-level meetings.

"The CUNA Mutual Insurance Society is a service affiliate of our movement, organized to provide credit unions loan protection, and (a little later) life savings insurance—nothing more," Morgan emphasized. "And yet, the organized credit union movement is threatening at this very moment to split itself asunder over its insurance problems.

"I think both the Credit Union National Association and the CUNA Mutual Insurance Society had better forget about organizing a casualty insurance company. I think (CUNA Mutual) had better get back to being the unique type insurance company it set out to be, providing credit unions loan protection and life savings insurance at the lowest possible cost.

"The Texas Credit Union League has an insurance affiliate, the Members Mutual Insurance Company. Members Mutual serves, and serves well, the insurance needs of those credit unions and those credit union members who wish to use its services. It is a service affiliate of the Texas Credit Union League, nothing more. I pray that we in Texas may never face the kind of dissension over insurance problems which has split the credit union movement on the national level. I honestly do not believe we ever will."

Morgan blamed the CUNA insurance feud on the tendency of some to try to complicate and corrupt the basically simple concept behind credit unions. "I am convinced," he said, "that the greatest danger the credit union movement faces today is the danger that we who preach the gospel of credit unions may forget the simple, basic truths upon which our movement is founded . . . that we may forget, in this complex world in which we live, what a truly simple thing a credit union is. Too many people, I fear, have already forgotten that the finest things of life are the simple things. If we in the credit union movement ever forget this, then the credit union movement is lost, and credit unions will be just another kind of financial institution, without a heart, a soul or a mission of service to mankind . . .

"All we have to do is to remember that credit unions are organized to help people help themselves by helping one another, and that we are here today to help ourselves by helping one another!"

Beginning in the early 1960s, a number of key changes in federal and state statutes were enacted that were to have a profound effect on the future of the TCUL and its member organizations. In 1959, the Texas Legislature had enacted a Non-Profit Corporation Act, which contained a number of advantages for the TCUL, advantages not afforded in the general law under which the League had been originally incorporated in 1945. The new law specified that eligible corporations would automatically come under the provisions of the law by September 1, 1961, unless they took action to place themselves under the law prior to that time. After determining that it did, indeed, qualify for non-profit status under the law, the League was brought under the act before the end of 1960.

In a special report on the Non-Profit Corporation Act, Barry outlined the law's advantages to the League as follows: "Over the years the League, as a corporation not for profit, has operated with very little law on the statutes to guide it . . . The new law is drawn in such a way that where we have only made provision for the handling of certain items in our Constitution and By-Laws, it appears that each of these provisions are authorized by the new law and can remain in effect. The new law also appears to be drawn in such a way that it is now inconsistent with many of our customs and practices which have never had the sanction of being incorporated in our By-Laws. Additionally, the new law provides for many contingencies, such as dissolution, for which we have never made provision. Finally, the new law grants many specific powers to the non-profit

194

corporation about which there has been some doubt at times in the past . . ."

Other important developments at the state level included the passage of a set of important amendments to the Texas credit union law in the spring of 1961. Introduced in the State Senate by Senator George Parkhouse of Dallas as S. B. 145 and in the House by Representative Don Kennard of Fort Worth as H.B. 354, the amendments package carried eight key changes in the existing law. When passed by the Legislature and signed into law by Governor Price Daniel, the amendments:

(1) Allowed credit unions engaged in making petty cash loans to levy a minimum service charge.

(2) Provided for branch operations.

(3) Set statutory requirements for the liquidations of credit unions.

(4) Provided that under special conditions the State Banking Department would have authority to require a a credit union to set up special reserves for delinquent loans.

(5) Permitted patronage refund payments after the statutory transfer to the guaranty fund had been made.

(6) Provided for the declaration of dividends by the board of directors of a credit union.

(7) Defined capital and surplus.

(8) Made it a criminal offense for anyone found guilty of circulating malicious, unfounded, or untrue rumors about credit unions.

The proposed amendments were all products of the League's Legislative Committee, headed by Jack Mitchell, who spent a great deal of his time during the early 1960s traveling back and forth between Austin and Washington. Indeed, Mitchell was right there, looking over Governor Daniel's left shoulder on April 6, 1961, as the state's chief executive signed the amendments into law. Barry also represented the League at the signing, which the *Bulletin* termed "another milestone in the ever-improving credit union situation in Texas."

At about this same time, the credit unions of Texas scored yet another legislative victory by successfully amending a bill that would have stymied the credit union life insurance program in Texas. Styled Senate Bill 212, the law would have prevented credit unions without life savings insurance from contracting for it and would have prevented credit unions from changing from one insurance carrier to another. Alertness on the part of the Legislative Committee was a factor in changing the bill, but if it had not been for a warning from CUNA's legal counsel about the bill's dangerous potential, the eleventh-hour amendment that excluded credit unions from its provisions might not have come in time. The close call caused League officials to call for obtaining legal counsel for the TCUL and Members Mutual by no later than January 1, 1962.

In Washington, meanwhile, both the TCUL and CUNA lent their support to a "Truth-in-Lending" Bill introduced in Congress in 1960 by Illinois Senator Paul Douglas. Along with other credit union leaders from around the United States, Morgan went to Washington to testify in behalf of the bill. "In interviewing thousands of people in connection with loan applications, all too often we find them to be deeply in debt—many times actually financially insolvent—due to their lack of understanding of the cost of credit," Morgan testified.

"I submit to you that it is bad enough for a person not to understand the legitimate charges for credit made by banks and reputable lending agencies. It is much worse when an unsuspecting consumer is deceived by an unscrupulous salesman or lender and when we permit a situation to exist which makes it impossible for the consumer to compare rates and shop for the most reasonable source of credit."

Writing in the July 1960 edition of the *Bulletin*, League Secretary-Treasurer Burdick further illustrated the need for the "Truth-in-Lending" Bill by citing a case that had occurred a short time earlier in Houston. As reported in the *Houston Chronicle*, a garbage worker for the City of Houston had borrowed $60 from a loan company on the condition that he repay $90 on payday— just four days later.

"I just got to wondering how that ("Truth-in-Lending") legislation would make this $30 interest for use of $60 for four days look when the lender had to advertise his true interest charges and true simple interest rate," Burdick said. "The lender in Houston—and there are more like him than most of us realize—would have had to advertise in much this manner:

"Borrow $60 for four days—total charges $30 or 4550 percent simple interest. Loan *not* insured without additional charges."

Burdick carried this idea a step further, clipping credit advertisements from various newspapers and using them to create a table showing simple interest rates charged by various finance companies and one major national retailer. The rates ranged from a low of 18 percent to a high of 31 percent, but credit union interest charges on all types of loans involved would have been a uniform 12 percent.

Despite the intensive efforts of the League and its Legislative Committee, there were powerful and well-financed opponents lined up on the other side of the issue, including some of the nation's largest retailers and lending institutions. The first time around, the state's powerful small loan lobby succeeded in tacking on a number of riders to the "Truth-in-Lending" Bill, including one authorizing "service" charges, and the bill bogged down and failed to pass.

But the move for a "Truth-in-Lending" statute to protect the huge numbers of citizens now living on credit did not end with this setback. Actually, the Texas campaign was one of 47 being waged in state legislatures in the nation's fifty states during the early years of the

Sixties. Even so, the main battle for a meaningful "Truth-in-Lending" law that would cover the entire nation was being fought at the federal level in Washington. Eventually, there would be such a law, but even after it was enacted, credit unions could expect increasingly bitter attacks from those who stood to lose billions of dollars in the high-stakes game of small loans and installment credit interest.

Changing the Guard

After two decades in which the key leadership positions in the Texas credit union movement had been occupied primarily by the same handful of people, the 1960s quickly developed as a period of significant change. This changing of the guard received major impetus when R.C. Morgan, who had served as League president since 1957—a relatively brief tenure in comparison to the lengthy administrations of Yates and Hudson—accepted nomination to the post of CUNA president early in 1961, leaving the TCUL presidency up for grabs.

In his four years as League president, Morgan had proved a highly effective, keenly perceptive leader. His presidency had begun in a burst of turbulence at the 1957 annual meeting, where delgates had given the Board of Directors an extremely hard time, consistently voting down board recommendations after vociferous opposition from the floor. When the board had met to elect officers, confidence was at a low ebb and, as *Bulletin* editor Quinlan phrased it in an editorial, "gloom was rampant." Their choice for this troubled time was Morgan, who assumed the presidency with quiet sincerity and diligence. "Through his efforts," Quinlan wrote, "he convinced the credit unionists of Texas that the League belonged to the credit union people of Texas, not to the Board of Directors. Through his sponsorship, new ideas were introduced to foster this

198

idea ... Based on his accomplishments and performance in Texas, directors of the Credit Union National Association could not go wrong with the selection of R.C. Morgan as president."

In his final report to the League at the annual meeting in Dallas on March 25, 1961, Morgan stressed the same themes he had emphasized so often before. "I hope ... that you will remember the aims and purposes of the Texas Credit Union League, and the principles of brotherhood, mutual aid and self-help which make credit unions unique among the financial institutions of the world," he said. "I hope you will remember, too, the achievements of the past 27 years. For if you remember these things, I think you need not fear for the soundness of your decisions."

Some six weeks later, on May 12 in Montreal, Canada, Morgan was sworn in as the new president of CUNA as he grasped the ceremonial gavel engraved with the names of all past presidents, including H.B. Yates of Texas. As president, Morgan became chief elected official of an international association which now served 15,000,000 individual credit union members in eleven countries. "The credit union movement is still the symbol of brotherhood and human dignity," he said in accepting his new office, as the strains of the "Eyes of Texas" echoed through the Grand Salon of Montreal's Queen Elizabeth Hotel.

"This election was a great personal victory for Morgan and his leadership abilities," said the *Bulletin.* "It was also a victory for Texas credit unionists, demonstrating the high regard that is accorded them throughout the recognition that has been granted a Texan ... With this honor also comes an obligation. This is an indication that Texans are considered the banner bearers of the credit union ideal, the guards of the guidons of basic credit union philosophy."

Back home, Morgan's successor as president of the TCUL was H.T. "Sandy" Sanderson of Corpus Christi, who had served on the League Board of Directors since 1946 and who had previously held the posts of first, second and third vice president. A versatile veteran of the movement, Sanderson had been associated with credit unions since 1939, and had served his own credit union, Corpus Christi Telco Federal, in many capacities. Since 1952, he had held the job of full-time assistant treasurer and manager. An active organizer in the Corpus Christi area, he had served as the first president of the League's Corpus Christi Chapter.

Other changes were also taking place in the League's leadership structure. Reflecting the emergence of women in the business and professional world (the first woman ever to hold a seat on the TCUL Board was Willie Martin of Waco, elected in 1950), the first woman member of the TCUL Executive Committee was named when the Board of Directors met on March 26, 1961. Mrs. Dyalthia Benson of the Hereford Federal Credit Union, who had been serving on the board for some time, was elevated to the office of third vice president. Serving with her and Sanderson on the Executive Committee were L.E. McMakin, who had succeeded C.E. Burdick as secretary-treasurer after the latter's record tenure of more than twenty years; Jack Mitchell, first vice president; and John Quinlan, second vice president. At the same time, two new directors, Oran Dill of the Texarkana Terminal Employees Federal Credit Union and Wayland L. Jones of the LeTourneau Texas Federal Credit Union of Longview, joined the board for the first time.

Women were also making their presence felt in various other leadership positions in the Texas credit union movement. Dy Benson had already set an outstanding example for other women to follow during her tenure as a League director and officer. And in 1958, Bessie Heard of Houston became the first female appointee to the Texas Credit Union Commission when she was named to that body by Governor Price Daniel.

Texas Gov. Buford Jester signs the credit union law of 1947 in Austin as top League officials stand by.

Texas credit union leaders visited Rep. Wright Patman in Washington in February 1965 to show their appreciation for his efforts in behalf of the credit union cause.

State Sen. George Parkhouse of Dallas (third from left) and leaders of the TCUL watch approvingly as Gov. John Connally affixes his signature to amendments to the state credit union law in 1963.

TCUL President R. C. Morgan (left) and U.S. House Speaker Sam Rayburn display a plaque commemorating the 50th anniversary of the founding of the nation's first credit union in 1959. Looking on are League officials (from left) Dyalthia Benson, Albert Henry, Jack Mitchell and Cecil Burdick.

Gov. Preston Smith signs more credit union legislation in 1970. That same year, Smith became the first Texas chief executive to address a TCUL meeting.

Mrs. Heard, a charter member of the Schlumberger Employees Credit Union of Houston when it was organized in 1946 and a full-time credit union employee since 1949, had already made her mark in Houston by becoming the first woman member of the Houston Chapter's board and then the first woman chapter president.

In all, she was destined to serve four four-year terms on the Credit Union Commission, which was strictly an advisory group with little power when she first was appointed to it, but which became the major authority governing state-chartered credit unions after the establishment of the State Credit Union Department in 1969.

"I think that women have as much a place in credit unions as anybody," Mrs. Heard said in a recent interview in Shreveport, Louisiana, where she now lives in retirement, "but I think the main requirement for anyone in a leadership position is that he or she do a good job, regardless of whether the person is a man or a woman. I'm not a 'libber' and I don't believe in quota systems."

Mrs. Heard credits her good friend Dy Benson with being "one of the real credit union pioneers in Texas," but refuses to take similar credit for herself, although many of her contemporaries believe her role has been at least equally important. Like Mrs. Benson, Mrs. Heard also served for a number of years on the League Board while serving as manager of the Schlumberger Credit Union. She retired in 1976.

Asked about her own contributions as a credit union leader, Mrs. Heard said candidly: "I asked rather blunt questions. I believe in doing things right or in not doing them at all. I got good results from my committees and I always tried to be a team player. I got along with almost everybody. I don't believe in just agreeing all the time, but I also think everybody deserves a fair shake."

Such exemplary leaders as Mrs. Heard and Mrs. Benson have paved the way for more and more women in key positions within the credit union movement, but they have done so, as Mrs. Heard observed, more in the role of "team players" than as "libbers" or revolutionaries.

The changing of the guard is, of course, an inevitability in any movement or organization. But the saddest example of that change is the death of revered and irreplaceable leaders. Thus, the late spring of 1960 was a time of mourning for credit unionists throughout Texas. On May 29, C.W. Hudson, one of the most colorful figures in the history of the movement in Texas, died suddenly at his Dallas home at the age of 56. At the time of his death, he was still serving as a national director of CUNA and was an ex-officio member of the TCUL board.

Possibly even more so than his predecessor Yates, Hudson had guided the League through a period of almost unbelievable accomplishment during his eight years as president. An ordained Baptist minister who had begun life as the son of a poor farmer near Rusk, Texas, Hudson was known across the length and breadth of the Lone Star State for his stirring speeches and dynamic personality.

"Even unto the great death inevitably comes," said the *Bulletin* in a special memorial tribute to Hudson. "Today we mourn the passing of one of our truly great credit union leaders, C.W. Hudson. His influence on the credit union movement was felt not only in his own city and state, but internationally. With his engaging personality, he counted friends in the credit union movement everywhere . . .

"Through his efforts and the application of his talents, the credit union movement in Texas has grown to be an outstanding one . . . and he will be remembered as a dynamic pioneer and leader forever."

In 1962, a more lasting tribute to Hudson was made in the form of a memorial scholarship fund established in his name by the joint boards of the League and Members Mutual.

A Birthday Party

July 1, 1962, marked the tenth anniversary of the first policy issued by a newborn insurance company named Members Mutual, and the occasion obviously called for both a celebration and an accounting of what the company had accomplished during its first decade of existence. It was also a time for looking back and reminiscing a bit. Many of those who had been instrumental in its founding were now gone, but a small corps of the original architects of the company were still on hand for the birthday party, and they had an abundance of memories to share.

By the time of the anniversary, T.J. Ford had been succeeded as president of Members Mutual by Saylors J. Mobley of the Amoco Employees Federal Credit Union of Texas City, who was elected at the company's tenth annual meeting in March 1962. Ford, however, remained a member of the Executive Committee, as did one other Texas credit union pioneer, Joseph A. Collerain, who continued to serve as secretary of the company. Other members of the Executive Committee as the tenth anniversary arrived were Duke Baker of Big Spring, vice president, and George Latz of Dallas, treasurer. Other members of the Board of Directors included oldtimer John L. Quinlan of San Antonio, former President Lester P. Shannon of Sherman, James H. Amis of El Paso, William R. Cash of Tyler, Ira L. Bone of Amarillo, Jerry Deering of Fort Worth, B.C. Eubanks of Dallas, M.A. Henderson of Waco, V.R. "Larry" LaRochelle of Corpus Christi, Joseph P. Murray of Houston and Fred M. Scantlen of Austin.

The management staff of the company, still headed by the indefatigable Jim Barry as managing director, had grown to include J.B. Browning as assistant managing director, Ted McGehee as investments and internal auditor, Lynn Matteson as director of research, Dan Smith as membership services director, Robert B. Ingram as claims manager, Clarence Rodgers as underwriting manager, V.R. Shirley as chief accountant and Jerry J. Jeter as data processing manager.

Every year since 1952 had seen major milestones in the company's growth and expansion. By 1953, its second year of operation, Members Mutual had passed the $1 million mark in assets and had nearly 13,000 policies in force for credit union members. In 1954, assets passed $1.5 million and by 1955, there were over 17,000 policyholders, and Members Mutual auto insurance coverage was extended to credit union members in Arkansas and New Mexico. When the company moved into its new home office in 1956, it had assets of more than $2 million and paid dividends of $269,000. In 1957, when service was extended to Oklahoma, Members Mutual ranked as the fastest growing casualty company in the Southwest with $2,246,000 in assets and more than 24,000 policyholders. In 1958, assets jumped another half-million dollars as more and more credit union members began doing business with "their" company. By 1959, when new coverages were added, assets reached $3.3 million and dividends totalled $425,000. In 1960 and 1961, the company again paid 20 percent dividends of more than a half-million dollars annually. And by early 1962, assets stood at nearly $4.3 million and the company counted 33,119 policyholders.

In his first report to the joint boards of Members Mutual and the TCUL on September 21, 1962, Mobley was able to point out that the growth of the company's first ten years was continuing without letup as its second decade began. "The growth of Members Mutual thus far in 1962 has been gratifying," he said. "In each of the first two quarters we have done more than a million dollars in business. By standards used in the insurance business, we are not a large company; however, in Texas we are now being considered as a competitor by the large companies in the automobile insurance field."

Chartered strictly to serve credit union members, administered by an unpaid Board of Directors and actually run by its policyholders, Members Mutual was something of an enigma both to the commercial insurance industry in Texas and to the State Insurance Department in Austin.

The interest of outside observers and competitors was heightened, no doubt, by the obvious fact that Members Mutual had no intention of settling into a nice, comfortable rut and staying there. Even as the tenth anniversary was being celebrated, leaders of the company were rapidly moving it into the homeowner insurance market, although only a few homeowner policies had yet been written. "It is my hope," said Mobley, "that we will be able to increase our sales and accelerate our service in this field ... I believe we have a great potential in this field. However, in the past very little has been done to promote our business in this area."

The move into the homeowner insurance market was part of an effort to broaden the base of the insurance company—a step that was appearing more and more advantageous to key officers of the company.

The feeling that something had to be done to keep Members Mutual practices in sympathy with credit union needs and the need for credit unions to gain a better understanding of insurance company needs and requirements were responsible for the formation of a Procedures Study Committee. Appointed by Mobley, the committee was designed to serve as a liaison to keep the company's operations as simple and as favorable to credit unions as possible.

"Members Mutual operations and credit union operations have a common goal—to serve the credit union movement of Texas and other states served by the company," Barry told the 16-member committee as it began work. "Through this group, we hope to fill a communications gap and coordinate our efforts."

The financial progress of the company, which had continued without major disruption since its very beginning, would continue. By early 1965, as the middle of the "Soaring Sixties" approached, Members Mutual was still soaring, too. Assets stood at about $7.5 million with a whopping operating surplus of more than $2.1 million as of the year just ended, and the total number of policyholders was approaching 50,000.

Despite its problems—and most of those problems were simply a byproduct of its tremendous growth— Members Mutual had proved conclusively by the time of its tenth birthday party that it could hold its own with anybody. Even the giants of the Texas insurance industry admired and envied its success.

In looking back to where it all began, with the issuance of that very first policy on July 1, 1952, the wisdom and foresight of the company's founders seemed little short of incredible. The five long years of study and preparation which had preceded the birth of the company had paid great dividends, as surely as the company had paid dividends of at least 20 percent each year since 1954.

In connection with the tenth anniversary, the *Bulletin* reprinted the same editorial it had published ten years earlier when Members Mutual started in business. And now, looking back, it was extremely prophetic.

"In years to come," it said, "credit unionists of Texas, perhaps the Western Hemisphere, should remember July 1, 1952, as the date when Members Mutual Insurance Company formally began business.

"It didn't just happen; it wasn't one of those ideas that suddenly occurred to League directors in March 1952. Rather, it resulted from years of study, and considerable experience with automobile insurance . . . To some, automobile insurance may seem far afield from the scope of the credit union movement. But it became a demanded item from credit union members who wanted one-package automobile financing. With the pioneering spirit of the Texan, with the faith of the true credit union member . . . Members Mutual was born.

"Members Mutual was created with but one idea in mind—the same idea that motivates the credit union movement—SERVICE! Better service to the credit union member—the best automobile insurance possible at the lowest cost consistent with financial safety. Not for profit—just for service."

If there was anything the founders of the company may not have foreseen with clarity, however, it was the company's colossal potential for profit. As noted earlier, only one solitary "nay" vote was cast when the proposal to form the insurance company was submitted to delegates at the 1952 annual meeting of the TCUL. But during the first ten years of Members Mutual's life, and for a long time thereafter, many a credit unionist might have paused to wonder just what that lonely dissenter may have known that all the other voting delegates didn't.

To some in 1952, insurance may, indeed, have seemed "far afield" from credit unions. But a decade later, when Members Mutual turned ten, it had become abundantly clear to all concerned that insurance was now an integral and inseparable part of the credit union movement in Texas, and it did not require a soothsayer to predict that it would become even more so. Probably, there were already those who could guess at just how much further "afield" Members Mutual might go in the days to come, and that the daring experiment begun in March 1952 would one day evolve into an entire family of insurance companies to serve credit union members and their families.

Tragedy in Dallas

In a very real sense, the handsome young President whom Americans had elected in November 1960 embodied the spirit of the public in those heady first years of a promising new decade. Urbane, sophisticated and wealthy though he was, John Fitzgerald Kennedy seemed to strike a responsive chord in the bosom of the common man.

Kennedy made good his promise to "get the country moving again." Fueled by freehanded spending at the federal level, the economy soon began to boom. As it heated up, the recessionary period of the late 1950s gave way to a new surge of prosperity. Inflation became a major concern of American wage earners and their families, but as long as wages kept rising, aspirations and hopes for the future seemed to follow suit. Somewhere ahead on this New Frontier awaited the elusive "good life," and more Americans than ever before were firmly convinced that they could find it.

Although it is highly unlikely that John Kennedy ever used or needed the services of a credit union, he, like so many other Presidents before him, recognized the great and growing role of credit unions in serving the working people of the country. He proved this through his support of a 1963 amendment to the Federal Credit Union Act which had been actively supported by both CUNA and the TCUL and which greatly strenghtened the original legislation and made it more applicable to modern times.

When Kennedy signed the amendment into law on October 17, 1963, one of the pens he used was presented to CUNA President Morgan. The pen had been given by Kennedy to CUNA Managing Director J. Orrin Shipe at the White House when credit union leaders went to the Oval Office on International Credit Union Day to witness the signing of the law. A second pen, which Kennedy gave personally to Shipe, was placed in the

Bergengren Memorial Library and Museum in Filene House in Madison, Wisconsin.

Slightly more than two weeks after the historic signing at the White House, President Kennedy came to Texas, along with Vice President Lyndon Johnson, for a series of major speeches and public appearances.

One of Kennedy's first major stops was in San Antonio, where *Bulletin* editor John Quinlan was able to obtain press credentials that allowed him to accompany the presidential party in its travels around the city. In recounting the events of that day, November 21, 1963, Quinlan captured the color and excitement of the presidential visit and offered a quick glimpse into the personality of JFK himself.

"The motorcade started at a swift pace, but slowed as the crowds thickened," Quinlan noted. "The President's car stopped momentarily to receive honors from the cadet corps of Texas Military Institute and at Incarnate Word College.

"Motorcycle-borne policemen swept by us interminably as the frantic voice of the Secret Service agent in the lead car came to us over our radio. He was pleading to keep the route ahead clear and to keep the cars in the entourage tightly spaced.

"Along the way, the crowds were friendly and smiling, displaying signs of welcome. One service station had a large sign stating, 'Double stamps for JFK.' One man stood with thumbs down, but a large smile wreathed his face . . .

"During our intimate association with the White House representatives, our admiration for President Kennedy was enhanced. Despite the tremendous load of his office, he found time to recognize his staff as individuals, and performed many acts of kindness. Endless anecdotes portrayed him as a person who had a great love for his fellowman, no matter what the station in life. This trait engendered an almost unbelievable loyalty in each those who served him."

That evening, Air Force One took the presidential party to Fort Worth, and the following morning, November 22, 1963, the President arrived at Dallas Love Field for a schedule motorcade through the city—very similar to the one described by Quinlan in San Antonio—and a speech at the Dallas Trade Mart. Again, as it had been the day before, the reception was warm and friendly. Tens of thousands of Dallasites lined the motorcade route, shouting greetings and waving "Welcome to Dallas" signs.

Then, as the presidential car turned onto Elm Street and moved down a slight incline toward the Triple Underpass shots rang out from a sixth-floor window of the Texas School Book Depository Building. Onlookers screamed and scrambled for cover. The President appeared to raise his hand to his throat as an expression of disbelief crossed his face. Then a second bullet struck him in the head and a shower of blood spattered the car and its occupants. Governor Connally also fell, seriously wounded. Police and Secret Service agents with drawn guns swarmed over the grassy knoll overlooking Elm Street as the presidential limousine sped away toward Parkland Memorial Hospital, where President Kennedy was pronounced dead a few minutes later.

The enormity of the tragedy and its aftermath—the slaying of a Dallas police officer, the arrest of an avowed Marxist named Lee Harvey Oswald as the accused assassin, and the subsequent murder of Oswald by Dallas nightclub owner Jack Ruby—left the city, the state and the nation stunned and sickened as it had seldom been before. The grief of credit union members everywhere was summed up in a telegram sent by CUNA President Morgan to the widow and family of President Kennedy. It read:

"The officials, volunteer leaders, staff and the other 17 million members of the organized credit union movement, in hearing of the death of John F. Kennedy,

President of the United States, join together in extending to you their greatest sympathy and understanding.

"We are deeply regretful that so tragic an occurrence had to put its black mark on the history of your family and on the history of these great United States of America. The worldwide membership of the Credit Union National Association will long remember President John F. Kennedy as being a staunch friend of the credit union idea.

"On October 17, 1963, President Kennedy affixed his signature to legislation passed by the Congress and thereby amended the credit union act. We will always remain deeply appreciative of the President's support in this vital matter. We join with the citizens of our beloved country and friends throughout the world in mourning the loss of our beloved President John F. Kennedy."

And a moving requiem in the *Bulletin* captured the mood of confusion, depression and sorrow that gripped the country in the days that followed:

"Half-masted flags, discharging rifles and cannons, tolling cathedral and church bells, the quiet crying of the populace, the rolling of muffled drums are external expressions of the mourning of the world and the nation.

"But there seems to be a groping—a gigantic question mark. WHY? This was a man who depicted the best that America could produce. He was well educated, fluent, gifted with an apparent phenomenal intelligence, with talents that were superlative. His patriotism was unquestionable as attested to by his war record. Besides an internal urge to serve his country and his fellowman, there was little apparent need to seek the presidency. With his personal wealth, he could have well been a sideline observer.

"We have no answers, but only questions and observations. Perhaps this man who was a hero in life is a greater hero in death. Perhaps this man whose lips are now mute in death has a silent message for our hearts more penetrating than any he uttered in life . . .

"His expressed aims were consonant with those of the credit union movement—to improve the status of his fellowman, regardless of race, religion, color or political inclination.

"We salute this martyr. We hope his aims, objectives and ideals live forever in our hearts."

Countless millions of words have been written about the Kennedy assassination in the years since. Innumerable critics and defenders have sought to define the character of the man, to determine the true meaning of his presidency and his death, to assess his proper place in history. But none, perhaps, is more revealing of the real John Fitzgerald Kennedy than a simple little story that emerged from the records of the White House Employees Credit Union in Washington, D.C., almost a year after the tragedy.

The records of the White House credit union were being checked by an examiner who became curious about the co-signer on one particular note. A new employee at the White House, working as a simple laborer, had needed a $100 loan to tide him over until his first payday. Because he was so new on the job, the credit union treasurer told the employee that he would have to have a co-signer in order to get the loan. Not knowing anyone at the White House, the employee had seemed rather dejected, but had taken the application form and vowed to try to find someone to sign it before the end of the day.

Five minutes before closing time, the loan applicant returned with the required signature. The treasurer glanced at the signature several times as though he had difficulty believing it, then nervously wrote out a check for $100. There was no doubting the validity of the signature, or the financial responsibility of its owner— John F. Kennedy, President of the United States.

More Milestones

By the mid years of the 1960s, it was apparent that the nation, the state and the credit union movement were entering a period of great change, both technologically and sociologically. For one thing, the computer age was dawning and bringing with it developments in the new science of data processing that would revolutionize the way credit unions—and everybody else—did business. Early in 1964, a report by a special Data Processing Study Committee of the TCUL, headed by Frank J. Kucera of Dallas, issued strong recommendations for taking the League and its member credit unions deep into the mainstream of computerization. At the center of the recommendations was a plan to establish a data processing cooperative within the League for the benefit of its members. To be known as TCUL Data, it was the beginning of the ultra-sophisticated computer information system designed to provide instantaneous data to credit unions in all parts of the state.

At the time, the state of the art was undergoing astoundingly rapid changes, however, and it was virtually impossible to predict what the next few years would bring in the data processing field. Jim Barry addressed this problem in his report to the joint boards of the League and Members Mutual in February 1964. "We foresee a possible new bottleneck developing in the future in data processing," he said, "and extensive planning is necessary to deal adequately with it. It may become advisable before long to start a two-shift day in Data Processing to keep up properly while an eventual changeover to a computer operation is planned out in complete detail ... There is a big investment in time and money needed to accomplish an eventual transition to a computer operation, and such a change must be predicated on future growth."

As exemplified by the League's entry into data processing, the entire year of 1964 could be characterized as the time of many important milestones for credit unionists in Texas. It was, of course, the thirtieth anniversary of both the founding of the TCUL and the enactment of the original Federal Credit Union Act.

President Lyndon Johnson took note of the latter occasion in a congratulatory message issued by the White House on June 16, 1964, in which he said: "I am pleased to greet the seven and a half million members of federal credit unions upon the thirtieth anniversary of the signing of the Federal Credit Union Act . . .

"Some 11,000 federal credit unions have been established with over four billion dollars in assets. I congratulate those thrifty Americans who have made this possible. And I urge renewed endeavors in the years ahead, particularly on behalf of men and women in lower income groups, who could greatly benefit from the services of federal credit unions."

And in designating October 15, 1964, as International Credit Union Day in Texas, Governor John Connally made mention of the fact that there were now 1,247 credit unions in the state with more than 840,000 members and assets totalling $470 million. "Credit unions not only promote the economic security of their members, but serve to strengthen democracy and encourage thrift and individual responsibility," Connally said.

But there were also some warnings mingled with the kind words. Congressman Wright Patman, for example, urged credit union executives at a Boston conference not to take their great successes of recent years for granted. A stalwart ally of the movement since its inception and one of the architects of the original federal law, Patman was now a veteran of 35 years on Capitol Hill and was known fondly as the "godfather" of credit unionism in the United States. Texas credit unionists deluged him with birthday greetings on September 6, 1964, and used the occasion to extend him a singular honor, as the TCUL's North Texas Chapter renamed itself the Wright Patman Chapter. But Patman made it clear that he did not believe credit unions had yet fulfilled their destiny in this country. He asked credit union leaders to "set as your goal access to a credit union for every person in the United States" and called for intensified efforts to organize new credit unions. "Next to safeguarding the laws, organizing must take its place as the most important activity of the movement," he said.

But not only was the TCUL interested in organizing new credit unions at this time, but was also taking key steps toward streamlining and upgrading its own internal organization in order to cope with the demands of an increasingly complex job. Under the leadership of Jack A. Mitchell, who replaced H.T. Sanderson as League president in 1963 and who was also named chairman of the joint Board of Directors of the League and Members Mutual, a modernized committee system was instituted. Mitchell's presidency also brought more new blood to the League's Executive Committee in the persons of Wilfred MacKinnon of the Humble Employees Credit Union of Baytown, who became first vice president, and Pete Gooch of the Texas & Pacific Fort Worth Credit Union, who became second vice president. Holdover members of the committee included P.D. Barziza of Peden Employees Credit Union in Houston, secretary-treasurer; Mrs. Dyalthia Benson of the Hereford Federal Credit Union, third vice president; and retiring President Sanderson, ex-officio member.

A past president of the TCUL's Dallas Chapter, Mitchell was treasurer-manager of the Dallas Teachers Credit Union, the largest in the state with more than 14,500 members and more than $12 million in assets. In a report to the Board of Directors in October 1964, he praised the "constant growth" and "healthy financial condition" of the League, but also warned that the competition now posed by the state's stronger credit unions was being keenly felt by other types of lenders.

"Recently, in one of our large areas, there was a rather wide distribution of a so-called 'fact sheet' to salesmen with automobile dealers which, to put it rather mildly, did not portray the true image and service of credit unions," he said. "Whether by intention or ignorance, the promulgation of this erroneous material vividly points to the increasing need for more and improved public relations by the League and individual credit unions in the future."

The year 1964 was also marked by a number of significant personal milestones for some of the most important leaders in the Texas credit union movement. Saylors J. Mobley stepped down as president of Members Mutual and was succeeded in the company's top post by Jerry A. Deering of Fort Worth on March 22. A board member of Members Mutual since 1961, Deering had served as assistant treasurer-manager of the Fort Worth Teachers Credit Union for a decade and was also a past president of the Fort Worth Chapter. (Deering is now President of the renamed Educational Employees Credit Union of Fort Worth.) A native of Alabama, a graduate of Texas Christian University and a veteran of the Air Force, Deering was also indicative of the "new blood" entering major leadership positions in the movement. In 1962, he had been named by Governor Price Daniel to the State Credit Union Advisory Commission, and was the youngest member ever appointed to that body.

In his final report as Members Mutual president, Mobley pointed "with a great deal of pride and satisfaction" to the accomplishments of the company during its recent past—not the least of which was a total of 42,655 policyholders as of December 1963. "The continued success of our company as a part of the Texas Credit Union League is proof that Members Mutual is not and never will be 'just another insurance company' that exists only for the profit of the few," he said, "but is a company owned and controlled by the credit union people who are the policyholders."

It was also time for Paul Mullins, who had served the League so ably for more than a decade as assistant managing director, to take his final bow, as he retired on September 1, 1964. As the date of his departure neared, Mullins was honored at a round of retirement parties and special ceremonies in appreciation for his long and dedicated service to the credit union cause. He was given a color television set by the Dallas Chapter at a special "Paul Mullins Night," which drew the largest crowd to attend a regular meeting in the chapter's history. He was also given a larger-than-life-size portrait of himself, complete with the full head of hair which nature had long denied him. A smaller, but more realistic portrait, accurately depicting Mullins' true state of baldness, was presented to Mullins by the International Association of Managing Directors, of which he had served as secretary from 1957 to 1961. A two-page spread of photographs in the *Bulletin* recaptured the high points of Mullins' career, and an appreciative editorial tribute said of him: "When you need that last yard or so for the fourth down, Paul would do the blocking so you could make it . . . Beneath a veneer of genuine sophistication, spiced with an acrid wit, was a real credit unionist, a friend of humanity, and a real expediter."

Succeeding Mullins as assistant managing director of the League was James T. Vest, a veteran member of the TCUL staff, who had first joined the League as a field representative in 1952. A native of Paris, Texas, Vest had served in the Navy and majored in business administration at East Texas State University. He had subsequently joined the Postal Transportation Service Federal Credit Union in Fort Worth and had become its assistant treasurer in 1950, later serving as manager of the Fort Worth Quartermasters Federal Credit Union. On the League staff, he had served as assistant director of education, director of field services and director of stabilization. In the latter post, he had been responsible

for getting an important new League program underway.

There was yet another notable milestone in that
year of 1964. Jim Barry, the man who had come to
epitomize the Texas Credit Union League, its growth, its
success and its expansion into new fields of service,
observed his twentieth anniversary as the League's
managing director on September 15. Barry and the
League had come an incredibly long way from the
war-weary world of 1944 and the modest duplex on
Hester Street. From the young husband and father
marching off to war, Jim Barry had evolved into the
white-haired "Old Faithful" of the Texas credit union
movement. Since 1952, he had, in effect, ridden two
galloping horses Roman-style as the managing director
of both the TCUL and Members Mutual. Somehow, he
had kept these two strong entities from charging off in
opposite directions and leaving him sprawled in the dust
behind them. It had been far from an easy ride. As Barry
himself put it in retrospect a long time later: "The politics
of it made it almost inevitable that there would be a lot
of friction. We wound up with two boards—sixteen
individuals on one and sixteen on the other, and nobody
on both—but we had one managing director, me, in the
middle."

As he observed his twentieth anniversary with the
League, Barry was still very much a "man in the
middle." Despite efforts to bring the straining horses
closer together and coordinate their movements, he was
still in danger of losing control or being torn apart. But
his unrelenting efforts to keep his charges in tandem
brought some well-earned words of appreciation from
Bulletin editor Quinlan.

"Under his (Barry's) guidance, both the Texas
Credit Union League and Members Mutual Insurance
Company have prospered," he wrote. "But it is difficult
to be 'all things to all men,' and this assignment as
managing director has been far from an easy one. There

have been times when the position appeared shaky. Attacks and criticisms have come both from the boards and the delegates in annual meetings. Jim Barry met them head-on and calmly. Despite these anxious moments, he is still managing director.

"And the Texas Credit Union League is looked on with respect and envy by the leagues throughout the world. Jim Barry has made a major contribution to this progress. So, after these twenty arduous years, we offer our sincere plaudits."

Some more arduous times still lay ahead, but "Old Faithful," with Board support, was still very much in the saddle, and he had no intention of relinquishing the reins just yet.

Fighting Complacency

The situation in which the credit union movement found itself as the middle of the Sixties arrived was very similar to that in which the typical individual American also found himself: Economically, times had been so good for so long that the long-held goal of working men and women simply to make financial ends meet no longer seemed enough. Like the public it served, the credit union movement was prospering. In a single twelve-month period during 1964, the nation's credit unions had increased their assets by more than a billion dollars and had enrolled more than a million new members. In Texas, credit union membership had tripled during the decade between 1954 and 1964, to more than 900,000.

The average American working person was doing equally well. Wages had never risen more rapidly, and although inflation was taking a big bite out of the buying power of those wages, Americans in general were still able to enjoy the highest standard of living in their history. Despite all this, however, stubborn pockets of hard-core suffering and deprivation remained resistant to the War on Poverty being carried out by the Johnson Administration. The racial minorities and other "have-nots" of the so-called Great Society were growing increasingly restless. And even those who had seemingly achieved the American Dream frequently found themselves feeling discontented, disenchanted and disoriented. Women were demonstrating particular dissatisfaction with a system that often kept them at home and family-bound and discriminated against them in the business and professional world. Consequently, "women's lib" was looming larger and larger as a major force reshaping the nation's entire social structure. The nuclear family was losing its influence on individual family members and long-hallowed family institutions were under attack. So was organized religion, big business and big government. The student revolution and the so-called "generation gap" between maturing children and their parents were already beginning to ferment. Young people were disillusioned with the materialism that had done so much to motivate their age group during the Depression and with the systems which so many had fought had died to preserve during World War II. With this disillusionment came alienation and also a strange type of complacency. It seemed as though the problems facing Texans, Americans and the world in general had become so huge and all-encompassing, so infinitely complex, that there was nothing anybody could do about them. And the public that now faced these problems no longer faced them as a united force, but as a melee of splintered factions squabbling over their own narrow self-interests.

With the successes of the past few years still fresh and glowing in their minds, the wealth of the present amply in evidence, and the promise of significant and relatively easy additions to that wealth and success in the immediate future almost undeniable, it was easy for credit unionists to feel complacent, too.

In one of his first official statements after taking over the League presidency from Jack Mitchell in March 1965 at the annual meeting in Corpus Christi, Wilfred S. MacKinnon squarely addressed this issue of complacency and strongly warned of where its continuation could lead.

"It would be very easy for us to take a complacent attitude at this time," MacKinnon said. "The League stands at an all-time high. We have more member credit unions than we have ever had. Our credit unions have more members than they have ever had. Some large credit unions, non-League members for many years, have come back into the League. Revenue is ample to take care of present and planned programs. All major staff positions are filled. Our proposed state legislation has passed without amendment. No other legislation has passed which will affect us unfavorably . . .

"These things are true, and yet we have cause for uneasiness."

Among the principal areas of concern cited by MacKinnon were (1) the lack of full-time legal representation that often made for "close calls" in the area of legislation; (2) the fact that, while credit union growth was undeniably continuing, the organization of new credit unions had slowed down markedly, and (3) a feeling that the movement in Texas was not responding adequately to the need for credit unions among the low-income groups which needed them most.

"People within our state are writing to the national association for help in organizing credit unions among low-income groups," MacKinnon said. "We have the know-how which would enable us to regain our momentum in (this) field . . . and to aid and guide new credit unions after they are organized . . . It is certain that if we fail to do this job, the national association or government will do it for us. It is our responsibility, and we do not want others to assume it for us."

At a time when the vast majority of working people were enjoying relative prosperity, it was important, MacKinnon said, for credit unions to turn their attention back to the less fortunate minority who had been left behind economically. These were, after all, the kind of people whom credit unions had been conceived to benefit in the first place. Now was not the time for the movement to become fat and self-satisfied.

And finally, MacKinnon said, there was yet another formidable reason for unease within the Texas credit union community. "Probably the single greatest reason for uneasiness must be the relationship of the League and Members Mutual, even at this time when this relationship has never been better," he emphasized. "We are concerned here with the whole field of mutual ties, responsibilities, management. We are concerned with insuring the continuity and stability of the close family ties that now exist, while at the same time providing for the continuity of the strong and aggressive management these two organizations have enjoyed. We are both growing fast and we have the responsibility to make the changes growth requires."

MacKinnon was a man well-equipped to take the lead in making such changes and in the fight against the complacency that threatened to creep into the movement. A native of Beaver Cove, Nova Scotia, and a magna cum laude graduate of St. Francis Xavier University in that Canadian province, the popular "Mac" MacKinnon had been a credit union manager for sixteen years and was now serving in that position with the Humble Employees Credit Union in Baytown. He had served as president of the Houston Chapter and had been a member of the League Board of Directors since 1962. In 1964, while serving as first vice president, he had also chaired the TCUL's Legal and Legislative Committee, been a trustee of the League Educational Foundation, and served on the Stabilization Committee.

Elected to serve with MacKinnon on the League Executive Committee were Pete Gooch of Fort Worth, first vice president; Mrs. Dyalthia Benson of Hereford, second vice president; R.C. Foster of Abilene, third vice president; and P.D. Barziza of Houston, secretary-treasurer.

For MacKinnon, his first election as president in 1965 was the beginning of a fourteen-year period of outstanding leadership during which he would become one of the strongest and most important figures in the annals of both the League and CUNA. He assumed his position at a time when the League had developed into a truly major institution in its own right. With a 1965 operating budget approaching $500,000 and representing roughly 90 percent of the 1,337 credit unions operating in Texas by the end of that year, the League had, in fact, grown larger than CUNA itself in terms of staff, budget and facilities. By mid-1966, individual credit union membership in Texas passed the one-million mark for the first time in history, and these members claimed combined assets of approximately $625 million.

By the time he delivered his first annual report to delegates at the League convention in Houston on March 24, 1966, MacKinnon could report significant progress in meeting several of the key areas of concern he had outlined the year before. The need for effective and successful credit unions among the low-income groups of the state was being attacked through a three-point program of of (1) organizational assistance, (2) special education for directors and committee members of young credit unions, and (3) a regular follow-up system of assistance after these initial steps had been taken.

Meanwhile, the number of credit unions organized in Texas had increased slightly and the number of liquidations had dropped sharply. A number of the new credit unions were those aimed at low-income groups, and this was a step in the right direction. In Washington, high-ranking federal spokesmen had served notice that they would not wait indefinitely for state and local organizations to produce results in this area. As Sargent Shriver, director of the Office of Economic Opportunity, told Congressman Patman in a letter: "I fully concur with you that credit unions can play an extremely valuable role in the war on poverty . . . For the past several months, we have had an informal agreement with CUNA . . . to provide technical assistance to communities interested in organizing credit unions as part of their local anti-poverty programs . . . You can be sure that in the future, as now, any community action program interested in organizing credit unions as part of its program will receive our whole-hearted backing in getting started. We hope for greatly increased activity in this field in the next six months."

But complacency and that disturbing feeling of unease which MacKinnon had singled out as major enemies of the credit union movement were destined to remain with the movement—and the U.S. public—for a long time to come. It could not be otherwise in a nation where the typical credit union member's position in life was so incredibly different from that of the typical victim of poverty and hopelessness at the bottom of the American economic ladder. As the *Bulletin* noted in a June 1966 editorial: "Credit union members generally have a little better car, a little better house, nicer household furnishings, more of the comforts of life, than others in the same income bracket. This margin is a gift . . ."

But it was a gift that was not extended to those struggling to survive on substandard incomes and still obtain access to credit unions. And it was a gift that was too often taken for granted by those who already had that access. In many respects, the Great Society was not only affluent, it was also prodigal. It was a society that would spend $300 million on mink coats in 1966. It was a society that would gobble down $40 million worth of exotic gourmet foods while its less fortunate members went to bed hungry. It was a society which was, in the words of Dallas Congressman Earle Cabell, "living more on what we borrow than upon what we earn or what we own." It was a society in which easy credit had become an addiction for many consumers, and in which thrift was no longer necessarily considered a virtue.

In such a society, the war against complacency would be no easier won than the War on Poverty.

Wages of Separation

As noted earlier, the TCUL and Members Mutual—while each remained inseparably linked to the credit unions of Texas—had been drawn along divergent paths in many respects from the day the insurance company was organized. From a purely financial standpoint, the new insurance company quickly overshadowed its parent service organization, and the vast amounts of money with which Members Mutual dealt gave it a different set of requirements than those of the League. As it grew, the insurance company required large amounts of space and great numbers of staff personnel, while the League's needs in these areas were much more modest.

But probably the most serious complications of all grew out of a move toward separate governing bodies for the two entities—a move which began with the formation of Members Mutual in 1952. At the time, the League was administered by a 13-member Board of Directors, all of whom also became directors in the new insurance company. But the disparity began when the three members of the League's Insurance Committee—the forerunner of the company—were named directors of Members Mutual only. This gave the company a total of 16 directors, while the League had only 13, and prompted the League to increase the size of its Board to 16 members as well. The problem was, however, that the

226

three new directors added to the League Board were not on the insurance company Board. And this began a trend.

Gradually, over a period of years, the two boards became totally separate, with no one person serving simultaneously on both, and such a situation made for an increasing number of differences between the two bodies. What was sauce for the goose was not necessarily sauce for the gander. What served the best interests of the League did not necessarily serve the best interests of Members Mutual, and vice-versa. As Jim Barry has noted: "Friction was inevitable."

By 1967, fifteen years after the birth of Members Mutual, that friction finally reached the unbearable point for Barry, who, as managing director of both the company and the TCUL, remained the last fraying link in the management chain that had once bound the two together. "The continual friction between the two boards," says Barry, "led to the situation where I had to choose between the League and the insurance company. I chose to stay with the League."

When Barry made his decision to step aside as managing director and executive vice president of Members Mutual early in 1967, the insurance company board appointed J.N. Nutt, a former State of Texas insurance commissioner, as his successor. In a further move to strengthen the company's management staff, Nutt immediately promoted former Assistant Managing Director J. Boyd Browning to vice president and former Assistant Secretary Ted J. McGehee to vice president and assistant managing director.

The choice of Nutt to fill the top executive job in the company seemed a sound one, especially from an insurance standpoint, although he had no real background in credit unions. A native of Granbury, Nutt had become a senior examiner for the Texas Board of Insurance in 1935 and had spent seventeen years in that position, before leaving in 1952 to help organize the

Mercantile Security Life Insurance Company and serve as its executive vice president and director. He had been appointed state insurance commissioner in 1963 and had served until November 1965. His resignation at that time brought forth plaudits from the State Board of Insurance for his "broad technical knowledge" and "unquestioned integrity."

Nutt appeared well-qualified to lead the company forward to new achievements in the insurance field and took office at an especially challenging time for Members Mutual, since new automobile insurance rates for Texas motorists were about to go into effect under a newly enacted "safe driver insurance plan." Under the plan, all auto insurance sold in Texas would begin including coverage against bodily injury caused by uninsured motorists, unless the buyer specifically rejected the coverage. In one of his first official communications to the credit union people of Texas, Nutt called August 1, 1967—the date when the new rate structure took effect—"among the most significant dates in recent history for Texas motorists," who would be "hit directly in the pocketbook" by the rate changes. "Members Mutual policyholders, like all insured motorists, will be affected," Nutt said. "But they have the advantage of Members Mutual's substantial dividends and the further advantage of dealing with a company guided by credit union principles."

Nutt soon encountered conflicts with the Board, however, and was ousted from his post in the fall of 1967 and replaced by Ted McGehee as acting president. In January, 1968, McGehee was made MMIC's new president of the Board. As this was happening, many of those who had guided the company during its first fifteen years were making their final departure. Within the space of a few months, two former company presidents, Saylors J. Mobley and Lester P. Shannon, were claimed by death, as was former director Joseph P. Murray. Meanwhile, three directors were added to the Members

Mutual Board: Duke Baker of Big Spring (a re-election), Roy Neidig of Austin and Marvin L. Wammack of Waco. Jerry Deering of Fort Worth, who had served as the company's president until that title was assumed by Nutt, then became chairman of the Board to put the company's management structure more in line with other major insurance companies.

Simultaneously, steps were being taken in the top echelons of the Texas credit union movement to alleviate the differences that were dividing the League and Members Mutual and forcing them onto separate paths. One of the most important steps in this direction was the formation of a Joint Management Committee with the task of resolving common management problems.

One of the committee's first major undertakings was an effort to locate a suitable tract of land for construction of a new and much larger home for the League and Members Mutual. The insurance company, in particular, was suffering from a space shortage in the old building on Ross Avenue, which was literally almost "bursting at the seams" by now. And although there was some temptation to let the company move into its own quarters while the League headquarters remained comfortably in the old location, it was decided that the two entities would remain together under the same roof, as they had from the first.

In considering which direction to move in seeking a new location, there were several options to be considered: leasing space in downtown Dallas or an outlying area, buying an existing building, having a landowner build a building and then leasing it, adding to the present building, or buying raw land and building a new headquarters/home office on it.

The Joint Committee settled on the last of these options, buying a ten-acre tract in far North Dallas near the small town of Addison. To the casual eye, the tract appeared to be "in the middle of nowhere," since there was nothing but bald, undeveloped prairie in all directions. Actually, however, it lay on the route of the new Interstate Highway 635 or the Lyndon B. Johnson Freeway, construction of which was already underway.

Since Members Mutual had the money to buy the land (and the League did not, at least at the moment), the insurance company became the purchaser and gave the League an option to buy 50 percent of the property. There were many within the League who were legitimately concerned over the TCUL's long-range ability to keep up its end of such an arrangement, and there was considerable pressure for the League to pull out of the deal.

In the midst of all this, deep-running efforts were being made to alter the structure of the Boards of Directors of both Members Mutual and the League, as well as that of the all-important standing committees which operated as a vital part of the boards. In one of his first messages to League members after he succeeded MacKinnon as League president in March 1967, Pete G. Gooch of Fort Worth, emphasized the importance of these reorganizational efforts.

"The committees have been appointed for both TCUL and MMIC," said Gooch, "and the structure of these committees, we believe, will give us more economical efficiency, and will utilize all of the talents of both boards, working together as credit union people for one purpose, to serve you better. It is a different structure, but we believe there is much to be gained from the change.

"The committees are already at work. Some of the items they are studying, among many others, are as follows:

"1. Space requirements and how to solve them for both TCUL and MMIC.

"2. A set of rules for policy-making decisions and management decisions.

"3. Personnel policy matters concerning the two organizations."

230

Under the leadership of Gooch, manager of the Fort Worth TELCO Credit Union as well as president of the TCUL, and others dedicated to preserving the strong traditional ties between the two organizations, a number of concrete steps were taken during 1967 and 1968 to avoid going any further down the road toward separatism. Before the end of 1967, a "joint operating agreement" was reached between the two Boards of Directors in what may have been the most significant of these steps. The agreement grew out of the work, beginning early in 1967, of a TCUL-MMIC Planning and Research Committee, chaired by R.C. Morgan and originally including Barry, MacKinnon, W.H. Goff of Port Arthur and Gooch as co-chairman. Gooch terms the agreement "the key to complete unity" between the two organizations—and "unity" became Gooch's principal theme during this difficult time.

"There are those of us who fear change," he said. "Many of us fear the unknown. We fear the future because it is unknown. We sometimes falter and fear our own abilities to meet the challenge. The way to overcome fear is to recognize it, to have faith in our credit union philosophy, and most of all, to have faith in each other. We can do this only if we work as one mind, one will, one organization and one body, with the strength that comes with unity . . .

"Let's not kid ourselves. We cannot divide our unity. We must be one. We must have faith. We must do our job. We can have no fear!"

(In December 1970, the items covered by the "joint operating agreement" were turned over to a special Coordinating Committee, which continues in operation today to deal with matters of mutual concern to the League and Affiliates.)

By following the unity theme, the stage had been set for the reversal of the divisiveness that threatened the credit union movement in Texas, for healing the rift that had gradually deepened and festered over fifteen years, and for halting the wages of separation before irreversible damage was done. By late 1968, the brewing controversy over the land in far North Dallas was brought to an end, at least temporarily. The ten-acre tract which had been purchased by Members Mutual was sold to the Rodger Meier Cadillac agency for an automobile dealership, and the League and Members Mutual signed a ten-year lease on a new building on Forest Lane near Marsh Lane in North Dallas, which adequately solved the space question for the moment and allowed the sale of the old headquarters/home office building on Ross Avenue as part of the Rodger Meier deal.

Perhaps even more important to the long-term future relationship of the League and Members Mutual, however, was the beginning of a move that would eventually reunify the Boards of Directors of the two entities—as well as the board of the newly formed TCUL Data Systems, Inc.—into one 32-member body that would administer the League and all affiliated organizations with no overlapping. By the early 1970s, each director of the League would also be a director of Members Mutual and other affiliates and vice-versa, and it would again be possible to guide the destinies of the partners on the basis of firm consensus, rather than constant conflict.

A lengthy report, representing two years of intensive effort by the TCUL-MMIC Planning and Research Committee, was submitted to the joint boards in March 1969 and became the keystone of the reorganization effort. It was this report which proposed in detail a totally revised organizational structure for the League and its Affiliates. With certain amendments added by the boards, it is the same basic structure in existence today. The introduction to that historic committee report reads in part:

> "What we are proposing in this report is a restructuring of the organized credit union movement in the State of Texas. We want to assure you, here and now,

that we have undertaken our deliberations, conducted our discussions and arrived a our conclusions with no motive or purpose in mind other than to recommend an organizational structure for the Texas Credit Union League and its affiliated organizations which will better serve the changing needs of Texas credit unions and their members. In this connection, we think the credit union world of the future can be a world far better than the world of today, but only if we move wisely and with good will and only if our decisions and actions with respect to the future are grounded in knowledge and reason and not ruled by emotion and passion."

Although the report went into great detail on many fine points, its basic recommendations focused on three key areas: (1) retaining the name and identity of the Texas Credit Union League as the "top" or parent organization; (2) creating a common board for the League and all organizations affiliated with it, and (3) providing that all boards and operating committees of the various Affiliates be elected by and from the 32-member TCUL Board. These were the basic components of the report and would become the cornerstones of a new guiding philosophy for the Texas credit union movement.

The report was signed by Morgan, as chairman, and seven other members of the committee, which had been enlarged and whose membership had changed entirely since its establishment. The members at the time the report was presented included James A. Chiarizio, Jerry Deering, James H. Amis, James W. Dodd, Beeman S. Jones, Harry A. Olson and John P. Parsons.

The deep philosophical concerns addressed by the report would, of course, not be resolved overnight, even by the most dedicated labor, careful planning and efficient management. Buford Lankford of the Bureau of Federal Credit Unions touched the very heart of these concerns in an International Credit Union Day address in Dallas on October 18, 1968, by posing a troublesome question: Were credit unions a "movement" or an "industry"?

Lankford defined an industry as a group of enterprises "engaged in the same line, producing the same product and selling that product for a profit." An industry, he added, is not bound closely together, because "competitive aspects work against close-knit organizations."

A movement, on the other hand, he said, consists of "a group of organizations banded together for the purpose of achieving a common goal or objective." The members of a movement benefit by their ties and the movement grows stronger as its units grow stronger, he added.

In the nearly three and one-half decades since the humble birth of the Texas Credit Union League, the state's credit unions had taken on many of the aspects of a true industry. They were now fully computerized, for example, through their access to the new TCUL Data Systems, Inc., which had gone "on line" as the League's newest service affiliate early in 1968. They were big and healthy and very wealthy, with 1,400 organizations and some 1,160,000 individual members with nearly a billion dollars in assets in Texas alone, and nowhere was their wealth and bigness more clearly manifested than in their insurance programs.

But were they still a true movement as well? And was it even remotely possible to function as both an industry and a movement all at the same time? These were troublesome questions—questions that only the future could answer.

A New Department

Culminating nearly a decade of efforts in that direction, Texas credit unionists finally succeeded in obatining their own State Credit Union Department in 1969 as an independent and separate agency not connected to the State Banking Department as credit unions had always been in the past.

The bill creating the new department as the chief regulatory and examining agency for the state's state-chartered credit unions was passed by the 61st Legislature as Senate Bill No. 317, under the sponsorship of State Senator George Parkhouse of Dallas, one of the movement's staunchest allies in the State Capitol. It was signed into law on May 13, 1969, by Governor Preston Smith and the department officially began functioning on September 1.

Its beginning was the conclusion of what new League President Walter V. Duncan of the Collins Radio Credit Union in Richardson, who had succeeded Pete Gooch that March, called "a rather busy period." Actually, the establishment of the Credit Union Department was just one key part of a new Texas Credit Union Act, which entailed the recodification and updating of all previous state laws pertaining to credit unions.

Duncan himself had taken a leading role in the preparation of the legislation, as chairman of the League's Legal and Legislative Committee. Assistant Managing Director Jim Young, former TCUL President Jack Mitchell and former League and CUNA chief executive R.C. Morgan also devoted countless hours of work toward the passage of the bill. As chairman of the statewide Credit Union Advisory Commission, originally organized in May, 1949, Morgan had called some 300 of the top credit union leaders in Texas to Austin early in 1969 to solicit their support for the proposed changes in the law.

The new law had been under active discussion at least since 1961 and a first attempt at drafting a bill had been made in 1967, but was judged to be premature and credit union leaders were sent back to do more "homework" before the bill was submitted.

John P. Parsons, who would move from a position as director of public relations and governmental relations for the TCUL to become credit union commissioner of the State of Texas and head of the Credit Union

Department in 1974, recalls some of the difficulties in designing the bill. 'Getting the legislation through to final passage was an interesting process," says Parsons. The first people who had to be convinced were the credit union managers themselves. They were going to have to pay more in examination fees in order to support a separate department, so they had to be convinced that the examinations would really be better.

The next step was to persuade Bruce Gibson, the credit union supervisor for the State Banking Department, that the idea of a separate department was sound and beneficial. Then others within the Banking Department had to be shown how the spinoff of a new regulatory agency for credit unions would benefit both the Banking Department and the credit unions, according to Parsons. "But once the support of all these parties were obtained, there wasn't really much of a problem once the bill got to the Legislature," he explains.

The creation of a new department meant that state-chartered credit unions would no longer be a sort of "stepchild" within the Banking Department, where, since they traditionally provided the least amount of dollars, they also received the least attention. Now credit unions would have their own commissioner—a post which was first filled by "borrowing" Gibson from the Banking Department and making him the first Texas credit union commissioner in history. In addition, credit unions also had a five-member independent commission chosen from their own ranks to administer the new department.

The State Credit Union Department began operation on a less-than-spectacular scale. Besides Gibson, the staff consisted in the beginning of a secretary, a part-time clerk and six field examiners. But the department quickly grew. Within a short time, the position of chief examiner was created, and in 1972 Tom Key became the department's first deputy commissioner when that post was established. Key resigned in 1974,

Bruce Gibson, first credit union commissioner of the State of Texas

Harry Hamilton, holder of the statewide record for attendance at the most consecutive League annual meetings — 44

R. C. Morgan, who left an indelible mark as both TCUL president and president of CUNA.

Bessie Heard's highly effective service on the TCUL Board helped to project women into an increasingly large leadership role in the League.

after serving as interim commissioner, following Gibson's retirement in October 1973. At that time, Parsons was named commissioner, a post he continues to hold, and John R. Hale became deputy commissioner, a position in which he also remains at this writing. Commissioner Parsons, a native of Galveston and a graduate of St. Edwards University in Austin, served as treasurer-manager of the University of Texas Medical Branch Credit Union in Galveston from 1957 until he joined the TCUL staff in 1972. He served as a MMIC director from 1968 to 1970.

In the meantime, the staff of the Credit Union Department had been steadily enlarged to its present authorized strength of 24, including 17 field examiners to serve the approximately 475 state-chartered credit unions operating in Texas as of late 1983.

In January 1979, dedication ceremonies were held for the Credit Union Department's own new building at 914 East Anderson Lane in Austin. To help pay for the $243,000 structure, the state's credit unions contributed one and one-half times their usual annual assessment. At the TCUL's annual meeting the year before, every state-chartered credit union present, with only two exceptions, voted in favor of the extra assessment, which was ultimately supported by 95 percent of the credit unions, according to Parsons. The building is designed to accommodate departmental operations through the mid-1990s.

As Texas was upgrading and changing its laws governing credit unions, similar changes were taking place at the federal level in laws pertaining to federal credit unions. In Washington, friends of the national credit union movement such as Congressman Wright Patman of Texas and Senator John Sparkman of Alabama were working with a CUNA Recodification Committee, of which Texas' W.S. MacKinnon was an active member, to draft a law incorporating these changes. By the end of 1969, the bill was ready to be submitted to

Congress as H.R. 2. When it was signed by President Richard Nixon on March 10, 1970, it became Public Law No. 91-206, making the Bureau of Federal Credit Unions an independent agency instead of a division of the Department of Health, Education and Welfare, as it had been previously.

The law also created a National Credit Union Board, which consisted at that time of a chairman and six members, one of whom was Texan Jim Dodd of Houston. Within a few years, however, this body evolved into today's National Credit Union Administration Board and its membership was reduced to three. Besides Dodd, two other Texans have served on the NCUA board. Wade Choate, a former TCUL director, former chairman of Members Insurance and former mayor of Big Spring, was named to the board in 1976 while serving as manager of the Webb Air Force Base Federal Credit Union (now Citizens Federal Credit Union of Big Spring). In 1982, Elizabeth Flores Burkhart, a former school teacher and officer of Houston's Texas Commerce Bank, was sworn in as the first woman member of the current three-person NCUA Board.

These law changes at the state and federal levels were a reflection of the increasing stature, strength and sophistication of the credit union movement as the pivotal 1960s drew to a close. As another new decade loomed on the horizon, both the total assets of Texas credit unions and the amount of loans granted during a single year surpassed the billion-dollar barrier simultaneously for the first time. After growing by more than 20 percent during 1969, savings reached more than $944 million. Individual membership in Texas credit unions stood at 1,352,682, and 1969 marked the first year ever in which more than 100,000 new members joined credit unions in the state.

But credit unions were far from alone in the growth and changes they were experiencing. Great social, economic and political changes were also taking place all across the country, touching every aspect of the average citizen's life. Complexities that would have staggered the human imagination only a few years earlier had now become commonplace.

Evidence of such change was found in the great growth and acceptance of TCUL Data Systems, Inc., which had been established as a major League affiliate in 1967 with its own Board of Directors, and which had signed up the Denton County Teachers Credit Union at the beginning of 1968 as the first credit union in the state to go "fully computerized." By the end of its first year of operation, TCUL Data Systems had converted more than 10,000 accounts to data processing, and would eventually offer data processing services for all sizes of credit unions all over the state. It pointed the way toward a new era of further diversification into specialized areas of service for the League. It also served notice that the only course for the League was to plunge ahead into such innovations, that there would be no going back to simpler times and methods.

TCUL Data was operated as a state-of-the-art system from the time of its birth and set a standard in data processing for the entire credit union industry. As the years passed, however, far-reaching technological changes in the computer field required near-constant updating of the system. By 1982, it had become obvious that the cost of keeping the system current with trends in computer technology was prohibitive. It is now operated by CUNADATA, a nationwide system of data processing for credit unions, which is operated by Electronic Data Systems of Dallas.

As the "Soaring Sixties"—a period that had begun with such lofty expectations, only to be marred by assassinations, massive alienation at home and a debilitating war abroad—finally gave way to the unknowns of the Seventies, it was a time to take stock. It was a time to review the accomplishments of the decade that had just slipped into the history books, and perhaps to wish for a

240

crystal ball with which to chart the course for the decade just ahead. As TCUL President Duncan observed in his report to the League directors as 1969 faded into memory:

"Growth is sometimes so fast that one has little time to chart it and no time to estimate what the future may hold. It is probably time to stop and take a good look at where we have been, where we are now, and above all, where we are going. Our task will not be completed tomorrow, next month or next year, but we must start defining today what the future holds for the next five years at least."

Reunification

If a crystal ball-gazer had, indeed, possessed the ability to foresee the events of the first half of the 1970s, he would have had plenty of reasons to smash his crystal ball and renounce his talent. He would have seen the Arab oil embargo and the first of the disastrous fuel shortages which crippled the nation and panicked motorists everywhere. He would have seen a President and a Vice President of the United States driven from office amid a cloud of scandal. He would have seen the collapse of South Vietnam, despite the outpouring of tens of thousands of American lives in a futile attempt to save it. He would have seen the most massive disillusionment ever felt by the American people in their government, their institutions and themselves. Even the toughest-minded crystal ball-gazer might have had trouble handling all this.

But the 1970s were also to be a time of great opportunity, great challenge and great growth. During the decade, Texas would come into its own as a major focal point of the tremendous migration to the Sun Belt, and cities like Dallas and Houston would take their place among the leading commercial centers of the entire world. As the cities of Texas became more

241

crowded, the state's farm population continued to dwindle. The number of farms dropped by nearly 60,000 during the period between 1960 and 1970, to about 190,000, and nearly 10 million acres of land were withdrawn from cultivation. On the other hand tens of thousands of new non-agricultural jobs were being created each year.

Clearly, the growing industrial strength of Texas was a prime factor in the growth of credit unions in the state. By 1970, it has been estimated that up to 40 percent of the 3.4 million households in Texas had access to credit union services through at least one household member. From these households and the changing lifestyles developing within them were emerging new demands for loans, financial counseling, creative systems of saving and other services which credit unions could provide. But only a unified, efficient and smoothly working organization could expect to meet these demands, and it was to the considerable task of reunifying its own ranks that the Texas credit union movement turned its major attention.

As the TCUL held its annual meeting in San Antonio in March 1970, it was significant that Governor Preston Smith became the first Texas chief executive ever to address a credit union meeting in the state. "Yours is an impressive organization of accomplishment and promise," he told the delegates, demonstrating by his statements and his presence the influence now wielded across the state by Texas credit unions.

But even more important, perhaps, than Governor Smith's kind words were the projections for the restructuring of certain League functions and the future expanding of services into new and uncharted areas which were outlined by President Duncan in his message to the delegates.

"During this annual meeting," he said, "we will review a report outlining further new concepts in services to include a trust company, a holding company for direct credit union service, and a mutual fund for Texas credit unions. As capitalization both now and in the future becomes a matter of essential concern, we are taking the first steps toward retaining resources in credit unions, toward further expanding our investment services to our members, and toward providing a way by which the direct services of the League and seed capital for other direct services can be handled in the future.

"The restructuring recommendations which will come before you embody a way by which we may separate the dues-supported functions and retain their tax-exempt status from two taxable subsidiary functions—insurance and directly paid-for services—but most importantly provide that control of tax-exempt and taxable services shall be in the hands of 32 directors elected by you, the member credit unions."

The man who would complete the restructuring and reunification process between the League and its Affiliates which had begun in the late 1960s was Wilfred S. MacKinnon, who took over the presidency of the TCUL in 1971 and who simultaneously became president of Members Mutual and TCUL Services. As the first chief executive officer of the League and its Affiliates, MacKinnon would exert a lasting cohesive influence on them during the seven crucial years between December 1971, when he officially assumed the combined position, and December 1978, when he retired.

MacKinnon was a man of tremendous strength, wisdom and foresight, and one who brought impeccable credentials to the job of cementing the divergent interests of the Texas credit union movement into a solid and united front. The position which MacKinnon now assumed was no mere honorary or "figurehead" post. Unlike all his predecessors in the presidency, MacKinnon was a well-paid, full-time executive. His job had been created by the combined Board of Directors to consolidate and coordinate every facet of the activities of the League and its Affiliates. The Board's action marked the change in the definition of the term "president". From this point on, the president's title would denote the highest League staff job in the state while the highest elected officials would become known as chairman of the board.

Duncan himself credits the changeover—and MacKinnon's strong leadership—as the salvation of the League and its Affiliates. "Mac and I hardly ever agreed on anything," Duncan recalls cryptically, "but if there was anybody who could have carried out the reunification we were striving for, it was Wilfred MacKinnon. There's never been any sentiment to go back to the old system, because the new system has worked so beautifully—thanks to Mac."

MacKinnon, of course, had already amply demonstrated the abilities he would use to make a success of his new job. Not only had he served as League president under the old organizational setup in the middle 1960s, but, at the time of his appointment to the combined presidency, was serving as president of CUNA as well—the third Texas credit unionist to hold that top national post. He was elected to the CUNA presidency in May 1970 during the organization's national meeting in Madison, Wisconsin, and thereby assumed the titular leadership of the credit union movement in the entire United States. (At the same meeting, former CUNA President R.C. Morgan, also of Texas, was elected to serve with MacKinnon on the CUNA Executive Committee as a vice president.)

MacKinnon thus became the first person to serve as president of a reorganized CUNA. The original national body had evolved into CUNA International with its expansion into other countries besides the United States. But in 1970, the name of the international body was changed to World Council of Credit Unions and the restructured CUNA again became a national organization.

From the spring of 1970 until the CUNA Executive Committee accepted his resignation "with regret" in November 1971 to allow him to assume his duties as chief executive officer of the League and its Affiliates, MacKinnon was unquestionably the most visible figure on the national credit union scene. He was a major force behind the passage of the recodification of the Federal Credit Union Act, which was signed into law by President Nixon on October 19, 1970, and which was hailed as one of the most important pieces of credit union legislation ever enacted. The new law enabled credit unions to insure member share accounts up to $20,000 and gave credit unions their own version of the Federal Deposit Insurance Corporation which protected bank deposits. "This . . . is a momentous occasion," MacKinnon said at the time. "The law will have a profound effect on the credit union movement and will materially add to our efforts in protecting our members' accounts."

As important as he was nationally, however, MacKinnon was even more important in the role he played at the state level. "The main objective," he said, after being named to the combined presidency of the League and its affiliates, "is the coordination of the total resources of the TCUL and its Affiliates . . . financial and personnel." With a "can-do spirit and a willingness to experiment," he said, "we will get the results stipulated by the board."

MacKinnon referred to a sweeping five-year plan that had been unveiled by the combined 32-member Board of Directors in June 1971 at a meeting in Dallas. The plan was designed to increase substantially the rate and quality of growth of the credit union movement in Texas for the next five years. It called for an "aggressive marketing" strategy, the reassignment of a large portion of the combined staff, a shift in public relations emphasis from the simple dissemination of information to more forceful, "hard-sell" PR, and other far-reaching changes. And now the man to implement those changes had been chosen.

"My first job was to attempt to consolidate the organizations so that they would work together for the betterment of credit unions," MacKinnon said in a 1979 interview conducted just a few months before his death in September of that year. "And this, I believe, we were successful in doing. The most important thing . . . was to have the use of management people from any one of the companies available for all; in other words, the management team consisted of people from insurance, services and so forth. We had the benefit of all these people's thinking in directing any one of the activities, and that was very valuable.

"Of course, in addition to that was the saving of money. For instance, we were able to establish one mail system for everyone, one receptionist and switchboard operator, and other minor benefits."

Under MacKinnon, long-range planning became the kind of continuous process that it remains today for the League and its Affiliates. And it was this planning that enabled the League to grow with the times and to institute so many needed new services and facilities. "You set your goals and then you review them," Mac-Kinnon explained, "to see that you're actually doing what you're supposed to do. We did that regularly, every six months."

With a well-organized management staff, the Board of Directors was able to remove itself almost entirely from the routine operation of the League, even as it and its growing family of Affiliates steadily expanded during the 1970s to include such huge entities as Members Life Insurance Company, Town North National Bank and the Southwest Corporate Federal Credit Union.

Organized in the fall of 1975 with deposits of just $35, Southwest Corporate had grown by December of 1983 to an organization of 1,525 credit unions in four states and had assets of $500 million. Its manager, John

Arnold, describes Southwest Corporate's four major areas of service to credit unions as "information, loans, investments and correspondence services." It serves primarily as a financial intermediary for credit unions and other institutions.

In March 1972, outgoing TCUL President Walter Duncan and this to say to delegates at the annual membership meeting in summing up the reunificiation effort:

"The Texas Credit Union League has just completed three years of change . . . Certainly the most important development has been the blending of our several organizations into a coordinated program of service to Texas credit unions and their members . . .

"Instead of three boards, we have one Board of Directors with the responsibility for all the Texas Credit Union League and all of its Affiliates . . .

"The second major restructuring was in management. The Board has established a single post of chief executive officer to be responsible for the coordination and direction of the personnel and financial resources of the League and its Affiliates. We have had our attorneys working with us to set up the position within the authority of the Board. And while we may want to change titles or other minor things, the directors are satisfied that an efficient, workable management system is now in operation."

In the twilight of his life, Wilfred MacKinnon would still look back on the long years of friction that he helped to end and recall his role in unifying and strengthening the credit union movement in Texas.

MacKinnon's philosophy of "strength through unity" had prevailed.

Branching Out

The 1970s were characterized by continuing expansion of the Texas credit union movement into fields that the movement's pioneers would never have dreamed of entering a few decades earlier—fields such as full-scale commercial banking, life insurance, tax-sheltered trusts, share draft "checking" accounts and credit cards, to name a few.

By early 1972, the League's Board of Directors and management were seriously looking into the possibility of operating a League-owned bank. Under MacKinnon's direction, a management team was actively researching the idea, although McKinnon emphasized to the Board that the League had no clearance at the moment for such a banking operation and that state approval would be required.

From the beginning, the idea was to purchase an existing bank. From the standpoint of the League's new long-range planning program, such a purchase made sense in many ways. First of all, owning a bank would help solve a fluctuating general liquidity problem, which troubled credit unions on a recurring basis. TCUL leaders envisioned the bank engaging in a thriving long-term first mortgage loan business on referral from member credit unions, while also functioning as the secondary market for credit union paper, buying loans of member credit unions as capital needs dictated, then selling them back when the interests of the credit unions could be best served by the transaction.

It was felt that the bank could also function generally as a corporate central credit union in the field of interlending, especially in amounts under $100,000. It could be utilized as a device to offer a third-party payment system to its members through correspondents in out-of-town areas, could provide mortgage financing for credit unions seeking to build or acquire their own office space, and perform other vital services.

TEXAS CREDIT UNION LEAGUE BOARD OF DIRECTORS

NAME	DISTRICT	YEAR OF ELECTION
J. E. Meador	Texarkana	1934†
W. O. Freeman	Fort Worth	1934†
W. E. Suddarth	Amarillo	1934†
Carl H. Bodine	Wichita Falls	1934†
B. S. Wallace	Waco	1934†
*R. H. Pitts °	Dallas	1934†
T. J. Ford °	Port Arthur	1934†
Adolph Anderson °	San Antonio	1934†
C. W. Thomas °	Tyler	1934†
G. W. Elder	Houston	1934†
A. T. Earles °	El Paso	1934†
C. T. Bergeron	Dallas	1934†
W. H. Edmonston °	Dallas	1936
*Joseph A. Collerain °	Houston	1936
*V. S. Judson °	Dallas	1936
Dr. L. Conrod	Denton	1937
H. E. Sherman	Houston	1937
S. H. Butler	Port Arthur	1938
*Guy V. Carroll	Houston	1939
A. Borofsky	Dallas	1940
W. D. Culbreath °	Houston	1940
W. R. Eddings °	Fort Worth	1940
W. J. Prejean °	Port Arthur	1940
H. W. Mecklenberg °	New Gulf	1940
B. F. Dooley, Jr. °	Port Arthur	1940
R. E. Miller °	Fort Worth	1941
*H. B. Yates °	Dallas	1941
O. F. Burgdorf °	Texarkana	1941
H. G. Turner °	Houston	1941
C. V. Anderson	Waco	1941
C. E. Burdick °	Tyler	1941
Phil Harvey	El Paso	1941
W. D. Turbeville °	San Antonio	1941
Frank McLain	Panhandle	1942
M. A. Worsham	Valley	1942
*C. W. Hudson °	Dallas	1942
E. E. Young	West	1945
G. B. Reed °	San Antonio	1946
Willie Martin	Central	1946
Arvin Eady	West	1946

° Known Deceased
* Chairman of Texas Credit Union League
† 1st Board

Continued on next page

NAME	DISTRICT	YEAR OF ELECTION
*H. T. Sanderson °	Valley	1946
C. W. McCoy	Southeast	1946
Sid D. Jackson	Houston	1947
C. W. Newman	Panhandle	1948
H. A. Davis °	Houston	1948
A. C. Black	Panhandle	1952
*R. C. Morgan	West (Far West-1959)	1953
Albert Henry	Southeast	1953
L. G. Pierce °	Panhandle	1954
Beeman Jones	North	1955
Dal A. Loe °	Dallas	1956
Dyalthia Benson °	Panhandle	1956
*Jack Mitchell	Dallas	1956
Oscar W. Dunn °	Fort Worth	1956
M. A. Henderson	Central	1956
Burton C. Eubanks	Dallas	1958
James W. Dodd	Houston	1958
Ben Levisee	Fort Worth	1958
J. W. Huggins	North Central	1958
W. L. Fannin	South Central	1958
Dr. Jule K. Lamar	South	1958
O. M. Fletcher	Midwest	1958
O. L. Cannon	North	1959
P. D. Barziza °	Houston	1959
Ted Mitchell	Dallas	1960
J. H. Dickerson	East	1960
Fred Scantlen	South Central	1960
Oran B. Dill	North	1961
Wayland Jones	East	1961
Rosemary Howison	South Central	1962
*Pete Gooch	Fort Worth	1962
W. A. Walker	San Antonio	1963
R. C. Foster	Midwest	1963
Juanita Williams	North Central	1964
Floyd Kelly	South	1964
Elton Smith	Dallas	1964
Cecil Allmand	Southeast	1965
*Walter Duncan	Dallas	1966
Wayne Hilton	Panhandle	1966
W. H. (Bill) Goff	Southeast	1966
Lois Hankins	Panhandle	1967
*Jim Chiarizio	North	1967
H. A. Olson	San Antonio	1967
Laura Lemon	Midwest	1967
Odell Dancak	South Central	1968
Kara Cooper °	South	1968
Bill B. Green	Dallas	1970
*Calvin Phillips	Dallas	1970

NAME	DISTRICT	YEAR OF ELECTION
Marvin Wammack °	North Central	1970
Jerry Deering	Fort Worth	1970
*Wilfred S. MacKinnon °	Houston	1970
Glenn D. Johnson	Houston	1970
Donald W. Rutter	Houston	1970
Tony Brasher	Panhandle	1970
Milton R. Durham	Panhandle	1970
*Jim R. Williams	San Antonio	1970
Robert W. Mitchell	East	1970
C. T. (Jake) Helpinstill	Southeast	1970
V. R. (Larry) LaRochelle °	Valley	1970
James Amis	Far West	1970
Ray Northrup	South Central	1970
*Roy Neidig	South Central	1970
Francis Cooper °	South	1970
D. Baker	Midwest	1970
Neva M. Spellman	Dallas	1971
Howard L. Andrus	Houston	1971
Bessie P. Heard	Houston	1971
Don R. Massie	North	1971
H. H. Marsh	Mid West	1971
Wilburn Dodson	Panhandle	1971
Wade Choate	Mid West	1971
Cecil Denison	North Central	1972
Barbara T. Skelton	East	1972
Jim W. Williams °	Fort Worth	1972
A. M. Davis	Houston	1972
Bert Miller	Houston	1972
Jack Hathaway	North	1972
Dan L. Cervenka	South Central	1972
John Arnold	South	1972
A. C. Doughty	Valley	1972
Dorothy Drattlo	Valley	1972
Dave W. Marr	Dallas	1972
E. C. (Ed) Rowland	Far West	1972
Carol Reagan	North Central	1973
Pat Edwards	Panhandle	1973
Ann McNallen	Valley	1973
Clyde Choate	Dallas	1974
Bob Morisey	South Central	1974
Peggy Holcemback Middleton °	Fort Worth	1974
Glenn G. Phillips	Panhandle	1974
Jimmy Sasser	Valley	1974
Carl A. Adkins	South Central	1974
*Ed Hale	Dallas	1974
*Ron Liles	Fort Worth	1975
A. L. Riley	Houston	1975
Wayne Lough	San Antonio	1975

NAME	DISTRICT	YEAR OF ELECTION
Virginia Trussell Warren	South Central	1975
Jesse Campbell	Houston	1976
Tony Lema	Houston	1976
Mark W. Taylor	North	1976
Wilfred Long °	Southeast	1976
L. Smith	Southeast	1977
Melody Lowery	South	1977
Gil Weston	East	1978
Billy Schaffner	Midwest	1978
Bea Herod	North	1978
Ruby Weinholt	San Antonio	1978
Roland Klar	San Antonio	1978
Billy F. Spivey	South Central	1978
Delton Moore	Southeast	1978
Mel Diamond	South	1978
Gary Base	Houston	1979
*Paul Mitchell	Houston	1979
Hal Thomas	Houston	1980
Mike Rusk	Far West	1980
Jim Gray	Mid West	1980
Fern Phillips	Dallas	1981
Barbara Clore	Houston	1981
Barbara Hall	Southeast	1981
Art Shaw	Far West	1981
Lee Feemster	Mid West	1981
Lynn Talbert	North Central	1982
B. Griffin	East	1982
Steve Rasmussen	South	1982
Curby Stech	Houston	1982
Gary Janacek	North Central	1983
Tommy L. Browning	Fort Worth	1983
Mary Nell James	North	1983
Fred L. Jewett	Panhandle	1983
Bob Piatkowski	San Antonio	1983
Rex McConnell	Southeast	1983
David Dowell	Dallas	1984
Artilla Patton	Valley	1984
Mike Marshall	South	1984
Larry Hertell	Central	1984
George Studdard	Fort Worth	1984
Sue Wilkerson	East	1984
Janice Ruyle	Central	1984

° Known Deceased
* Chairman of Texas Credit Union League
† 1st Board

252

Originally, the ownership of a bank was also seen as a way to give credit unions a toehold in the type of "checkless, cashless society" which many leaders of the nation's financial industry had begun to envision in the late 1960s. At the time, it was felt that this might be the on yway for credit unions to obtain access to the electronic funds transfer systems which were becoming prevalent through bank-operated automated clearing houses.

"Such leaders as Duncan, MacKinnon and Morgan considered the advent of these clearing houses as a distinct threat to credit unions, recalled Southwest Corporate Manager Arnold in early 1984. "The clearing houses were private concerns, which were closed to both savings and loan associations and credit unions. In the early 1970s, the credit unions tried to gain access and were denied. That's when the idea of owning a bank evolved."

(Later, however, a Colorado anti-trust lawsuit filed by a credit union against an automated clearing house in Denver helped force the clearing houses to serve credit unions. Meanwhile, in 1974, the U.S. Central Credit Union was formed, paving the way for the development of regional corporate credit unions such as Southwest Corporate—the first such regional institution in the U.S. when it was chartered in 1975. These new regional entities gave the credit unions their own system of electronic funds transfers. And in 1980, a further change in the law allowed regional corporates to set up an independent funds flow system without any bank involvement whatever. "In the 1980s, this has given the credit union movement real independence for the first time," Arnold said. "We now have 17 Texas credit unions which don't even have bank accounts at all." In Arnold's view, it has also effectively removed much of the impetus felt by credit unionists of a decade ago to acquire banks. In fact, only Texas, of all states, still has a credit union-owned bank today.)

With such a lengthy list of key reasons for the acquisition of a bank before it, the TCUL Board of Directors took a major step in that direction in March 1972. They authorized James A. Chiarizio, who had been elected to fill the new post of TCUL board chairman; Donald W. Rutter, board chairman of Members Insurance, and Calvin Phillips, board chairman of TCUL Services, to negotiate for and purchase a bank on behalf of the League and its Affiliates. They were authorized to pay up to $3.2 million for the bank, and given full authority to handle all details relating to the transaction.

But finding a bank that could be acquired by Texas credit unions proved to be a long and time-consuming task. It was to take more than three years to complete this key expansion project with the purchase by a group of 51 state-chartered Texas credit unions of Town North National Bank in the Dallas suburb of Farmers Branch in April 1975. In the transaction, 99 percent of the bank's shares (some 40,750 shares altogether) had to be purchased from more than 100 shareholders. The shares were bought by a group of ten individuals, then resold to the 51 credit unions, none of which received more than 4.9 percent of the shares.

Later the same year, after receiving notification that federal credit unions could participate in ownership of the bank, a holding company known as CU Bank Shares, Inc., was formed and a number of federal credit unions became shareholders. By mid-1976, the bank was owned by 155 Texas credit unions, including 86 federal and 69 state-chartered organizations. But a later NCUA ruling excluded federal credit unions from bank ownership and it is now owned by 87 state-chartered credit unions (CU Bank Shares, Inc. is currently the only bank holding company in the U.S. owned by credit unions.)

Under credit union ownership, Town North National Bank experienced impressive, immediate and continuous growth. During the first year after its purchase, the bank's assets grew by an impressive 30 percent, and this was only the beginning. By July 31, 1978, the bank's deposits had grown from $9.9 million at the time of its acquisition by the credit unions to $32.2 million—an increase of more than 300 percent in just over three years. Under President Fred Ferguson and Board Chairman Clyde Johnson, Town North National had amassed total assets by that time of more than $34.8 million, had added credit card services through VISA and Master Charge, and had written loans in excess of $18.8 million.

The move to acquire a bank by the TCUL and its member credit unions proved that the pioneering spirit was still alive and well among Texas credit unionists.

It also proved to be one of the most financially lucrative ventures ever entered into by participating credit unions. By September 1983, Town North National Bank's assets had soared to $70 million and its total deposits had reached $63 million. And with its advantageous location in the heart of a fast-growing North Dallas suburb, it is continuing to grow at a planned rate. Although the bank has not proved a workable vehicle for many of the programs which the League had originally visualized for it, Town North National Bank was instrumental in allowing the TCUL to set up America's first experimental credit card system for credit unions in 1976. This program involved over 200 credit unions at year-end 1983.

On July 1, 1972, the League and its Affiliates officially entered the life insurance business with the formation of Members Life Insurance Company as a wholly owned subsidiary of Members Mutual. The new company was formed to provide a needed service to credit unions and their members and was authorized to write life and health and accident policies. The first policy was issued to Don Rutter, board chairman of Members Insurance Companies. Elected to the company's first Board of Directors were MacKinnon, R.C. Morgan, V.R. (Larry) LaRochelle (who served as a

Members Mutual director from 1961 to 1972 and as MMIC chairman from 1970 to 1972), James Chiarizio and Jim R. Williams. MacKinnon was appointed president of the new company. Other officers included Ted J. McGehee; Barbara Skelton; and Marvin L. Wammack.

The company actually began issuing policies in January 1973, concentrating on a basic family protection policy designed exclusively for Texas credit union members and available at an extremely low fee of $5 a month, which provided benefits of up to $8,000 for the head of the family, $4,000 for the spouse and $1,000 for each child.

The growth of Members Life was nothing short of phenomenal. By July 1974—after just 18 months in business—the company had issued more than 7,000 policies and was writing new policies at the rate of 160 per week. New types of coverage were steadily added, and by the time Members Insurance Companies celebrated Members Mutual's silver anniversary in 1977, more than 20,000 Texas credit union members had purchased life insurance policies through Members Life. Between 1976 and 1977, the amount of claims paid out by the life insurance company skyrocketed from just $170,000 to $742,000.

Overall by 1977, Members Insurance Companies were paying more than $21 million in claims to 35,600 property/casualty policy owners. More than 132,000 credit union members had property/casualty coverage through the companies. Impressive as they were at the time, however, even these figures would be dwarfed by developments of the next few years, as Members Insurance continued on its way to becoming one of the genuine giants of the insurance industry. The story of MIC's journey toward that status will be told in detail in a later chapter.

Along with the moves into banking and life insurance, the TCUL took steps in the early 1970s to set up a special trust company to protect the assets of credit union people in Texas. The TCUL Trust Company, which was formed in late 1971, was designed to act as trustee for credit union members and to manage their estates for the benefit of their beneficiaries. Because of its tax-sheltered status, a trust could save credit union members significant amounts of federal estate taxes and other levies. The trust company could also provide professional estate planning and expert help on complicated estate tax matters.

When it was established, the TCUL Trust Company was the first credit union-owned organization of its type in the United States, operating as a branch of TCUL Services, Inc. It added a total new dimension in credit union services to which most credit union members might otherwise never have had access.

Initially, however, the trust company ran into problems with the Texas Securities Commission, from which it had to obtain clearance before it could begin operating, and it did not actually start doing business for nearly two years after it was established. "At one point," confessed MacKinnon, "we were beginning to fear this company would never be in operation." But by mid-1973, the trust company was finally operational.

Under the direction of Ted McGehee, its vice-president and general manager, TCUL Trust proved that trusts were no longer a luxury that only the super-rich could afford. It put professional estate-planning and management services within easy reach of the 2 million credit union members in Texas. Through the trust company, any credit union member could now establish either a living trust or a testamentary trust (which comes into existence when the grantor dies and assures that his wishes are carried out) without paying any initial fee. The company then charged a small annual fee to manage the trust.

Later the trust company, as a full-scale Affiliate of the TCUL, expanded its services to include a home mortgage lending program for Texas credit union members, enabling them to obtain home loans with as little as 5 percent down payment and for periods of up to 30 years. For the first time, a credit union member could obtain a mortgage loan from something other than a commercial lending institution. It was yet another desirable breakthrough for the typical credit union member, but it was also yet another example of the increasingly competitive nature of the modern credit union. With interest rates on the way up and the national economic situation growing more and more volatile and less and less stable, other segments of the financial community could be expected to resist this new source of competition with all their might. (The TCUL mortgage program was merged in 1981 with the CUNA mortgage program. Since then, the trust has been inoperative.)

One of the most utilized services of the League is "Information Central," which was started in April 1972. Utilizing a toll-free WATS line in the Dallas office, the service handled calls from credit union staff personnel around the state asking questions about day-to-day operations and management areas. At first, all calls were handled by one person, Tony Gehring, and by the end of 1972, the service was averaging 238 calls per month. By late 1983, a three-person "Information Central" staff composed of Gehring, Chuck Korioth and John Heusman was processing a monthly average of 1,186 calls.

Another service that was being used by nearly every Texas credit union on a continuing basis was the League's supply department, organized in 1954. Of the 1,232 credit unions in Texas at year-end 1983, 1,198 had ordered some type of supplies from this department during the year.

As Texas credit unions and their League established footholds in new fields and new functions, some of the TCUL services that had been most vital to member credit unions in the past were now rendered unneces-

General Texas Credit Union Data, 1977-1983

Credit Unions

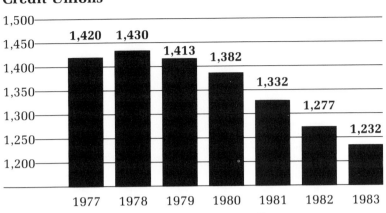

Year	Credit Unions
1977	1,420
1978	1,430
1979	1,413
1980	1,382
1981	1,332
1982	1,277
1983	1,232

Assets (in billions)

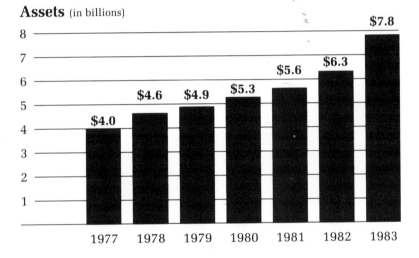

Year	Assets
1977	$4.0
1978	$4.6
1979	$4.9
1980	$5.3
1981	$5.6
1982	$6.3
1983	$7.8

Members (in millions)

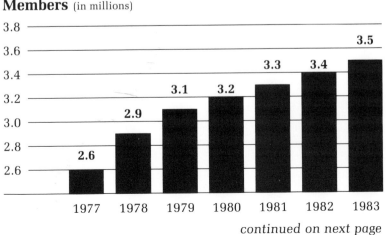
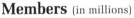

Year	Members
1977	2.6
1978	2.9
1979	3.1
1980	3.2
1981	3.3
1982	3.4
1983	3.5

continued on next page

continued from previous page

Loans (in billions)

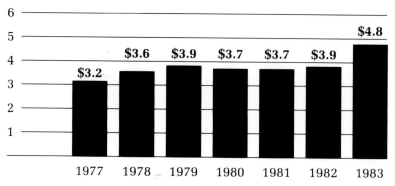

Savings (in billions)

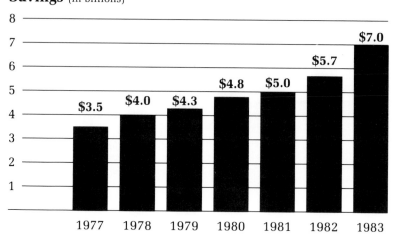

sary. A classic example of a once all-important function that became totally obsolete during the mid-1970s was the League's Stabilization Fund. The fund had been established during the early 1960s with Assistant Managing Director Jim Vest in charge of it, and the fund had proved a godsend to thousands of credit union members over the years.

According to Vest, the fund was set up to purchase the assets of any credit union entering liquidation, thereby guaranteeing that members could retrieve their savings at one hundred cents on the dollar. On occasion, if the fund did not have enough money to purchase all of a credit union's assets, it would arrange to sell outstanding loans to another credit union and guarantee that the purchasing institution would suffer no loss on the loans. This was the case in 1970, when the Ford Motor Company permanently closed down its Dallas assembly plant, not only throwing some 1,900 employees out of work but wiping out a credit union with $1 million in assets.

But in July 1975, all Texas credit unions came under the protection of insurance programs through either the Texas Share Guaranty Credit Union or National Credit Union Administration. Suddenly, there was no longer a need for stabilization service where shareholders' protection was concerned, and the Stabilization Fund was changed to the Credit Union Progress Fund, aimed at the development of new practices and services, rather than at reacting to financial crisis. One of the catalysts in getting share insurance approved in Texas was the collapse of the $3.3 million Amarillo Air Force Base Credit Union in early 1973, resulting in the subsequent indictment of four credit union officials and action by the 1973 Texas Legislature.

Slowly—indeed, almost imperceptibly at times — the credit unions had moved over the span of some forty years into one area after another that had once been reserved for the "professional" bankers and other big-money interests. By the mid years of the Seventies, credit unions were poised to move into head-to-head competition with the banks and savings and loans in virtually every field where they had not already penetrated, the home mortgage field, checking accounts and credit cards being prime examples.

Inexorably, the battle lines were being drawn for a great financial free-for-all.

Pioneers, New and Old

"Progress Through Unity: Forty Years of Pioneering" was the highly appropriate theme of the fortieth annual meeting of the Texas Credit Union League and Affiliates in San Antonio on March 20-23, 1974. Without doubt, phenomenal progress had been made by the credit union movement in Texas over four decades. And with the successful amalgamation of the League and its Affiliates into one cohesive entity under one overall chief executive and one Board of Directors, an unprecedented measure of unity had also been achieved within the movement.

But the early to mid-1970s were a highly crucial period for the "pioneering" aspect of the credit union cause in Texas. In a sense, each new success made it more difficult to keep the fervor of the pioneering spirit alive. And this was a period in which the League was losing, through retirement or death, most of the key figures who had embodied that pioneer spirit during those first forty years.

Indeed, as the San Antonio convention opened, amid much hoopla and congratulatory speeches by Governor Dolph Briscoe and Congressman Henry B. Gonzalez, a number of familiar faces were missing from the ranks of the 2,500 delegates. Such outstanding leaders as H.B. Yates, Joe Collerain and Cecil Burdick were now gone, and the void left by their passing would be difficult to fill.

John Pete Parsons (left) is sworn in as the second credit union commissioner for the State of Texas by Chief Justice Joe Greenhill of the Texas Supreme Court.

Past League President Jack Mitchell strikes a happy pose with Rep. Wright Patman.

Buford Lankford, longtime NCUA regional director

Cecil Burdick of Longview served as the TCUL's secretary-treasurer longer than any other person — some two decades — and was involved in many of the most critical decisions in League history.

Yates, the tough, taciturn Texan who had become the first from his state to rise to national prominence in the highest echelons of credit unionsism, died in May 1973 at the age of 82. His death ended 42 years of active credit union work, which had begun when he helped organize the Dallas Teachers Credit Union in 1931 and extended through his long term as president of the TCUL, followed by his years of leadership at the national level as president, managing director, vice president and secretary of CUNA. Although Yates had been out of the limelight since the 1950s, he had remained a strong and inspiring figure, even in the background of the movement. And those who knew him realized that, while other capable leaders had arisen and would continue to arise within the movement, there would never be another H.B. Yates.

The same could be said of Joe Collerain, who preceded Yates in death in June 1972. Collerain's service to credit unions predated even that of Yates, since Collerain had been an organizer of the state's first known credit union in 1915. Later a founder of the Humble Houston Credit Union, Collerain and his dedicated leadership had helped keep the struggling movement afloat during the dark years of the 1930s, during which he had served as the League's second president. In the intervening years, he had held a series of top state and national positions and remained an active, visible figure in the movement up until the time of his death. And even then his influence remained. As the *Bulletin* noted: "Joseph Collerain's shadow lives; he will walk the historical hall of Texas credit union leaders."

In November 1972, death also claimed Cecil Burdick, who was remembered both for his outstanding leadership qualities and his keen sense of humor. Burdick served as secretary-treasurer of the League for nearly twenty years, from 1941 to 1960, while also serving as treasurer-manager of Humble Employees Longview Federal Credit Union, where he was a charter member. He became an honorary League director when his company transferred him from Longview to Houston in 1960. He had served as a director and vice president of CUNA, had organized more than thirty credit unions, and had been widely recognized for his civic and community involvement.

And finally, on May 7, 1976, the Texas and national credit union movements lost an irreplaceable friend as death claimed Congressman Wright Patman in Washington, D.C., at the age of 82. During his 47 years in Congress, the East Texas lawmaker had been an active sponsor of every single piece of credit union legislation introduced on Capitol Hill, and at the time of his death was strongly backing legislation that would have granted broad new powers to credit unions. On March 10, the day of his funeral in his hometown of Texarkana, the board of directors of the House Credit Union in Washington voted unanimously to change its name to the Wright Patman Congressional Federal Credit Union.

Retirements also depleted the ranks of the movement's pioneers during the first half of the 1970s. Buford Lankford completed 31 years of service to the cause in April 1972 when he retired as regional director of the National Credit Union Administration, although he was to remain active for a long time to come in other capacities. And Boyd Browning, who had become known as the credit unions' "insurance man" during more than two decades of service to Members Insurance, stepped aside as senior vice president of Members Mutual in June 1975. Browning had previously served as claims manager, assistant managing director and vice president of the company, and had served as president of the Southwestern Insurance Information Service. Since he had joined the company in 1954, Browning had seen Members Mutual become one of the fifteen top casualty underwriters in Texas, with assets of more than $30 million.

And in February 1975 came what must be considered one of the most historically significant retirements in the annals of the Texas Credit Union League, as the venerable Jim Barry concluded a spectacular tenure of more than thirty years as the League's managing director. It was appropriate that the League's annual report, presented at the annual meeting in Fort Worth in April 1975, was dedicated to Barry. It was also appropriate that the TCUL Board voted to retire the title of managing director along with Barry. For more than three decades, Jim Barry had personified that title, and it was now a title that had seemingly outlived its time under new concepts of management.

Adjusting to the complexities of a new management system caused some problems with titles during the early 1970s. Most people were in general agreement that the old managing director's title had become something of an anachronism. But this was not the only problem where the matter of titles was concerned, published records of League activities during that period indicate. For instance, when MacKinnon took over the combined leadership of the League and its Affiliates, he continued for some time to be referred to as "president" as specified in 1973 bylaw amendments. But when James A. Chiarizio, manager of the Red River Employees Federal Credit Union in Texarkana, succeeded Walter Duncan as the elective head of the League in 1972, he was also referred to more often than not as "president" in League publications. Over the next year or so, this confusing duplication of titles was gradually eliminated. The elective heads of the League and the various Affiliates assumed the more appropriate title of "chairman of the board" of their individual organizations, and MacKinnon was frequently indentified as "chief executive officer" until all concerned became accustomed to the change and the new definition of the term "president." Other chairmen of the board during this time included Donald W. Rutter, chairman of Members

Insurance, and Calvin C. Phillips, chairman of TCUL Services.

Part of this problem in semantics may have been related to the fact that the official publication of the League was itself in a state of flux at the time. John Quinlan, who had edited and directed the monthly *Bulletin* since the 1940s, had quietly retired in 1969, and his departure had set off a number of changes, both in the style and format of the publication and in the personnel who produced it. Too, the responsibilities of the League's Public Relations Department, under which the publication was placed after Quinlan left, became many-faceted, ranging from the production of television commercials to legislative communications. In 1970, the publication's name was changed from the *Bulletin* to the *Texas League Newsletter*. With a newsletter format of short, typed paragraphs instead of lengthy articles with headlines, the revamped publication was somewhat less thorough in dealing with the detailed functions of the League and its Affiliates, and although the *Newsletter* won several awards, it was not particularly well-received among rank-and-file credit union people. Another total changeover in personnel followed in the Public Relations Department during 1971, and the *Newsletter* was again redesigned and returned to a newspaper-style format. Since the *Newsletter* name was no longer appropriate, it was changed in 1973, during the tenure of John Pete Parsons as TCUL public relations director, to *Texas Leaguer*, and has remained the same since.

Fortunately for the League and the credit unions of Texas, as the early pioneers of the movement faded from the picture, they were replaced by equally capable and dedicated leaders who refused to let the pioneer spirit fade away with the "old guard." In the professional management field, some of the key "rising stars" of the period included Ted McGehee, a Sweetwater native who had joined Members Mutual in 1958 as an underwriting manager and had risen steadily in the company management structure to the post of senior vice president. In 1973, McGehee was named to the newly created staff positions of vice president of the League and vice president of TCUL Services, becoming a principal assistant to MacKinnon in all three areas.

In the meantime, Jack L. Eaker, a native of Waco who was reared in Greenville, assumed McGehee's former responsibilities in the operation of Members Insurance, in his position as executive vice president of the combined companies. Eaker had been with Members Mutual since 1965, when he joined the company as claims supervisor. He later served as claims manager and vice president of claims before being elevated to the executive vice presidency of Members Insurance Companies. (Eaker's rise through the company ranks and his contributions to the League and the credit union industry will be detailed in subsequent chapters.)

Among the elective leaders of the League and Affiliates, there was also an impressive crop of rising stars. Jim R. Williams, president of the Government Employees Credit Union of San Antonio, succeeded Chiarizio as TCUL board chairman in March 1974. A native of Magic City, Texas, Williams was only 39 years old at the time, and his election was a major step in a career of credit union service that would take him to the top elective position in CUNA within a few years.

Chiarizio, who had served as a field representative for the League from 1960 to 1964, was the first former TCUL staff member elected to the chairmanship of the League. After leaving the post in 1974, he continued to serve as a TCUL director until 1983, when he concluded a 16-year tenure on the Board. He has also been honored with enrollment in the CUNA Founders Club for organizing ten credit unions.

Don Rutter, a native of Pennsylvania, served as Members Insurance board chairman from 1972 to 1975. He is president of Ethyl Employess Credit Union of Pasadena, a position he has held since 1962.

Calvin Phillips, president of the Dallas Postal Credit Union, has been a TCUL director since 1966. In addition to serving as board chairman of TCUL Services from 1972 to 1975, he also served as board chairman of the League from 1976 to 1978. In 1979, he was appointed to the Texas Credit Union Commission and was elected chairman in 1983, succeeding Walter Duncan, who had held the chairmanship from 1975 to 1983, and who continues to serve as a member of the commission, as he has since 1969.

Coinciding with Williams' election were wholesale changes on the combined Board of Directors, as eight new faces joined the body in 1974. The newcomers included Marvin Wammack of Waco, Clyde N. Choate and S. Edward Hale, Jr. of Dallas, Peggy Holcemback of Fort Worth, Glen R. Phillips of Amarillo, Jimmy F. Sasser of Edinburg, Robert L. Morisey of Austin and Carl R. Adkins of Wharton.

Almost simultaneously, Parsons left his post as TCUL public relations director to assume the all-important role of credit union commissioner of the State of Texas, effective February 1, 1974.

And, of course, there were still enough of the older credit union pioneers around to help ease the movement through this critical period of transition—a period described by Chiarizio as "a turning point" and "a new beginning." Former League President Pete Gooch, for one, was still around and still going strong. In May 1973, he was elected chairman of the board of CUNA Mutual Insurance Society, while still serving as full-time president-manager of the 5,500-member Telco Credit Union of Fort Worth and as a member of the Texas Credit Union Commission.

And in May of 1972, after retiring from one major position as assistant regional director of the National Credit Union Administration, Clyde Johnson joined the staff of the TCUL as special projects administrator. The following year, he was named vice president of the

League, assuming the responsibility of heading both the Members Services Department and the Education and Training Department. A Cooper native with 34 years of credit union-related federal service behind him, Johnson, too, was still going strong.

In taking note of the many changes taking place within the leadership ranks of the credit union movement in Texas during the first half of the Seventies, MacKinnon summed up the transition in these terms: "It is with regret that we see expert people leave. On the other hand, we are proud of the fact that we have been able to attract many young people into our management group, and we hope we will be able to use their services in a manner that will be most interesting and challenging to them, while profitable and rewarding to them and to the Texas Credit Union League and Affiliates."

Times change. So do lifestyles and public priorities. So does the cast of characters upon the human stage. But the need for pioneering—and for dedicated men and women to serve as pioneers—remains as timeless as the pyramids.

Battling the Banks

Virtually ever since their inception, credit unions had been the objects of periodic sniping attacks by bankers and the banking lobbies at the state and federal levels of government. But until the midway point of the Seventies, banks had generally continued to view credit unions as a relatively minor irritant—in the nature of a troublesome pimple—rather than as a serious danger. Most of the "heavy fighting" within the financial community had remained between banks and the savings and loan institutions which were their nearest and most visible rivals. To many within that community, credit unions still had the image of a step-child, a minor entity which deserved less than full attention of the banks— and less than a full-scale assault from them.

But by 1975, astute observers could see that the great growth of credit unions, and their appetite for still greater growth, were leading them on a collision course with the American banking industry in general. A year earlier, in 1974, NCUA had authorized several federal credit unions nationwide to offer their members a novel new service called "share draft" accounts on a test basis. To many credit union leaders at the time, the main purpose of share drafts was to give credit unions the capability of handling the increasing number of electronic funds transfers resulting from the rapid move into data processing, especially by government agencies. But it quickly became apparent to credit unionists and bankers alike when the test was complete and NCUA allowed all 13,000 federal credit unions nationwide to offer share drafts, that this system boiled down to a new kind of interest-bearing checking account for credit union members. Since banks were prohibited by law from paying interest on checking accounts and historically opposed to such a consumer benefit, their reaction to share drafts was predictably bitter. Across the country and at every level at which they could make their influence felt, the banks began an all-out campaign to have share draft accounts outlawed.

As with any new concept, it took a while for share drafts to catch on among credit unions and their members. But in his annual report in the spring of 1975, the TCUL's MacKinnon gave share drafts prominent mention in regard to a new Electronic Funds Transfer System which the League was developing as part of its long-range planning program. A number of key League employees were spending a "good deal of time," said MacKinnon, on such aspects of the Electronic Funds Transfer System as "plastic cards . . . the automated teller system . . . (and) the share draft systems."

Of all the League staff members involved in work on share drafts, John Dunagan was the chief figure in translating this new concept into reality. Dunagan, who served at the time as vice president of information services, noted that a number of Texas banks were treating share drafts as "collection items" and not giving depositors credit for them until the drafts cleared.

To combat this practice, the League asked the U.S. Department of Justice to conduct an anti-trust investigation of five banks in the Tyler area which were routinely holding share drafts for collection. "This was a common tactic at the time," Dunagan says, "but that investigation helped put a stop to it."

Later in 1975, after hearing proposals from eight or nine major Texas banks, the League awarded a contract to the First National Bank in Dallas to service the first share draft accounts for Texas credit unions under a program known as Credit Union Instant Cash (CUIC). Later, because of the heated opposition by bankers to the share draft accounts, the First National found itself in an admittedly "awkward" position, but did not elect to stop servicing CUIC accounts. By the end of May 1976, the *Texas Leaguer* was able to report that "well over a half million CUIC drafts, as they're known officially, have been written by Texas CU members." At the time, only about a dozen credit unions were participating in the system, however, with about 112,000 drafts being cleared monthly by the First National Bank. This was a mere "drop in the bucket," but it was a beginning of a bold new era in credit union history. The TCUL took over First National Bank's share draft clearing operation in February 1980 and became the first league in the U.S. to clear share drafts. By October 1983, volume topped seven million drafts per month, cleared from 185 credit unions on the system.

Dunagan points out that the League's takeover of the share draft clearing operation was not carried out merely to benefit the League financially, but to save Texas credit unions and their members a great deal of inconvenience, since the First National Bank "was pulling out anyway." Subsequently, thirty First National employees joined TCUL Services to handle the clearing operation. By early 1984, the operation employed about 100 persons and had become the largest "end point" in the entire Eleventh Federal Reserve District, handling more items per month than anyone else.

But in the summer of 1977, a pitched battle was raging over the share draft accounts—A battle that suddenly caught the full attention of the nation's financial media, which, in turn, seemed to suddenly discover just how big the credit union movement had become. As the *Wall Street Journal* reported in its edition of June 22, 1977:

> "Nearly 34 million persons, or about one out of every six Americans, belong to a credit union—double the number a decade ago. The cooperatives' assets have more than quadrupled since 1966 and now exceed $47 billion. And credit unions hold $36.7 billion in installment loans, 19.5% of the total outstanding.
>
> "Credit unions were founded to provide cheap credit and encourage savings among individuals sharing a common bond, such as employment. Depositors own a credit union by holding shares in proportion to their savings—usually one share for each $5—and they are paid annual dividends rather than interest on amounts deposited.
>
> "But lately, the cooperatives have begun to expand into traditional banking areas. In April, President Carter signed a bill extending such banking functions as long-term mortgages, savings certificates and credit cards with unsecured lines of credit to the 13,000 federally chartered credit unions. Another 10,000 credit unions, regulated by individual states, already had most of those privileges.
>
> "Another new service is the share draft account—basically an interest-bearing checking account. Introduced in late 1974 by five credit unions, they now are available at . . . more than 850 others in 46 states. About 225,000 members wrote an estimated $1 billion of share drafts last year."

From the banks' viewpoint, this was $1 billion in lost checking and savings account funds. They called the new competition from credit unions "unfair," and bankers across the country were, in the words of the *Wall*

Street Journal, "hopping mad about the aggressive invasion of their turf by the credit unions."

Among the first shots in the battle was a lawsuit filed by the American Bankers Association against the NCUA, contending that share draft accounts were illegal, since credit unions did not pay taxes or meet the same reserve requirements as banks. After the NCUA temporarily halted the spread of share drafts, the ABA dropped the suit. But local bank groups in 11 states, including Texas, challenged share drafts with their own lawsuits or by seeking legal rulings by regulatory officials in the various states.

In addition to their lawsuits against a state-chartered and federal credit union in Texas, the Texas Bankers Association and the Independent Bankers Association both lodged protests with the Texas Credit Union Commission. When these were rejected, they asked Attorney General John Hill for an opinion on the legality of the share draft accounts under Texas law. In November 1977, the bankers lost this round, too, as Hill ruled that state-chartered credit unions could legally engage in share draft programs. Adding to the bankers' woes, Hill also ruled that credit unions were not in violation of the Texas Constitution's ban on branch banking by doing business in more than one place.

Credit union officials celebrated their victories and steadfastly defended themselves against charges of unfair competition. "We aren't really moving into competition with the banks," said TCUL Public Relations Vice President Dick Williamson. "They are getting into competition with us. Nobody wanted the average consumer's financial business. Now banks realize there is tremendous potential there and are getting into our market."

Texas Credit Union Commissioner Parsons, meanwhile, emphasized that the dawning era of electronic funds transfers made it imperative for credit unions to develop the share draft system. "The federal govern-

A half-century after it began, 2,467 participants turned out to celebrate the TCUL's 50th anniversary in Houston in April 1984. They paid tribute to representatives of six Texas credit unions which had themselves recorded 50 years of service to their members. They also saw impressive exhibits detailing the growth and strength of Members Insurance Companies and other League Affiliates, watched dancers commemorate "50 Golden Years" in the finale of Training Day activities, and shared a huge 50th birthday cake.

ment and many corporations are encouraging direct deposit of paychecks to the payee's account at the financial institution of his choice," Parsons explained. "But credit unions felt there must be a convenient way to get the money out again. If they were not able to provide a way, credit unions would be at an unfair disadvantage and unable to compete for those direct deposits."

And former TCUL President Pete Gooch, claiming that credit unions had already moved ahead of banks in a number of key areas, noted that his own Telco Credit Union of Fort Worth had been invited to join the Southwest Automated Clearing House Association, an entity set up to facilitate the transition of banks into electronic funds transfer. "There may come a time when we don't need banks to clear share drafts," he said.

These and other statements by credit union leaders pointed up the increasingly competitive spirit—and the strong urge for independence—within the Texas credit union movement. There were now more than 2.5 million individual credit union members in the state, and their leaders left no doubt that their ultimate goal was to extend share draft privileges and other new kinds of service to every last one of them, no matter what toes might get stepped upon in the financial community in the process.

Much of that community was clearly surprised by the muscular new stature which credit unions had assumed in what the *Wall Street Journal* dubbed "the battle for the buck." "The recent gains of credit unions seem surprising, because they played a minuscule role for so long," the *Journal* noted.

One major reason for those gains, however, was the effective communication and outstanding level of rapport achieved by credit unionists at the statehouse level in important, populous, wealthy states such as Texas, as well as at the congressional level in Washington. Over the years, the movement had developed a corps of strong backers in the state legislatures and in Congress. Even such less-than-friendly publications as the *American Banker* candidly gave their competitive rivals credit in this area.

As Joseph D. Hutnyan wrote in that publication in April 1977, as pro-credit union legislation was sailing through to passage despite attempts to kill it by the banks:

"Lobbies for banks and savings and loan associations must be feeling a bit like the tough kids who just found out the hard way that the new skinny kid on the block has taken boxing lessons."

"The skinny kid in this case is the credit union lobby. This week Congress approved a bill granting broad new powers to the CUs despite opposition from the commercial banks and the Treasury, and despite the fact the bill could be criticized because no hearings were held on it in the Senate, and the House hearings were stacked with only CU witnesses.

"Obviously, lobby power was a factor, and the credit unions have been adding more muscle to their lobbying apparatus in recent years. But the CUs also benefited from a combination of circumstances that helped make their bill almost impossible to stop.

"One of them was the fact that it was tacked onto legislation extending deposit rate ceilings. This helped in two ways. First, it was a bill that had to be passed because Congress believes that to end savings rate ceilings at this time could cause serious disruption in the housing market. Secondly, the rate issue diverted the attention of commercial bank and savings and loan lobbies from the CU part of the bill.

"The banks and the S&Ls were so busy battling each other, they lacked the time and energy to mount an all-out effort to defeat the section dealing with the new CU powers.

"If the CUs had tried to pass the bill separately, they would not have had these advantages, and probably would have had a much rougher time. But it might have made it anyway because credit unions have developed an amazingly friendly and positive image in Congress. The word support almost is too cold to describe this relationship. Fellowship might be a better one.

"One perceptive observer of banking politics went so far as to suggest the CUs are the new political darlings in the financial community. . ."

The share draft controversy and its ultimate resolution, in which banks and savings and loans were allowed to offer interest-bearing checking accounts if they chose, but in which credit unions permanently moved into the checking account picture, marked an important watershed for the entire financial community. It forced the gray-haired patriarchs of that community to make room for an upstart newcomer. It proved conclusively that sheer economic resources alone—the $925 billion in banks assets versus the "mere" $50 billion or so in credit union assets—could no longer decide the victor in any head-to-head confrontation. And it set the stage for a completely new approach for the entire financial community, under which banks, savings and loans and credit unions could become more and more similar in the services they offered—it they desired such similarity and the competition it entailed.

At any rate, the share draft battle represented an overwhelmingly successful extension of credit union services into a field that had heretofore remained closed to the cooperatives. By the end of 1977, the share draft program in Texas was a *fait accompli*. Between December 1976 and December 1977, the number of participating credit unions in the TCUL system soared from 18 to 32. The number of drafts cleared per month reached 851,876, compared to just 292,659 twelve months earlier, and the dollar value of these drafts more than tripled, from $12.4 million in 1976 to $41.4 million in 1977. And this was merely the beginning. By year-end 1983, more than 230 of Texas' larger credit unions were offering share draft services to their members, and 79.5 million drafts (190 credit unions) were processed by the TCUL payment system during the year.

The credit unions had taken on the "big boys" and won a decisive victory.

The Legislative Front

As we have seen from the very beginning of this history, and as the preceding chapter clearly demonstrates, friendly and practical legislation has always been the key "life force" without which the credit union movement could neither have survived nor expanded. As part of the credit union chronology in Texas, we have examined certain "watershed" pieces of legislation at the federal and state levels, as well as vital non-legislative changes in governmental regulations affecting credit unions. But as the interwoven system of laws and regulations has become more and more complex—and as credit unions have plunged competitively and aggressively into new fields—the legislative front has become the scene of continual and ongoing action, rather than simply a stage for periodic skirmishes as it once was.

The level of legislative activity has increased steadily over the past decade, during which the TCUL, other state leagues and CUNA have been required to keep their constant, unflagging attention focused on the major lawmaking bodies, the regulatory agencies and the courts of the nation. Cooperation has been the key to legislative success during the 1970s and early 1980s, not only between state and national organizations, but between state-chartered and federally chartered credit unions. State-chartered credit unions have frequently journeyed to Washington, D.C., to assist the federals in their legislative quests, and the federal credit unions have, in turn, lobbied legislators in Austin on issues of consequence to state-chartered credit unions.

279

To further facilitate legislative activity in Texas, a Credit Union Political Action Committee (CUPAC) was established by the League Board of Directors in January 1977. By interpretation of the Federal Election Commission, CUPAC and similar state organizaions became affiliated with CUNA's Legislative Action Council (CULAC), since CUNA and the various state leagues constituted a federation of trade associations. The role of CUPAC in Texas involved making direct contributions to state candidates. In addition, an agreed-upon portion of the funds collected by CUPAC were to be transmitted to CULAC for future contributions to candidates for federal offices as recommended by the TCUL trustees to the CULAC trustees.

After the 61st Texas Legislature approved the creation of an autonomous Credit Union Department in 1969, the enabling legislation remained in effect for six years with only minor changes. But in 1975, the Legislature approved a recodification of the Texas Credit Union Act, designed to give credit unions not only more specifically defined authority, but a great many more "implied" powers. It was this recodification, strongly supported by the League, that signaled the beginning of the most intensive period of legislative activity in the movement's history. The broad and loosely defined new powers given credit unions under the recodification alarmed other financial institutions—especially banks—who mounted fierce opposition to the credit unions' invasion of "banking functions."

One banking ploy in 1977 involved a proposed amendment to the Texas Constitution—called Proposition Six—which would have permitted the state's banks to participate in inter-bank systems of electronic funds transfer. The wording of the amendment was such that credit union leaders feared that the bill, if passed, would exclude credit union participation.

Taking his appeal to the public through the mass media around the state, Calvin Phillips, TCUL chairman at the time, explained that the proposition could not only be in violation of anti-trust laws, but was certainly not in the best interests of all Texas consumers, especially those without banking connections who might be excluded from future electronic funds transfer access. The proposition was soundly defeated by a two-to-one margin and represented the growing impact of credit unions in the legislative process. (In 1979, this amendment was finally passed by Texas voters, but only after the banking industry amended its position to include a "sharing" concept among all financial institutions in the field of electronic funds transfers.)

Also in 1977, the Legislature passed a "Sunset Law," which was described as an act to cause a periodic review of all state agencies and the restructuring, consolidation or outright elimination of agencies whose functions were found to conflict, duplicate or overlap. It was obvious that the Credit Union Department would be one of the agencies coming under the closest scrutiny. And it was equally obvious to both the League and the department that legislative steps must be taken to prepare for the agency's scheduled review by the Sunset Commission.

There had already been several attempts to place the Credit Union Department under that State Finance Commission, thereby creating a single regulatory body for all state-regulated financial institutions—a body which, not coincidentally, would be disproportionately made up of members friendly to the banks.

Failing this, the banking industry launched a series of attempts in the Legislature in 1979 to strip away specific services offered by credit unions unless they were explicitly authorized by law. The major focus of these efforts was to get rid of share draft accounts, which were simultaneously being attacked through various lawsuits filed in the courts, as noted in the previous chapter.

When the U.S. Supreme Court finally issued a ruling in April 1979, stating that unless they were specifically authorized by law within one year share drafts could no longer be used by credit unions, it appeared to be a crushing blow. But in retrospect, many observers now see this setback as a major turning point in getting credit union members at the grassroots involved in the legislative process. Over the next few weeks, an outpouring of more than 100,000 letters from credit union members nationwide—including some 30,000 from Texas alone—helped to convince members of Congress that these members liked share drafts and strongly believed that they should be paid interest on their money left in checking accounts.

This massive reaction from credit union people paved the way for the Monetary Control Act of 1980, which not only authorized credit unions to continue their share draft programs, but also established Negotiable Order of Withdrawal (NOW) accounts for all financial institutions. This, in effect, removed the banks' argument that credit unions had an unfair advantage and put them in the position of having to compete with credit unions for interest-bearing demand deposits. The same act also raised the maximum allowable interest rate on loans by federal credit unions from 12 to 15 percent, and further stipulated that the NCUA Board could increase the maximum rate above 15 percent for periods of up to 18 months.

Since then, this authority has been used twice by the NCUA Board to increase the allowable rate of interest to as much as 21 percent. But the current authority under the act is scheduled to expire on April 1, 1985, unless it is extended. This means there can be no rest in the meantime for the governmental affairs arm of the credit union movement.

On the state level, equally important legislative battles are being fought and won by credit union forces. One such battle was staged during the Texas Legislature's 1981 session, when it became apparent that state-chartered credit unions had to obtain immediate interest rate relief if they were to survive. The crisis also affected most other types of lending and financial institutions, however, and it gave all concerned an opportunity to prove that they could cooperate—rather than just squabble among themselves—when issues of mutual concern were involved. After discussing the interest crisis with key legislators, a single bill was produced to grant relief from the existing hodge-podge of maximum interest rates allowed under Texas usury laws—which were stifling the state's economy. (State-chartered credit unions were limited to a 12 percent rate that could be charged on loans.) Wayne Lough, vice president, governmental affairs, represented the League on the legislative team while Walt Bondies and John Lederer, TCUL staff attorneys, assisted in drafting the parts of the final bill that involved credit unions. All played a major role in the successful passage of the final bill.

As part of the overall effort, a comprehensive statewide public relations campaign was launched to convince the press and the public of the pressing need for reform in the usury law. Dick Williamson was one of the key contributors to this campaign from a public relations standpoint. His selective use of credit union leaders and members in certain areas added credibility to the campaign with the media. It was soon obvious that the high level of public trust in credit unions because of their cooperative, non-profit philosophy would be a vital factor in the campaign's success.

In debate on the House floor, 57 amendments were offered, but all but one were defeated. The single surviving amendment lowered the maximum interest ceiling from 28 to 24 percent.

There was virtually no doubt that the legislation would be approved, but because of the gravity of the economic situation, the sponsors were desperately striving to obtain a two-thirds majority approval in both houses, which would allow the bill to take effect immediately. In the intensive lobbying for a two-thirds majority, credit unions again put their credibility to the test and carried a major share of the load.

The first vote in the house produced only 94 "ayes" out of the 100 needed. A second vote produced a margin of 114-27 in favor of the bill, which had already obtained the necessary two-thirds support in the Senate, passing by a comfortable 26-4 margin. On May 8, 1981, HB 1228 became the official law of the State of Texas after being signed by Governor Bill Clements.

Even as this was happening, though, credit unions were pressing on with other important legislative matters. Practically unnoticed amid the flurry of activity over interest rates were companion bills introduced by Representative Gerald Hill and Senator Hector Uribe, confirming statutory authority to the Texas Share Guaranty Credit Union and establishing three public members of the Credit Union Commission.

The review of the Credit Union Department began in the summer of 1982, and through a process of interim committee hearings, testimony and negotiations with the Sunset Commission, workable solutions were found in most areas. The League was able to convince the Commission that the proposed consolidation of the Credit Union Department under the Finance Commission would not serve the best interests of credit union members. A proposal to ban any League director from serving on the State Credit Union Commission was modified so that only the League chairman, first vice chairman and secretary-treasurer were excluded.

In January 1983, a new 78-page State Credit Union Act was introduced by Representative Bill Messer and Senator Craig Washington. After hearings, only six minor changes in language—none of which affected the intent of the bill—were made in the House, and a single amendment was added in the Senate. The bill passed both houses on a voice vote and was sent to Governor Mark White for his signature on May 27.

This new Texas Credit Union Act is considered a model for the rest of the nation and immediate past TCUL Board Chairman S. Edward Hale, Jr. feels it was the "crowning achievement" of his two-year tenure, 1982-1984, as the state's top elected leader. Again, an all-out effort by Wayne Lough, Walt Bondies, John Lederer and other key TCUL staff contributed to the success of this most recent legislative achievement. It reconstitutes the Credit Union Department and Commission as an autonomous agency and extends their existence until 1995, when they will be scheduled for another review by the Sunset Commission (which means, of course, that the legislative efforts which produced the bill may have to be repeated a decade from now). A far cry from that original crude and unworkable credit union law of 1913, this new act stands as a tribute to the tireless and tenacious efforts of the League's legislative efforts.

During the same time period in which the Sunset Commission's review was taking place, credit union forces were also engaged in a bitter fight in Washington over a law passed by Congress that would require all financial institutions to withhold ten percent of all interest earned on members' savings and turn it over to the Internal Revenue Service.

The TCUL and other state leagues worked closely with CUNA to convince members of Congress that this damaging law should be repealed and to educate individual credit union members about what this federal invasion of their savings accounts would mean. Thousands of irate letters from Texas credit union members reached Texas congressmen, and most of the state's lawmakers became co-sponsors of repeal legislation.

By July 1983, both Texas senators and 24 of the 27 Texas members of the House had co-sponsored repeal legislation. A compromise bill passed the House by a vote of 392-18 and the Senate by a vote of 90-7.

It was a major victory, not only for credit unions and their members, but for small savers everywhere. The final version of the bill was not perfect, but under the circumstances, it was hailed by credit union leaders as the best possible solution to a very bad law.

There was little time for celebrating, however, among those who fight the unending legislative battles for the credit union movement. After catching their breath, they began preparing for those struggles still ahead. Even as this book was going to press, events were taking place in Washington, D.C., that could have a profound, long-term effect on all credit unions—taxation.

One example that surfaced early in 1984 was the taxation of credit unions.

Faced with huge budget deficits in an election year, House and Senate committees were exploring ways to reduce the federal deficit by increasing revenue sources.

Although the taxation of credit unions was never formally introduced into the legislative system, there was sufficient behind-the-scene discussions to alarm credit union lobbyists in Washington, D.C., and ask for action from the grassroots.

Texas responded by calling on Chairman Ed Hale, Ted McGehee, Wayne Lough and Assistant Vice President for Governmental Affairs Kathleen Miller to make a hurried trip to the nation's capital seeking legislative support concerning the tax issue.

The overall effort was successful. Taxation of credit unions was temporarily delayed. But, it is an issue that will return as the administration and U.S. legislators struggle to control budget deficits. Compounding the problem will be pressure from credit union competitors who will be seeking "a level playing field" as their tax status is being evaluated.

On the legislative front, as has been stressed, it is seldom quiet for very long.

Insuring Success

Ever since the establishment of Members Mutual more than 30 years ago, observers have been straining to find sufficiently powerful and glowing adjectives to describe the growth of the insurance arm of the Texas credit union movement. Time and again in this book, we have referred to that growth, using such terms as "phenomenal," "incredible," "amazing" and "fabulous." But while all these words are certainly applicable in a sense, they still fail somehow to convey the full impact of the Members Insurance Companies growth story.

Figures, too, reveal part of that story. They tell of huge gains in the number of policyholders, the amount of premiums paid and the amount of insurance in force year after year. But they alone also fail to tell the whole story.

Much of the MIC story can also be told only in terms of people. The story would not have happened if it had not been for inspired, imaginative, innovative leadership and a high level of professionalism among those who have guided the fortunes of Members Insurance. They have built it into a complex, yet cohesive, family of companies capable of serving virtually every insurance need of credit union members. And yet, just as important, they have never forgotten that those credit union members are themselves part of the TCUL-MIC family and should be treated as such. One of the most important—and most appropriate—slogans used during the insurance companies' period of most rapid growth has been keyed to that very idea: "We are family!"

As MIC Board Chairman Paul A. Mitchell emphasized to delegates in his report at the 1983 annual meeting: "Innovation is Members Insurance Companies' response in serving credit unions and their members . . . a family growing stronger."

Working in a spirit of close family harmony has made such innovation possible. And while the insurance companies have developed into giants in their respective fields, the talents of their executives and personnel and the financial support they have generated have been indispensible factors in the success of the League, as well as in the success of the companies themselves. In countless ways, today's League and its member credit unions benefit from the vast resources of Members Insurance Companies and from the skills of the companies' more than 700 employees (some 600 of whom are concentrated in the Dallas headquarters).

As impressive as the MIC growth story has been from the beginning, the most dramatic events in that story have taken place within just the past eight or nine years. By the mid-1970s, for example, Members Mutual and its affiliated casualty companies were already the largest credit union-related insurance operation in their field—by far. But their rate of growth since that time has, in effect, dwarfed everything they had done up until that time. As Members Insurance Senior Vice President Allen Hudson explains: "In 1975, the casualty companies showed a total of $18 million in premiums. By 1983, that annual figure had risen to nearly $100 million in premiums."

One key to this kind of growth lies in the continued diversification of Members' casualty product line and in innovative approaches to new types of coverage. But an aggressive, hard-hitting marketing program has been another important factor, and it was only in 1975 that this program began to be developed, as a result of a joint decision of MacKinnon, the League's chief executive, and Jack Eaker, the man destined to succeed him.

The most immediate result of that decision was the hiring of Hudson, an Alabama native and a veteran of eleven years as regional sales manager for Allstate Insurance Company, to become the chief architect of the marketing program. "It's only been in the last seven or eight years that we've become a full-fledged insurance company," Hudson says, "and the biggest factor in this

288

Helen Wood MacKinnon, who served as the TCUL's first fulltime secretary, later played an important unofficial role as the wife of League President Wilfred MacKinnon.

The leadership of Wilfred S. MacKinnon, both at the state and national level, has left a lasting mark on the credit union movement in America.

Members Mutual Chairman Jerry Deering (left) and TCUL Chairman Pete Gooch (center) congratulate Ted McGehee after McGehee was named president of Members Mutual in 1968.

Wayland Jones, representing the East Texas District, has served continuously on the TCUL Board since 1961.

has been putting our marketing program on a professional level."

Eaker, in particular, is credited with setting the stage for the new marketing strategy and with creating an atmosphere in which it could be carried out. "He (Eaker) couldn't have come on the scene at a more important time," says Hudson. "It was a time when things were happening faster in the financial world than most people could understand. Since his own expertise was in claims, he went outside the company for a marketing strategist. He made a lot of far-reaching management decisions and applied a professional businessman's approach when it was needed."

Today, Members Insurance constitutes the largest credit union-related casualty insurance operation in the United States—even larger than CUNA Mutual's—and is the only such operation to offer such full-service features as drive-in claims centers, statewide telephone claims service and special catastrophe teams to write on-the-spot checks for damage claims at the scene of major disasters. "Our philosophy," says Hudson, "is to provide competitive insurance products for credit union members, and to deliver service to members with a credit union flavor. Evidence that we must be doing something right showed up in a recent survey when 94 percent of our customers surveyed expressed satisfaction with Members Insurance services."

They cover the full spectrum of automobile insurance, regardless of what risk group a credit union member may fall into, three affiliated companies have been created over the years in addition to Members Mutual, the original company in this field. As the "granddaddy of them all," Members Mutual had more than 130,000 policies in force with average-risk drivers and had annual premiums of more than $53.5 million as of December 1983.

Other companies in the field include: Members Insurance, a preferred-risk carrier organized in 1970, with nearly 28,000 policies and almost $11 million in premiums; Members Service Insurance, an average-risk carrier organized in 1974 with some 27,000 policies and about $10 million in premiums; Foremost County Mutual, which has supplied special or high-risk policies since 1969 and now has some 5,800 policies and about $4.7 million in premiums. With the four companies, MIC is capable of insuring any credit union member, regardless of his risk group as a driver, and never finds it necessary to turn away a credit union member applying for coverage.

Today, of course, automobile insurance is only one of a large and steadily growing group of products offered by the MIC casualty companies. Other types of coverage include homeowners, renters, mobile home, fire, theft, personal liability, boat owners, Texas multi-peril, workers compensation, commercial fire and commercial liability.

Although the casualty companies do not actively market their products outside Texas, they are licensed to write insurance in six other states—California, Arizona, Colorado, New Mexico, Oklahoma and Arkansas. This allows MIC to continue to serve the insurance needs of Texas credit union members who move into one of these six states.

As described earlier, another principal chapter in the MIC success story is Members Life, now a husky 12-year-old company with more than 40,000 policies and more than $875 million insurance in force. And here, too, innovative marketing and a continuously expanding line of life insurance products have contributed mightily to the company's acceptance and growth. Today's Members Life offers a full line of coverage including whole life, annual renewable term, mortgage cancellation, joint mortgage cancellation, family plan, guaranteed insurability option, accidental death and dismemberment and hospital income plan insurance.

In addition, it is one of the first 100 life insurance companies in the entire nation—and the only credit union-related company—to offer the newest and most versatile type of life insurance. Known as a universal life policy and marketed by Members Life as "Uniflex" coverage, this new kind of life insurance offers a wide range of advantages to the policyholder. Because it offers adjustable protection, one policy can be maintained for a lifetime and periodically altered to meet the policyholder's changing needs. Other advantages include tax benefits, guaranteed performance, annual reports, low mortality charges, first-dollar interest, etc.

"With Uniflex, a person has the option of putting in as much extra money as he wants into annuity or investment programs under the policy, and he can also skip premiums if he wants to," explains Hudson. "It's the most flexible kind of life insurance available." Since the first Uniflex policy was issued in February 1983, more than 1,000 of the new policies have been written by Members Life.

To keep credit union members informed on such important developments within their insurance companies, and to make insurance service convenient and easily accessible to them, MIC operates a total of seven service centers across the state and also operates an agency program in 30 Texas credit unions. In addition, the companies also have seven complete financial centers in the state, each of which offers financial planning services, discount stocks, individual retirement accounts (IRAs) and, of course, a full range of insurance services.

Direct mail is widely used as well to keep credit union members abreast of MIC's ever-widening field of insurance and related services. For example, nearly six million pieces of literature will be mailed by the companies during 1984.

And the search for descriptive adjectives is far from over where Members Insurance is concerned. In the

Growth of Members Insurance Companies

Policies in Force

Year	MMIC & CPI & Foremost	MIC	MSIC	MLIC	Total
1952	—	—	—	—	—
1962	—	—	—	—	—
1972	—	—	—	—	80,876
1975	89,666	9,432	1,981	9,167	110,246
1976	98,308	12,459	8,864	14,904	134,535
1977	110,593	13,049	8,826	19,753	152,221
1978	117,837	14,303	11,331	25,971	169,442
1979	115,759	24,141	15,632	30,032	185,564
1980	121,801	24,325	21,475	34,589	202,190
1981	130,137	27,456	23,435	36,438	217,466
1982	133,427	28,643	25,621	38,466	226,157
1983	125,555	31,151	17,740	40,566	215,012

Gross Written Premiums

Year	MMIC & CPI & Foremost	MIC	MSIC	MLIC	Total
1952	$ 466,221	—	—	—	$ 466,221
1962	$ 4,060,373	—	—	—	$ 4,060,373
1972	$16,133,111	$ 658,730	—	—	$16,791,841
1975	$20,688,540	$ 1,720,188	$ 438,137	$ 543,540	$23,390,405
1976	$27,322,450	$ 3,003,314	$ 2,885,764	$ 916,958	$34,128,486
1977	$33,946,819	$ 3,391,937	$ 1,919,425	$1,541,263	$40,799,444
1978	$37,924,900	$ 3,926,431	$ 2,785,441	$2,094,395	$46,731,167
1979	$40,438,581	$ 7,042,711	$ 4,748,407	$2,417,093	$54,646,792
1980	$44,346,546	$ 8,062,595	$ 6,345,044	$2,926,183	$61,680,368
1981	$50,177,421	$ 9,595,355	$ 7,045,001	$3,290,336	$70,108,113
1982	$60,679,238	$12,440,648	$11,133,111	$3,657,557	$87,910,554
1983	$64,129,758	$15,174,177	$ 8,896,572	$4,037,225	$92,237,732

Notes:

Members Mutual Insurance Companies organized March 1952

Members Insurance Companies organized February 1970

Members Life Insurance Companies organized July 1972

Members Services Insurance Companies organized October 1974

Assets

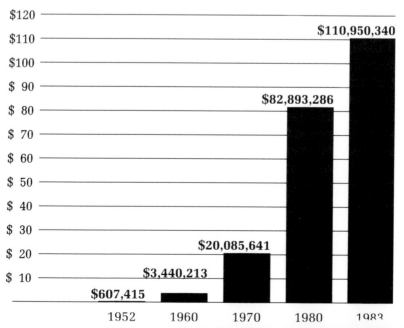

view of Hudson and other key leaders in the companies' management, the real growth story has barely begun. "Ten years from now," Hudson emphasizes, "I think we'll be triple our size today. I see us as a $300 million company in the casualty field, and operating across a major portion of the nation. This expansion could come in the form of a joint venture with CUNA Mutual or in some other form. If we don't fill this void, somebody else will. Either we'll go backwards and dry up or we'll progress into new services and new areas and be forced to diversity. The key decisions on what directions that diversification will take will probably come within the next five years."

But the MIC leadership also stresses that, regardless of how large or diversified the insurance companies may become, they will always remain an inseparable part of the credit union "Family," both in spirit and in fact.

"I think our insurance companies and our credit unions will continue to grow and to serve—but in different ways than before," Hudson says. "We once served people who couldn't get service anywhere else. Now the challenge is to serve someone who can get service anywhere."

For a future whose successes will outshine even those of the past and present, meeting that challenge head-on is the only effective insurance.

"Family Financial Centers"

During the final years of the 1970s, the credit union movement embraced a bold new goal—to develop credit unions into sophisticated full-service family financial institutions capable of offering every type of financial service needed by the average family. Share draft accounts were, of course, one vital aspect of this goal, but there were numerous others. Many of the legislative tools necessary to attain the goal were handed to America's credit unions and their 33 million members in the spring of 1977, when President Carter signed into law the first major expansion of federal credit union powers since the passage of the original Federal Credit Union Act of 1934. Under the new law, credit unions were able to offer their members such expanded services as:

(1) Home mortgage loans of up to 30 years (previously, state-chartered credit unions had been able to offer mortgage loans, but federal credit unions had been effectively shut out of the home mortgage market by a ten-year limit on loans they could provide).

(2) Home improvement and mobile home loans of up to fifteen years (again removing the ten-year limitation).

(3) Unsecured loans of up to twelve years and of any amount, as fixed by the individual credit union (removing previous limits of $2,500 and five years).

(4) More savings instruments, such as "share certificates," similar to the certificates of deposit issued by other financial institutions.

(5) Revolving lines of credit, in the form of credit card or charge accounts with major retailers, thereby offering a system of continuous borrowing within established credit limits (instead of having to get the approval of a credit committee or loan officer for each new advance as in the past).

(6) Participatory loan arrangements between credit unions, making funds for long-term loans more available to all credit union members and especially benefitting newer credit unions.

(7) Automatic participation in federally guaranteed or insured loans (instead of having to continually amend the Federal Credit Union Act to extend investment authority to credit unions).

In a number of these areas, Texas credit unions and the TCUL were setting the pace for the rest of the nation. Through their ownership of Town North National Bank in Dallas, Texas credit unions had been able to launch an experimental credit card program, which included federal credit unions, as early as March 1976. Approved on an experimental basis by the National Credit Union Administration, the program gave thousands of Texas credit union members access to Master Charge through their state and federal credit unions long before such a service was available elsewhere in the United States. Under the Program, a member filed a credit card application with his credit union. If approved, a maximum credit limit was set by the credit union and the application was forwarded to Town North National Bank, where it was processed and authorization given for a card to be issued. "When the card is 'cut,' showing the name of TNB on its front and the CU's name on its reverse, it becomes ready for use just like any other credit card," explained the *Texas Leaguer*.

Once the new federal law went into effect, the program was removed from its experimental status, and by the late summer of 1977, a VISA card program had been added, allowing Texas credit union members to take their choice between the two most widely used credit card systems in the world—or they could apply for both cards. Meanwhile, under the leadership of Texan Jim R. Williams, who had been elevated in 1976 from his post as chairman of the TCUL to the top elected job at CUNA and who subsequently became the president and chief executive officer of CUNA in 1979, (the second Texan to do so—Yates was first) the national organization launched revolutionary programs in financial services and innovative data processing procedures.

An example of one of the newest CUNA systems will be piloted in the Texas League in 1984. Called Internet, meaning the National Credit Union Information Network, this sophisticated data-processing and telecommunications network will eventually link CUNA, its service affiliates, U.S. Central and the Corporates (Southwest Corporate Federal Credit Union is already on the corporate system), Leagues, League service corporations and credit unions into a single communications network.

The Texas League test program will involve three functions of Internet: the Information Resource, Product Service Delivery and the Personnel Administration systems.

(President Jack Eaker chaired the CUNA Information System Task Force that was instrumental in changing the Internet idea from a concept into a reality.)

As president of the huge Government Employees Credit Union of San Antonio, with assets of more than $200 million in 1976, (year-end 1983 assets totaled $500 million) Williams was able to see clearly the full-service role that could be played by larger credit unions in the future, and he was eager to see CUNA move decisively into many new areas. Williams' own credit union, for example, had been among the first in the country to install automated teller machines (ATMs) in its branch offices around San Antonio, and he could envision the time in the future when statewide and even nationwide networks of ATMs could enable a credit union member to transact business at any time anywhere.

In addition to Williams, Texas was also represented in national credit union leadership circles during this period by former CUNA President R.C. Morgan of El Paso, who was again filling a key role as vice chairman of CUNA's Governmental Affairs committee. As such, Morgan was actively soliciting the support of Texas credit union members for the Credit Union Political Action Committee. He was instrumental in helping CULAC to build a $185,000 "war chest" to aid in the fight to establish credit unions competitively in the financial community. Morgan was also serving as a member of the Federal Reserve Board's 25-member national Consumer Advisory Council.

At home, meanwhile, a strong corps of new leaders was rising within the Texas credit union movement to guide it through this crucial period of expansion. In the spring of 1976, Calvin C. Phillips, president of the Dallas Postal Employees Credit Union, was elected chairman of the board of the TCUL, succeeding Williams, and was re-elected to the chairmanship in 1977. The 1977 League elections were also notable for producing the first elected female head of a major TCUL Affiliate. Board members had named Mrs. Carol Reagan as chairperson of TCUL Services and CU Trust company in mid-1976 as successor to Roy Neidig, who had resigned to become first vice chairman of the League, and during the regular elections of 1977, the board reaffirmed their choice of Mrs. Reagan by naming her to a full term in the combined chairmanship. The first woman to achieve such high office within the League leadership structure, Mrs. Reagan had served as director since 1973 and is treasurer-manager of the Hoodview Federal Credit Union in Killeen. She later became the first woman president of Southwest Corporate serving in that capacity in 1982 and 1983. Also in the 1977 elections, held in conjunction with the TCUL's 43rd annual meeting in Dallas April 14-16, Ronald L. Liles of Fort Worth was named chairman of Members Insurance, succeeding Wade Choate, who had served two terms as Members' chairman and who remained a member of the board.

As a symbol of their new competitive spirit, credit unions were also mounting the most extensive advertising campaign in their history through the mass media during the latter years of the 1970s. Because research had shown that most credit union members still viewed their credit unions as a secondary, rather than a primary, source of family financial service, the national advertising campaign sought to change this situation through a new theme: "Discover your credit union. We're doing more for you." Full-page ads appeared in such widely circulated national magazines as *Time, Newsweek, People, Redbook and Sports Illustrated* and thirty-second commericial spots appeared on prime-time network television. It marked the first time that credit union advertising had stressed something more than mere membership. The idea now was to make members aware that, under the new law, credit unions could perform virtually any service that a bank or savings and loan could perform.

One service that Texas credit unions were especially interested in was mortgage loans. Although a few state-chartered credit unions already had millions of dollars in home mortgage loans on their books by 1977, most credit unions had done little or no mortgage financing before the passage of the new federal law that year lifted the restrictions under which federal credit unions had been operating. Now many larger Texas credit unions were eager to follow the example of Williams' Government Employees Credit Union of San Antonio, with $50 million worth of real estate mortgages on its books, or the Texins (Texas Instruments) Credit Union of Dallas, with $18 million worth. As *Financial Trend*, a Southwest business publication, explained: "If sharedrafting has caught the attention of the commercial bankers, home mortgage lending by the CUs ought to attract the attention of others in the financial community. The program is in the embryonic stages at the moment, but the elements are in place for CUs to go after the home mortgage business at full tilt in the near future."

There was a problem, however, and for many credit unions it loomed as a serious constraint on their ability to make mortgage loans in large numbers. Essentially, the problem was one of tying up funds for long periods of time when the demand for shorter-term consumer loans remained at record high levels. The problem had already forced the Texins Credit Union to stop writing mortgage loans temporarily and would undoubtedly have a similar effect on other credit unions unless some solution could be found.

The instrument with which the League planned to solve the problem was the Credit Union Trust Company chaired by Mrs. Reagan. In anticipation of the booming demand for mortgage loans from credit unions that would soon follow, the trust company applied, in June 1976, to become a seller-servicer for the Federal National Mortgage Association (FNMA). That October, the FNMA—familiarly known in the real estate trade as "Fannie Mae"—approved the application for conventional single-family home mortgages. This meant that the Credit Union Trust Company could originate single-family loans for sale to FNMA, and it also opened the way for the trust company to get into mortgage banking on a full-scale basis in the secondary market. And for the individual members of Texas credit unions, it meant it would soon be possible to finance 95 percent of the purchase price of a new home for thirty years through their credit union.

"A home loan program was always part of our long-term goal to assist credit unions in becoming full financial service institutions," said Ted McGehee, vice president of the trust company. "State law permits only 25 percent of a credit union's deposits in real estate mortgages and many credit unions have found they were at their limit in real estate loans. We had to find a way to utilize the secondary mortgage market. Eventually, we hope to be able to go to a credit union with a million dollars in assets and say, 'You make forty real estate loans, instead of four, and you keep ten percent of them, and we'll take the rest.'"

By January 1977, the "Credit Union Home Loan Plan" devised by the trust company was being offered in various parts of the state, and the response from credit union members was almost instantaneous. Within a few weeks, the trust company was processing as many as six home loan applications per day. Under the plan, loan applicants could finance up to $42,000 for thirty years with as little as five percent down payment, or up to

$55,000 for thirty years with ten percent down. Within a year, steps were being taken to include federally insured FHA and VA mortgages in the trust company's program, and the goal of making credit unions into full-scale "family financial centers" had become another giant step closer. By the end of 1983, several Texas credit unions qualified as such centers, offering a full range of insurance, stocks and mortgages, in additon to regular financial services.

All in all, it was a time of heady success and remarkable gains for credit unions in general. And yet it was also a perilous time, a time fraught with sophisticated new dangers, mind-boggling new complexities and nagging questions as to the true identity of modern credit unions. Despite efforts to include them in the revolution that was sweeping through the financial community, the small credit unions of Texas were particularly at peril in the new competitive, no-holds-barred atmosphere.

It was these small institutions—those with 300 members or less—which R.C. Morgan called "the backbone and the life blood" of the credit union movement. But many of them were caught in the "crunch" created by the very growth and prosperity of their larger counterparts. Many of them lacked the trained management and skilled personnel needed to cope with the complicated financial gadgetry of the modern age—data processing, electronic funds transfer, automated tellers, share drafts and credit cards, government red tape, increased competition and so on.

If credit unions were to be able to compete shoulder-to-shoulder in the complex world of the future, one thing they would need would be a higher level of capital reserves to protect them against potentially catastrophic turns of events. By early 1981, leadership at the national level recognized the growing need for credit union capital (defined as retained earnings and other reserves) at all levels of the movement. In January of that year, the ratio of capital resources to total assets among credit unions stood at only 6.1 percent. By mid-1982, it had risen to 7.2 percent, but it was still felt that additional capital would be needed to: (a) develop new products and services which were becoming more expensive all the time; (b) weather unexpected losses or setbacks caused by sponsor layoffs or bankruptcies, and (c) bolster earnings in the event of sharp increases in the future cost of funds.

A National Credit Union System Capitalization Committee (NCUSC) was organized to study the problem and make recommendations. During the following 18 months, the commission (with Jack Eaker as its vice chairman) held meetings and regional forums around the U.S.—including one in Dallas in January, 1982—and examined the problem in detail.

A comprehensive analysis of the capitalization question, containing 39 recommendations including a 10 percent goal of capital to assets, was completed in the spring of 1982 and was adapted for implementation at the national level in May. The TCUL Board took similar action in August.

"There is a long-range capitalization opportunity within the credit union system," Eaker emphasized in his report to the Board. "The commission believes that its recommendations for increased capitalization will promote the growth and stability of the credit union movement to the benefit of all credit union members."

Credit unions had come a long way since the days of Raiffeisen, or even since Filene and Bergengren. The distance they had covered could be measured in light-years. But they had not outgrown or outdistanced the need to retain those founding principles for which Raiffeisen, Filene and Bergengren had stood—principles perhaps still best embodied in those small credit unions that no one would ever mistake for banks.

As Texas Credit Union Commissioner Parsons observed in a speech in Fort Worth in the fall of 1977: "Credit unions need to stop and take stock. Each credit union should examine its own conscience. Credit unions are still, in 1977, what credit unions were in 1849—only with different tools . . . credit unions are riding the crest of a wave. They should be careful not to fall off.''

Community Spirit

While the triumphs of the second half of the 1970s were considerable, credit unions were not "riding the crest of a wave" in every area, however. For one thing, liquidations and mergers were beginning to deplete the ranks of the state's credit unions, particularly the smaller ones, and the total number of credit unions in Texas began to decline for the first time since World War II, from a high point of nearly 1,450 in the mid-1970s to today's total of less than 1,200. For another thing, credit unions still found themselves largely stymied in their efforts to make credit union membership available to the great majority of Texans who could benefit from it. Despite the monumental advances of the past seventy years, credit union membership remained confined to about 20 percent of the total population of the state in 1983, and there were millions of Texans who had no access to credit union services. As veteran TCUL employee Betty Danyluk explained: "People call us all the time looking for a credit union to join, but they simply aren't eligible.''

One of the most fervent hopes of the Texas credit union leadership as it looks toward the middle years of the 1980s is that methods can be found to put credit union membership within reach of a significantly larger percentage of the public. At the same time, ways need to be found to make the organization and operation of credit unions more feasible in the scores of smaller communities in the state where there are presently no credit unions at all, or perhaps only one or two serving employees of small companies. In the minds of many leaders, the community credit union—a concept that has been in limited practice ever since the 1930s, but which is still very much in an experimental stage—offers one opportunity for accomplishing both these purposes.

At first glance, the community credit union, in which membership is open to anyone who lives within the geographic boundaries defining a certain community, seems an ideal vehicle for spreading credit union benefits to a wider audience. It would seem an especially useful vehicle for forming credit unions in the kind of isolated farming communities and rural areas where the founders of credit union philosophy first envisioned them blossoming.

As community credit unions have developed, so have widely divergent opinions on expanding fields of membership and how this issue should fit within the total framework of the movement in Texas. This became apparent during the early 1980s, when a League task force conducted an intensive study of the community credit union concept and issued a detailed report to the Board of Directors in December 1981.

Appointed in response to a resolution presented by the Wichita Falls Chapter early in 1981, the task force was chaired by James Chiarizio and included Jimmy Sasser, Cecil Denison, Delton Moore, R.C. Morgan, Ruby Weinholt and Gilbert Weston. At the time, credit unionists in Wichita Falls were concerned over plans by the Sheppard Area Federal Credit Union to change its charter to include the entire population of the West Texas City in its field of membership. Since the move was viewed as a threat to other credit unions in Wichita Falls, it was vigorously opposed by the local chapter, which asked the NCUA to disapprove the charter change.

But after its lengthy and in-depth study and a statewide public forum on the issue, the task force concluded in its report that the League should not oppose such moves toward community charters as the one proposed by the Sheppard Area Federal Credit

Dyalthia Benson of Hereford helped pioneer the community credit union idea by employing it successfully in the small West Texas farming town.

Walter Duncan, who served as League chairman from 1969 to 1972, heads the Richardson Community Credit Union, the largest in Texas to utilize the communitywide service concept.

James A. Chiarizio, TCUL chairman from 1972 to 1974, served as chairman of a statewide task force on community credit unions in the early 1980s.

The thriving community credit union in the tiny hamlet of Windthorst is headed by Albert Ostermann (right), its president, and Louis Schroeder, its treasurer-manager.

Union. (The charter change was, in fact, granted on October 8, 1981, even before the report was issued by the task force. The only stipulation was that primary members of other credit unions in Wichita Falls be excluded from Sheppard Area's field of membership. Subsequently, other credit unions in the area have found that the threat of being overshadowed or swallowed up by a large community credit union was largely non-existent, at least in this particular instance. "It's worked out better than we could ever have expected," said John Christoff, vice president for branch operations of Sheppard Area, in early 1984. "The other credit unions didn't lose their members. Instead, they took care of them. The threat simply wasn't there.")

Although there was much disagreement with the task force report's conclusions, it helped to define for the first time the Texas credit union movement's position, not only on community charters themselves, but on such closely related matters as competition between credit unions, protectionist policies to prevent such competition, expansion into unlike fields of membership, and the increasing tendency toward mergers.

Among the task force's key conclusions were these:

"We believe, as a practical matter, the field of membership of a credit union cannot be protected from competition, including competition from other credit unions.

"We believe reasonable competition between credit unions—chartered equally—is healthy and beneficial to the member.

"We believe all credit unions should have an equal opportunity to merge with credit unions of unlike fields of membership and to expand into unlike fields of membership.

"We believe that the community charter is a definite asset to the credit union movement."

The fears of smaller credit unions faced with the emergence of large community credit unions capable of serving everyone in a given geographical area were effectively summed up at the League's annual meeting in April 1982 by Mary Nell James, president of the

Wright Patman Chapter, headquartered in Texarkana. The directors of her own Lone Star Steel Federal Credit Union, she said, "do not believe the future of credit unions lies in large centralized public institutions."

Mrs. James, who was elected to the League board in April 1983, pointed out that if the 15 credit unions in Bowie County were permitted to expand their fields of membership to serve the entire county, all would become "public institutions with no common bond as we know it today." She added: "We do not feel it to be in the best interest of our chapter, of the League or even of the individual credit union member."

The opposing view was expressed by such officials as Sheppard Area's Christoff, who said: "Over 56 percent of our citizens do not have access to a credit union. We feel that these people as well as the people in this same situation across the state and nation have a right as well as a need to be served. . . We feel that the proof of any damage caused by a community charter is non-existent. Much of the objection that we hear is unfounded speculation."

For those who favored it as well as for those who opposed it, the task force report represented a historic watershed in credit union philosophy. And it is worth noting that, when CUNA itself conducted a similar nationwide study in 1983, its conclusions were virtually identical to those reached by the TCUL task force.

The debate undoubtedly is far from over. But in cities, suburbs, rural communities across Texas and in those credit unions looking for opportunities to expand their field of membership, the concepts as defined in the task force report are continuing issues. The whole idea of how to increase the membership of individual credit unions or how to organize successful credit unions could emerge as one of the most important issues affecting the movement during the final one and one-half decades of the Twentieth Century.

But the classic example of a successful credit union in a non-urban setting is the Hereford Federal Credit Union which serves residents of the West Texas town of Hereford (population 16,000) and a surrounding radius of 25 miles. Chartered in 1936, when the TCUL was barely two years old, the Hereford Credit Union was for years the only one of its kind in Texas and one of the largest community credit unions in the world. Under the direction of its dedicated manager-director, Mrs. Dyalthia "Dy" Benson, it achieved nationwide acclaim.

As Pauline Howard, current assistant manager of the Hereford Federal Credit Union, explained: "Our credit union was organized at a time when the low-income people here had to have some help. Bankers didn't trust people who had no assets, but Mrs. Benson found out you *could* trust them. She worked without pay for years and years to build this credit union and help these people."

Under the direction of Mrs. Benson, who also served as a director and officer of the TCUL, the Hereford Credit Union grew spectacularly. In 1936, it issued loans of just $86, but by the time it celebrated its 25th anniversary in 1961, the credit union had loans outstanding of $1,393,000. Originally organized with 22 members as an outgrowth of a discussion at a meeting of the Hereford Business and Professional Women's Club, the credit union had assets of just $125 at the end of 1936. By 1960, its assets totaled $2,247,000.

When the Hereford Credit Union was recognized in 1958 as the nation's largest federally chartered community credit union, Mrs. Benson's response was: "We have achieved this goal without actually aiming for it. We aim to be the best, not necessarily the biggest."

Today, under the leadership of Jimmy C. Rowton, its manager since 1978, Mrs. Howard, and its board of directors, the Hereford Credit Union is continuing its phenomenal story of growth. Its membership now stands at 7,280 and its assets at more than $13.5 million.

Offering complete share draft services, a Master Charge Card program and operating a branch office in nearby Dimmit, the Hereford Credit Union is as modern in its approach to family financial services as any institution in the state. Yet it adheres firmly to the same principles of personalized assistance that have guided it from the beginning. "Many of our members are farm people, and even those that aren't derive their livelihood from agriculture," said Mrs. Howard. "We're now into our third and fourth generations of membership in some families."

The success of the Hereford Credit Union extends far beyond mere dollars and cents—and even beyond the confines of its own community and its own membership. It also serves as a sterling example for people in other communities who want to start community-based credit unions of their own. Within the past few years, the number of community credit unions in Texas has increased sharply, to about forty, and some of the newer ones have far outstripped even the Hereford Credit Union in growth.

And community credit unions are proving conclusively that they can work equally as well in populous urban areas as in small towns and rural communities. The state's best example of a successful community credit union in an urbanized setting is the giant Richardson Credit Union, which serves the populous suburbs of Richardson and Plano, north of Dallas. Managed by former TCUL President Walter Duncan, the credit union became a community-type institution in 1972 and is the successor to the old employees' credit union at Collins Radio Company in Richardson, which was once a major employer in the area, but which was later absorbed by Rockwell International.

Under Duncan's leadership, the Richardson Credit Union has enjoyed explosive growth over the past decade, and has evolved into one of the larger financial institutions in the Dallas Metropolitan Area, with 36,468 members and more than $100 million in assets as of the summer of 1983. Today, with full-service facilities including drive-in tellers in both cities (eight in Richardson and five in Plano), it epitomizes the kind of "family financial center" which the planners in the credit union movement envisioned in the 1970s.

Like the Richardson Credit Union, many of today's community or areawide cooperatives have been converted to their present form after beginning life as company credit unions. There are notable exceptions to this rule, however, both in the state's large cities and in isolated rural communities.

In the words of TCUL veteran Tony Gehring, who spent many years traveling the highways and byways of Texas organizing and assisting credit unions, the little hamlet of Windthorst is just a "wide place in the road," but the community credit union there has shown what a small group of dedicated people can do by pulling together and working hard. As a fieldman for the League, Gehring helped get the Windthorst Federal Credit Union established in 1964 in a town of 400 people that had never had a bank.

Amazingly, the Windthorst Credit Union today boasts well over three times that many members (a fact that is accounted for because of its authority to enroll members within an eight-mile radius of the town itself, located some 25 miles south of Wichita Falls). Many of its 1,412 members, as of the fall of 1983, are children and teenagers, since it is routine practice for whole families to join the credit union, rather than just a single member of a family, according to Louis Schroeder, who has managed the thriving institution for 19 years. The Reverend Cletus Post of St. Mary's Catholic Church in Windthorst was a principal organizer of the credit union, which now serves as a focal point for the parish's financial needs. Windthorst Postmaster Albert Ostermann served as president of the credit union for 18 years before turning the office over to Tommy Berend in 1982, and continues to serve on the board of directors. By 1983, the credit union had assets of more than $3,233,000 and had moved into its own office after 15 years in Schroeder's home. In serving its closely knit, predominantly Catholic community—composed mainly of families of German descent—the credit union has had to charge off only one bad loan, for $144.

Will the concept of community credit unions—a concept that is still being "explored," in the words of Jack Eaker—become the avenue to a dramatic new breakthrough for the credit union movement in Texas? Will it become the device through which credit union services will at last become available to a large segment of Texans who desire them? Perhaps, but the verdict of history is still not clear and there are not, as yet, any hard-and-fast answers to these questions.

Community or area credit unions have, overall, met with greatly varying degrees of success. Where they have failed or proved to be only marginally successful, it has been felt that they lacked the "common bond" which has played such a vital part in the development of credit unions over the decades.

Part of the formula for success for those community credit unions that have flourished, according to Tony Gehring, has been a "common bond" of an economic variety among the memership. "What makes a successful community credit union is a situation in which there is a regular, steady income from an identifiable source," Gehring explained. "It's very important in a farming community that money be coming in steadily and on a predictable basis, rather than just a time or two each year. In Windthorst, for example, the source of steady income is dairying. Without it, the credit union couldn't sustain its programs and services."

Eaker and other leaders feel that community credit unions deserve a thorough examination and extensive testing, but that the search for new ways to expand and improve credit unions services should not be limited to them. "In the past 24 to 36 months," Eaker said in an August 1983 interview, "the move toward community credit unions has accelerated greatly because of the parity situation between financial institutions. This has caused credit unions to re-examine themselves and look for new avenues of growth. These include community credit unions, but are not confined to them by any means. One of our goals is to see that every citizen of Texas has access to a credit union. The community credit unions are helping to put that goal within reach."

Living and Learning

Because the credit union movement—both in Texas and elsewhere—originated out of the efforts of unpaid, non-professional volunteers, it was generally assumed during the early years of the movement that credit unions could be successfully managed by the same people. And, indeed, many of these early volunteer leaders did prove to be capable and adept managers, despite their lact of specialized training.

But beginning in the 1950s, it became more and more apparent that some type of organized educational programs were needed for the managers and other fulltime personnel who handled the day-to-day operation of the state's credit unions. Since there were no such programs available in any of the schools and colleges in Texas, it was up to the leaders of the credit union movement to formulate their own, which they did. The first training classes for Texas credit union people were held at Southern Methodist University in Dallas from September to December 1959 under the direction of TCUL Assistant Managing Director Paul Mullins. And the SMU classes marked the start of an educational effort that would lead to a statewide system of seminars and training sessions, a separate Education and Training Department within the TCUL, and eventually, to a

312

number of college programs leading to degrees in credit union management.

In 1967, eight years after Mullins had conducted the first school in Dallas, the League launched an annual Texas School for Credit Union Personnel at the University of Houston. Patterned after and sanctioned by the nationally known CUNA School, the Texas version offered a week of resident instruction each summer to interested credit union employees, who could obtain a recognized graduation certificate from the school after attending for three years. Classes were taught by University of Houston professors in such subjects as principles of finance, marketing, public relations, collection procedures, socio-economics of credit unions, interviewing techniques, budget methods, personal finance, consumer credit, financial analysis, etc.

By the early 1970s, the name had been changed to the Southwest CUNA School for Credit Union Personnel, and it was one of only four such schools in North America. In 1975, the school's already high standards were raised still farther with the establishment of a "Project Review Board," which was empowered to approve each candidate for graduation following a special oral examination. The program was renamed Southwest CUNA Management School in 1984.

Meanwhile, the League's Education and Training Department, under the direction of Joseph Wasaff, was also staging a statewide series of other training conferences and seminars for credit union personnel. Wasaff and his assistant director, Jim Henderson, traveled to all parts of Texas as the demand for educational services grew with amazing rapidity. As Jim Barry noted in his report to the League's annual meeting in March 1972:

"The use of services offered by the Education Department to member credit unions increased substantially during 1971. Chapter demands on the department's services practically doubled: more programs, both on the state and chapter levels, were conducted during 1971 then ever before."

Some of these various schools, seminars, conferences and clinics on the statewide level included a Managers' Seminar, a Family Financial Counseling Clinic, a Management Conference and an Employees' Conference. Working through the annual Chapter Presidents' Conference, the department also initiated numerous programs dealing with specialized training needs at the chapter level. And in an effort to make the TCUL and Affiliates' annual meeting more informative, Wasaff and his staff designed a special Training Day program, including seminars conducted by top authorities from all over the country in such fields as marketing, investments, financial counseling, cash management, data processing, auditing, collections, etc., plus a "Grand FINALE" about key issues impacting credit unions.

As another step insuring a continuing supply of well-trained management people for Texas credit unions, the Texas Education Agency, beginning in late 1978, approved a number of college programs leading to an associate degree in credit union management. At this time, Alexene Crow had risen through the Education and Training Department ranks to become a Department officer; and a staff member had been hired to install and foster the CU Associate Degree Program in Texas' community colleges.

The first programs of this kind in the state were offered at McLennan Community College in Waco and at Amarillo College, beginning with the spring semester of 1979. For the convenience of credit union employees, both colleges offered the program in evening classes, using texts and materials from the national Certified Credit Union Executive (CCUE) program. The four-semester degree plan required 66 class hours, twelve of them in credit union courses.

By 1981, seven community colleges had included the CU management degree program in their curriculum, adding another vehicle for the League to reach and better educate credit unions.

"Getting these programs started was a monumental task," said Wasaff. "From this point on, it is very important that credit unions . . . recognize their responsibility to give full support and take every advantage of these programs, so that they will not only sustain themselves, but improve in quality in coming years. There is a strong need for professional development among credit union employees if credit unions are to stay competitive in a highly competitive industry."

Initially, many of those who enrolled in the college courses were present credit union employees encouraged by their credit unions to return to school to further their own careers and strengthen their institutions. One of these, Rhonda Shelley, teller supervisor at the Hoodview Federal Credit Union in Killeen, drove 120 miles round trip to attend the first classes at McLennan Community College. After six years of credit union employment and fifteen years away from the books, her enthusiasm and determination were typical of many other credit union personnel. "I want to be a better employee," she said simply, and promptly talked three other Hoodview co-workers into enrolling at the college.

The annual Wright Patman Scholarship, established to honor the Texas congressman who had done so much for the credit union movement and first awarded in 1972, helped call attention to these efforts. The $2,000 scholarship was awarded to an outstanding student at the master's level in finance at the School of Business Administration of the University of Texas at Austin. (This program was dropped in 1980 because all of the nine recipients went to work for banks and insurance companies, not for credit unions.)

By the early 1980s, with increased educational staff, the League's newly named Human Resource Development Department had in place many diversified and sophisticated educational vehicles which gave credit unions of all asset sizes, offering full or limited financial services, located in different areas of the state, with employees and officers of different educational backgrounds and levels of experience, the opportunity to become better educated in CU management and operations. The following list demonstrates the variety, diversity and sophistication of the League's educational service in the early 1980's:

- textbooks.
- easy-to-read, inexpensive, self-study manuals.
- manuals for self-study or group study.
- audiovisuals/manual programs.
- cassette tapes/manual programs.
- inexpensive mini-programs with cassette tape and manual.
- videotape programs.
- videotape subscription program with text.
- evening workshops.
- Saturday workshops.
- correspondence courses.
- League Annual Meeting main sessions, seminars and Grand Finale.
- 1-day special interest seminars.
- ½-day special interest seminars.
- 1½-day conferences.
- 2½-day conferences.
- chapter meetings and chapter mini-seminars.
- teller and loan officer training series held in the evenings.
- special interest CU association educational meetings.
- management consultant services.
- non-accredited continuing education programs.
- CCUE clinics.
- CCUE workshops.
- the Southwest CUNA School Alumni Seminar.
- the Southwest CUNA School Student Seminar.

- customized in-office training for the employees or officers of a particular credit union.
- schools on both state and national levels.
- the Southwest CUNA Management School with standards and requirements.
- the CU Associate Degree Program with standards and requirements.
- the CCUE with standards and requirements.
- experimentation with teleconferencing on the national level.

With this kind of educational variety and diversity, over 6,500 credit union persons from 800 Texas credit unions participated in the League's educational workshop, schools, clinics, seminars and conferences in 1983.

Time of Transition

Change, of course, is a continuous process, one that goes on unceasingly in every aspect of human endeavor. Everything is constantly changing, and yet most of us think of the more noticeable and significant changes in life as taking place abruptly and at a precise point in time. These are the times of great transitions, and the closing months of the 1970s were just such a time for the Texas Credit Union League and Affiliates.

On May 10, 1978, with TCUL Board Chairman Roy Neidig, Members Insurance Board Chairman Dave Marr and TCUL Services Chairman Carol Reagan officiating, ground was broken for the new $15.5 million Texas Credit Union Center on a ten-acre tract fronting the LBJ Freeway in suburban Farmers Branch, just north of Dallas. Farmers Branch Mayor Bill Binford was among the speakers for the occasion. Calvin Phillips, immediate past board chairman of the TCUL, offered the invocation at the outdoor ceremonies, which included the planting of a symbolic oak tree by two young members signifying the stability and future growth of Texas credit unions.

317

"We are, in effect, testifying to the continuing growth and prosperity of the credit union movement in our state," Niedig told a crowd of 135 dignitaries, credit union leaders and guests. The twelve-story, 315,000-square-foot building that would rise on the site to house the League, Members Insurance, TCUL Services, Southwest Corporate Federal Credit Union and Town North National Bank "reflects the fact that credit unions have become an indispensible financial service for so many people throughout Texas," Neidig said.

The building enterprise sped on under the direction of Jack Eaker, whom MacKinnon had assigned the awesome task of coordinating the total project from concept to conclusion.

Just a day short of one year later, on May 9, 1979, the new building was officially "topped out" as the final beam was hoisted into place, accompanied on its ride to the top of the structure by an evergreen tree for good luck. League Vice President Harley Barrett, building projects manager, Board Chairmen Neidig, Marr and Jimmy Sasser (who had by this time succeeded Carol Reagan as chairman of TCUL Services) were equipped with hardhats and given a special tour of the center, as were members of the Board of Directors.

Eaker had been occupied with the expansive building project for nearly a year and a half before construction actually began. Directors had approved the general concept for the parallelogram-shaped structure in January 1977, based on a study conducted by the architectural-engineering-planning firm of Swanson, Hiester, Wilson and Claycomb, Inc. The Board wanted to try to make sure that the building would accommodate the needs of the League and its Affiliates through 1996, and planned to build enough reserve space into the building to meet this goal and lease what was not immediately needed. An equally important step by the Board was a firm reaffirmation that the League and all its Affiliates remain together under the same roof. Members Insur-

This building on Forest Lane in North Dallas was the home of the TCUL and Affiliates for several years prior to the completion of the new Texas Credit Union Center in 1980.

The planting of an oak tree symbolizing the strength of the credit union movement was part of the groundbreaking ceremonies for the new Texas Credit Union Center. Assisting the young tree planters (from left) are Dave Marr, Roy Neidig and Carol Reagan.

Cutting the ribbon to officially open the new 12-story home of the League and Affiliates are (from left) Clyde Choate, Ron Liles and Jimmy Sasser.

ance Companies, it had been decided, would be the actual owner of the building. Financing was handled by the Government Employees Credit Union of San Antonio; and the Vantage Companies of Dallas were named as both the general contractor and the leasing-management agent.

As work on the new building was about to begin, there was some sentiment within the TCUL leadership to name it "Town North Bank Building." The rationale behind this was that lease space in a bank building would be more attractive to potential tenants. But in April 1978, the Board of Directors took a firm stand against this idea, voting to call the new structure Texas Credit Union Center, thereby emphasizing the multiple identity of the building as the house of the entire TCUL "family."

Eaker summed up his sentiments in completing the building project during open house ceremonies at Texas Credit Union Center, June 14, 1980.

> "Without a doubt, this is a particularly proud moment for all of us here and all credit unions around this great state. It is here where the Texas Credit Union League and its Affiliates, under one roof, will develop the new services that credit unions can use to meet the challenges of the 1980s.
>
> "This building is a symbol for all to see. It is a symbol of the strength and credibility of credit unions and the Texas Credit Union League. It is a symbol of the unity of Members Insurance Companies, TCUL Services, Town North National Bank, Southwest Corporate and all the people working here that support Texas credit unions.
>
> "This building is a lasting symbol to remind us of our acomplishments and what we have left to do."

Before the transition to new quarters from the old leased headquarters on Forest Lane, which the League and Affiliates would actually occupy until March 1980, came a momentous transition in leadership. W.S. MacKinnon, the man who had led the reunified TCUL as the first chief executive officer and president of the League and all its Affiliates, was now in failing health

320

and in the fall of 1978, as workmen were completing the foundation for the new building, he made the decision to retire.

The impact of MacKinnon's leadership—not only his seven years at the helm of the League and Affiliates, but his earlier presidency of the League under the old system and subsequent presidency of CUNA—can hardly be exaggerated. As the *Texas Leaguer* noted: "MacKinnon's tenure the past seven years as president of the Texas Credit Union League and Affiliates has spanned perhaps the greatest forward thrust of the credit union movement since he entered the field almost 40 years ago as a manager."

MacKinnon was a vital part of that thrust, but he was also a master of understatement and a leader who was never inclined to "beat his own drum." In assessing his seven years in the TCUL's highest post, he attached the most importance to the very consolidation and "pulling together" that had put him there in the first place. "Anything like this is a matter of opinion, personal judgments and all that," he told an interviewer in April 1979," (but) I guess the most important thing . . . was to pull the organization together."

He was gratified by the situation of the League and its Affiliates as he departed, but that gratification was tempered somewhat by the challenges and yet-unsolved problems that he could see ahead. "In the last seven years I am most pleased about the financial situation in which the League finds itself—without dues increases and yet with a continuing succession of surpluses," MacKinnon told the *Texas Leaguer*. "The Members Insurance affiliates and TCUL Services, Inc. operations are all financially in good shape and making money in 1978—and this despite the fact we have had many new programs: Master Charge, the home loan mortgage program, share draft development, the development of the life insurance company, Southwest Corporate Central FCU and the purchase of Town North National Bank for credit unions."

MacKinnon viewed the new technology and its various forms of specialized expertise as the "primary challenge" facing individual credit unions. At best, it would be difficult to stay abreast of technological changes in the field, he said, but this was the only way to "be sure members will have the same opportunities for service as other financial institutions provide for their customers." Unfortunately, he added, credit unions had not characteristically taken the lead in technological changes. "I'm afraid the tendency is that credit unions wait and let everyone else start a new program, and then we come along and inaugurate it in good time. Unfortunately, that means we are not providing services on a timely basis."

MacKinnon urged credit union managers to "do their homework" by attending seminars and reading literature made available by the League and other credit union organizations, to be careful in the areas of cash flow and cash handling, to be concerned about any investments they made, and to make themselves aware of new services."

He was not worried, however, about any dearth of leadership for the League after his retirement. He pointed with pride to the "development of leadership that directs TCUL and Affiliates, through a program of hiring good people and providing backup support for top management individuals." And Jack L. Eaker, a veteran of 13 years with the League and the man to whom MacKinnon was turning over his position, was an outstanding example of that leadership-building program.

With thirteen years of exerience in claims adjusting before he joined Members Mutual in January 1965 as claims supervisor, Eaker advanced steadily through the ranks of the company, being named claims manager, then claims vice president in the late 1960s, and being

Growth of Texas Credit Unions (Dollar Amounts In Thousands)

Year	No. CUs	No. Members	Assets (000)	Asset Growth
1929	11	1,405	$	
1934	63	8,048	$ 535	
1940	401	96,568	$ 8,296	
1941	439	98,394	$ 10,146	22.3%
1942	456	89,496	$ 9,741	−4.2%
1943	447	80,773	$ 10,175	4.5%
1944	350	77,952	$ 10,634	4.5%
1945	334	76,217	$ 11,795	10.9%
1946	331	82,078	$ 14,180	20.2%
1947	333	99,404	$ 18,032	27.2%
1948	353	121,564	$ 24,025	33.2%
1949	436	151,122	$ 33,238	38.3%
1950	499	179,956	$ 44,216	33.0%
1951	540	214,454	$ 54,033	22.2%
1952	634	260,360	$ 72,991	35.1%
1953	749	317,523	$ 96,846	32.7%
1954	856	374,669	$ 122,241	26.2%
1955	926	432,548	$ 152,205	24.5%
1956	991	487,319	$ 182,760	20.1%
1957	1,040	542,503	$ 215,676	18.0%
1958	1,094	591,261	$ 248,425	15.2%
1959	1,129	641,689	$ 287,740	15.8%
1960	1,171	706,655	$ 323,737	12.5%
1961	1,186	745,292	$ 369,307	14.1%
1962	1,222	790,433	$ 413,596	12.0%
1963	1,247	844,475	$ 471,230	13.9%
1964	1,282	902,881	$ 542,643	15.2%
1965	1,320	976,961	$ 623,642	14.9%
1966	1,362	1,063,631	$ 698,168	11.9%
1967	1,378	1,159,183	$ 777,922	11.4%
1968	1,403	1,243,750	$ 903,887	16.2%
1969	1,427	1,345,577	$1,034,062	14.4%
1970	1,439	1,452,416	$1,178,701	14.0%
1971	1,418	1,575,795	$1,431,141	21.4%
1972	1,421	1,625,691	$1,670,121	16.7%
1973	1,408	1,850,100	$2,009,200	20.3%
1974	1,401	2,025,748	$2,269,219	12.9%
1975	1,411	2,216,168	$2,561,948	12.9%
1976	1,413	2,373,438	$3,296,856	28.7%
1977	1,420	2,609,563	$3,968,762	20.4%
1978	1,430	2,876,419	$4,626,201	16.6%
1979	1,413	3,067,117	$4,852,913	4.9%
1980	1,382	3,212,168	$5,306,235	9.3%
1981	1,332	3,296,400	$5,608,791	5.7%
1982	1,277	3,367,001	$6,283,916	12.0%
1983	**1,232**	**3,487,000**	**$7,759,000**	**23.5%**

elevated to executive vice president of Members Insurance in 1970. In November 1976, he had been named first vice president of the League and Affiliates and became the first person to hold this position.

Eaker was appointed to the presidency of the League and Affiliates at a special meeting of the Board of Directors in Dallas on November 9, 1978, the same meeting at which MacKinnon announced his retirement, effective December 31. Eaker formally assumed the presidency on January 1, 1979, becoming only the second man to hold the post.

Eaker brought to the presidency a style and approach all his own and one that was, in many respects, far different from MacKinnon's. He was quieter, more reserved and somewhat less outspoken, but he was also highly effective in his new role. As one key TCUL executive who worked with him during this transitional period observed, "Jack took control and made the hard decisions that had to be made. He has become one of the strongest leaders in the credit union movement."

Ed Hale, who also has worked closely with Eaker during his tenure as TCUL Board chairman, explains both the differences in Eaker and MacKinnon and the advantages of those differences in these terms: "Mac was the first to see the need for professional management, and he started assembling that kind of staff. Jack is an outstanding example of this new professionalism. The type of leadership we had before was appropriate at the time, but it wouldn't be appropriate now. Today, we need the business approach that Jack Eaker exemplifies. Jack has gotten everything working together in a way that very few other people could have done."

Hale cites two major Eaker contributions in particular. "For one thing, he got credit unions involved in the political process on every level and welded the movement into a truly powerful political force. For another, he has taken many important steps in extending new League services to credit unions and their members

324

without the credit unions having to do costly research and development."

From both his staff and the elected leadership, Eaker draws especially high praise for his role in reversing the fortunes of TCUL Services. As Hale puts it: "Jack Eaker should get the bulk of the credit for turning around TCUL Services, which had a negative net worth of more than $300,000 in 1973, to a financially sound service corporation just ten years later."

From a fiscal liability, TCUL Services has developed into a strong and vital arm of the League under Eaker's direction. In 1983, ex-TCUL Chairman Ron Liles was designated by Eaker to manage the rejuvenated service Affiliate. Today, the six divisions of TCUL Services provide services to credit unions in any area not related to insurance, including: (1) share draft processing, (2) auditing, (3) marketing/communications, (4) printing and mailing, (5) discount brokerage services, and (6) supply.

"We help credit unions provide a wider range of service for their members by eliminating costly up-front expenses and the potential for errors associated with any new service, "Liles says. "Our three goals are providing needed products, quality service and competitive pricing."

Evidence that this emphasis on quality is well-received by Texas credit unions can be found in the larger number of credit unions using the share draft payment system and utilizing what Liles calls "the best in-house audit assistance service in the U.S."

Overall, the success of TCUL Services is a graphic example of Eaker's distinctive style of leadership, and a clear indication that the League's helm remains in strong and dedicated hands.

Passing the Torch

In the inexorable march of time and events, the passing of the torch to new leaders is an endless and essential process. Some leaders are afforded more time upon the human stage than others, and those with the least time, perhaps, must endeavor to move the fastest and furthest in the shortest amount of time. Such may have been the case with Wilfred MacKinnon, who gave so totally of himself to the credit union cause.

Tragically, MacKinnon did not survive long in retirement. On September 29, 1979, he died at his Dallas home at the age of 57 of the heart ailment that had forced him to step aside well before normal retirement age. He was mourned throughout the movement he had served, but even as they grieved at his passing, his fellow credit uinonists realized that MacKinnon had left an indestructible legacy behind.

"In my lifetime I have never met a person quite like Wilfred MacKinnon," said former TCUL President Walter Duncan. "It was very difficult to know him, but when you did, you knew him to be a person dedicated to his profession . . . a person never to cower . . . a person to stand erect and a person to call a friend."

Added CUNA President Jim Williams: "In some ways, he was one of the least understood credit union leaders of our generation. The side most people saw—a strong-willed and determined individual—was one I always admired. He set out to accomplish what he believed in and did it. He was forceful and had a bulldog tenacity . . . But there was a side that many people didn't know. Mac was also a kind and compassionate individual. He had a keen perception not only of political moods but of other people's personal problems, and he could recognize these things when others couldn't."

And former TCUL Board Chairman James Chiarizio put it this way: "I have been accused of thinking that Mac hung the moon. I guess I did as far as credit unions

TCUL Chairmen (1974-1984)

Jim R. Williams, 1974-76

Calvin Phillips, 1976-78

Roy Neidig, 1978-80

Ron Liles, 1980-82

S. Edward Hale, 1982-84

Paul Mitchell, 1984-

go. He had the foresight to see what we needed long before the rest of us. He had the knack of getting those needs accomplished."

The MacKinnon-Eaker transition was only one of many personal changes that were taking place within the League and its Affiliates as the Seventies dissolved into the Eighties. There were other retirements, other new faces in major leadership positions and other examples of the continuing high caliber of men and women rising to fill these positions. In June 1979, Clyde Johnson retired as the League's executive vice president. He had served continually on the board of Town North National Bank since its purchase by Texas credit unions and was the bank's board chairman from 1975 to 1980, when he was succeeded by Eaker. Al Jones, the League's director of governmental affairs and a key figure in credit union legislative concerns for more than a decade, retired in September, 1980, and was succeeded by his assistant of two years, Wayne Lough.

Meanwhile, newly elected leaders were succeeding old ones on the Board of Directors. Liles replaced Roy Neidig as TCUL board chairman in April 1980 and Clyde Choate was elected chairman of Members Insurance, succeeding Davis Marr. Two years later, in April 1982, Liles was, in turn, succeeded in the TCUL chairmanship by Hale; Paul A. Mitchell took over as chairman of Members Insurance, succeeding Choate; and Delton Moore became chairman of TCUL Services, a post held in 1981 by Mitchell, who had replaced Jimmy Sasser. Carol Reagan became first vice chairman of the League in 1982, moving into the post vacated by Hale's elevation to the chairmanship, and Choate meanwhile took over her old post as secretary-treasurer. This was far more than a mere game of "musical chairs" where the chief leadership positions were concerned. Instead, it was continuing proof that a solid and growing corps of highly capable leaders had firm control of the reins of

328

the League and Affiliates as they pressed resolutely on into the uncertainties of yet another new decade.

Although these leaders of the 1980s tend to hold their various elective postions only for a relatively brief period in comparison to some of the League oldtimers, they do not usually pass from the scene when their terms of office expire, but move on to serve the credit union movement in other capacities. Their ability to serve in many different positions with expertise and integrity has proved one of the great strengths of the modern credit union industry.

Liles, for example, continues to serve as senior vice president for member services for the League, although he is no longer on the Board of Directors. The Wise County native and former assistant manager of the Carswell Credit Union in Fort Worth, is a second-generation credit unionist, whose father was active in the movement for many years, and whose brother, Gary, is assistant manager of the LTV Federal Credit Union in Grand Prairie. Liles represents a mixture of the old-style idealism and the new professionalism in the movement. "I'm totally committed to the unity of our organization," he says. "To improve our level of service, we won't hesitate to create new entities within that organization as they are needed."

Hale, Liles' sucessor as TCUL chairman, is a New Yorker by birth, who adopted Texas as his home, earned a law degree from the University of Texas at Austin and has been active in credit union work for nearly a quarter-century. Since he was hired as an employee of Dallas Teachers Credit Union, which he now serves as president, by H.B. Yates himself, Hale stands as another living link between the past and present of the TCUL. He, too, stresses the theme of unity. "Unity has been my goal," he says. "Collectively, all the credit unions in this country are smaller than the Bank of America ($94 billion versus $103 billion in assets), but our strength is in our unity. I don't see any cracks in it at this point."

Mitchell was elected first vice-chairman of the League in 1983. President of the Food Industry Federal Credit Union in Houston, Mitchell is a former TCUL staffer and a former president of both the Houston Chapter and the Southeast Texas Managers Association. "We need to stick together within the movement and avoid a go-it-alone attitude," says the Houston native, echoing the sentiments of Liles and Hale. "In this coming age of financial giants, we need all the unity and cooperation we can get."

Neidig, president of Austin Municipal Federal Credit Union, not only served as TCUL chairman for 1978-79, but was also president of Southwest Corporate from 1975 to 1978. The native Texan from Elgin served on the TCUL Board from 1967 to 1984.

Delton Moore, who became MIC board chairman in 1983 and who serves as general manager of Texaco PAW Employees Federal Credit Union of Port Arthur, has been a TCUL board member since 1978. A native of New Iberia, Louisiana, and a veteran of more than 25 years in credit union work, he is a past president of the Sabine Area Chapter.

After serving two terms as chairman of Members Insurance (1980-82), Clyde Choate has also served as secretary-treasurer of the League. Born at Cooper in East Texas, he has been a TCUL director since 1974 and has been associated with Enserch Federal Credit Union in Dallas, where he serves as president since 1967. He has also served as treasurer of the Texas Credit Union Political Action Committee.

Billy Spivey, president of the Public Employees Credit Union of Austin since 1972, became chairman of TCUL Services in 1983. He is also a past member of the Texas Credit Union Commission and has served on the League Board since 1978. On January 1, 1984, he assumed the presidency of the Texas Share Guaranty Credit Union, succeeding Buford Lankford, who retired at the end of the 1983.

The following have worked for the League and Affiliates for 25 or more years in 1984:

Betty Danyluk — 31 years (April)
Jim Vest — 31 years (November)
Tony Gehring — 30 years (June)
Jeanne Hardin — 29 years (November)
Mary Ogden — 27 years (August)
Nancy Clark — 26 years (June)
Ted McGehee — 26 years (August)
Clarence Rodgers — 26 years (September)
Myrtle Johnson — 26 years (October)
Gladys Yarbrough — 26 years (June)
Dan Smith — 25 years (April)

1983 CHARTER ANALYSIS

Federal CUs	770
State Chartered CUs	462
	1,232

DISTRIBUTION BY ASSETS, 1983

	No. CUs	% of Total
$0 - 100,000	95	7.7%
$100,001 - 250,000	132	10.7%
$20,001 - 500,000	178	14.4%
$500,001 - 750,000	103	8.4%
$750,000 - 1,000,000	74	6.0%
$1,000,001 - 2,000,000	172	14.0%
$2,000,001 - 5,000,000	222	18.0%
$5,000,001 - 7,500,000	63	5.1%
$7,500,001 - 10,000,000	40	3.3%
$10,000,001 - 20,000,000	73	5.9%
$20,000,001 - 50,000,000	50	4.1%
$50,000,000 & Over	30	2.4%
	1,232	100%

DISTRIBUTION BY COMMON BOND, 1983

		No. CUs	% of Total
Associational		168	13.6%
Occupational (Total)		1,023	83.1%
Manufacturing	391		31.7%
Whse & Retail Trade	71		5.8%
Government	219		17.8%
Education	112		9.1%
Other Occup.	230		18.7%
Residential		41	3.3%
		1,232	100%

By the time the League's 46th annual meeting convened in Houston on April 9, 1980, the hundreds of employees and myriad functions of the TCUL and Affiliates had been relocated to the new Texas Credit Union Center and were in full operation there, although the formal opening ceremonies were not held until June 14.

By this time, too, five Texas credit unions had already celebrated their fiftieth anniversaries, and seven others were planning their own golden anniversary observances. This particular annual meeting marked a dramatic confluence of the past and the present. But whether those in attendance were more concerned with the new look and new leadership of the League and Affiliates or with the celebration of a half-century of service, the theme of the Houston meeting seemed extremely appropriate: "The Time is Now."

One great period of transition had been completed. It undoubtedly would not be the last.

And Now, The Future

This story has no end. Even as this book is being written and published, new chapters in the continuing history of the credit union movement are being created in Texas and elsewhere. As the late 1970s witnessed the share draft revolution, the early 1980s saw credit unions, now totally deregulated on the savings side, plunging into such new financial fields as money market accounts, certificates programs and Individual Retirement Accounts (IRAs). By August 1983, the League had established operating relationships with both major automated teller machine (ATM) networks in Texas—Pulse and MPACT—providing operational links betwen these vast systems and member credit unions at an extremely low cost. And, as more sophisticated technology has been added, so have more specialized and expert personnel. Dr. Charles Idol, for example, became the first full-time staff economist to be employed by any state league when he joined the TCUL, also in August 1983. And between now and the mid-point of this decade, other dramatic innovations within the financial marketplace will almost certainly bring more challenges for credit unions and more opportunities for expanded service.

And yet, as much as times and concerns have changed in the seventy-plus years since Texans first began to experiment with credit unions—and as much as they will surely change in the future—some things about credit unions remain constant.

The vast majority of credit union people realize that credit unions have won their place in today's financial community not by virtue of the fact that they were richer or stronger than their competitors, but because they were—and *are—different*. As credit unions meet the challenges and crises of the Eighties and Nineties and beyond, whether in the form of a business calamity such as the collapse of Braniff International Airways and the loss of thousands of jobs by credit unions members, or in the form of a natural disaster such as Hurricane Alicia, the most costly insurance loss ever handled by Members Insurance, with $18 million in claims paid, they must retain this difference.

As TCUL President Eaker explained: "Banks may have the world-at-large as their marketplace, while the credit union marketplace is more restricted and aimed at relatively small common-bond groups. But the main advantage of credit unions is that they are democratic, member-owned institutions that are really dedicated to serving the average consumer. Banks didn't even want this kind of business until credit unions made something of it."

As important as are the bridges now being built toward the future by the Texas Credit Union League and Affiliates and the member institutions they represent, there are equally important bridges that must continue to link the movement to proud traditions of its past, and to the underlying principle upon which that movement continues to rest: "Not for profit, not for charity, but for service."

Fortunately for the credit union movement, as it expands and as today's styles and customs give way to those of tomorrow, there remain some strong physical links with earlier, less sophisticated, more austere times. The Yates, Hudsons, Patmans, and MacKinnons are no longer here to guide the movement they once led. And other pioneer leaders, such as John Quinlan, have passed from the earthly scene even as this book was being written. But there are still survivors of those other times. There are the "elder statesmen" of the movement in Texas, such as Buford Lankford, Jim Barry, Jimmie Parker, Phil Davis, Paul Mullins, Jack Mitchell and others, who are still active on the sidelines and who provide an important frame of reference. There are venerable leaders such as R.C. Morgan, Jerry Deering, Jim Williams, Pete Gooch, Walter Duncan, Calvin Phillips and others who continue to hold leadership positions and to exert powerful influence within the movement. And there are veteran employees of the League and Affiliates such as Mary Ogden, Jim Vest, Tony Gehring, Betty Danyluk, Danny Smith and Clarence Rodgers, whose careers stretch from the present back across the decades to a time when TCUL functions were carried out by a tiny handful of staffers operating out of a small, obscure office.

Today's upper-level staff management of the League and Affiliates consists of a Mangement Council composed of ten individuals: Eaker; John Arnold, manager of Southwest Corporate; Walt Bondies, vice president, general counsel; John Dunagan, senior vice president finance and administrative services; Allen Hudson, senior vice president, insurance; Ronald L. Liles, senior vice president, members services; Carol Luebke, vice president, corporate activities; Ted

These four key leaders of the Texas Credit Union League and the state's credit union movement represented nearly 40 years of outstanding service to the Texas credit union cause when they met for this historic photo in 1979. They are (from left) Jimmie Parker, former TCUL managing director; Jack Eaker, present League president; Jim Barry, former managing director, and Wilfred MacKinnon, immediate past president of the League.

Symbolizing the growth of the credit union movement, the striking new Texas Credit Union Center is shown as it nears completion in 1979. Opened in 1980, the 12-story building rises from one of the highest geographical points in Dallas County and is visible for miles.

McGehee, senior vice president, credit union services; and Mrs. Ogden, administrative assistant to the president. (In September 1984, Liles was promoted to First Vice President of the League and affiliates, the second to hold that post after Eaker and Bill Hamilton was named to Liles' old post in member services in October.)

In a very real sense, these people—and countless others who have contributed along the way—are the foundation upon which the modern credit union movement in Texas rests. Just as the new Texas Credit Union Center stands as a monument to the courage and foresight of all those pioneers who risked their time, their energies and their meager financial resources on a new and unproven concept, these human links with the past are living monuments to what that movement has accomplished.

The center, magnificent as it is, will one day be outgrown, just as all the previous homes of the TCUL have been. That is part of the price of progress. "The new building was originally projected to be capable of handling all League and Affiliates functions until 1996," noted Eaker recently, "but rapid growth has made this projection obsolete already."

Thus, the long-range planning process for a future that will inevitably arrive must continue. The decision must be made within the next few years whether to remain at the present site, where a second office tower could be constructed, or seek larger quarters somewhere else. Whatever happens, though, the League and its Affiliates are expected to remain under the same roof, according to Eaker. "Separating any of our functions would be a most undersirable alternative," he emphasized. "Keeping them all together is mandatory to maintain a cohesive internal operation as well as to project an outward appearance of unity."

Between now and the dawn of still another decade—call it the "nebulous Nineties" for now—many urgent questions must be answered: Can the small credit

336

union survive in an atmosphere of increasing complexities and competition? Will the erosion of the spirit of volunteerism in America signal the end of the missionary zeal with which the pioneers of the movement organized so many thousands of credit unions across the country? Will the overriding goal of extending access to credit union membership to every citizen of Texas become a reality or an "impossible dream"? And, if this goal is realized, will credit unions evolve into mere banks under another name?

Only the future holds the full answer to these questions, but each is receiving the careful attention of the TCUL's leadership. "I feel there is still a viable place for the small credit unions, even though the organization of them has declined sharply in recent years," said Eaker. "There are still many small towns with no credit unions and no access to them. If we are to reach our goal of access for every citizen, we must organize credit unions in these places. We need to devise ways in which larger credit unions in an area can help the small ones, and we have to remember that a credit union's needs can vary greatly, depending on the needs of its individual members. We aren't all stamped out of the same mold, and we don't want to be."

But credit unions, whether large or small, must stand up and compete, Eaker stressed. "The main challenge facing credit unions today is competition," he said. "Whether we sought it or not, we've been placed on the same footing with the rest of the financial community. This has caused us to make changes and reposition ourselves in some areas, but I'm optimistic that we can meet the challenge. We *can* compete on every level, as long as we respond to the needs of the credit union membership, as long as we keep the lines of communication open between members and their credit unions and between credit unions and their League."

As the late Wright Patman said so often, and as he believed so firmly: "Next to the church, credit unions

are the most powerful force for good in America today."
Next to the church, the credit union movement has
almost certainly won more converts over the past half-
century than any other. But like the church, the job of the
credit union movement is far from finished. In a very
real sense, there is just as much to be done today as there
was on that day in 1934 when a few dozen men met in
Fort Worth to organize the Texas Credit Union League.

A noble beginning has been made. But only by the
same self-sacrifice and the same unrelenting effort put
forth by those pioneers can credit unions claim the
future to which they aspire. Only by reaching firmly out
to grasp that future can this irrepressible movement, and
the humanitarian philosophy that undergirds it, expect
to maintain the momentum that has taken it so far and so
fast in the past fifty years.

The exciting excursion into the future begins today,
as the journey from yesterday to tomorrow goes on. Bon
voyage!

THE END

*Postscript:*The League and Affiliates 50th annual meeting was held in Houston's Albert Thomas Convention Center, April 12-13-14, 1984. Coincidentally, TCUL's 25th annual meeting was held in the same city. Theme for the convention—which included 2,467 registrants and 524 delegates representing 343 credit unions—was "50 Golden Years, Shaping Tomorrow Together."

Chairman Ed Hale, in his report to the delegates stated, "The fiftieth anniversary of an organization bears testimony to its purpose which has enabled it to survive and clearly demonstrate its ability for serving its members. This occasion in the history of the Texas Credit Union League is significant to many people.

"First, of course, are the pioneers of what credit unions could do for mankind.

"Secondly, are the leaders and the countless volunteers who developed and nurtured this vision for the past fifty years . . . bringing us to today. It is now the responsibility of each one of us to carry on that idea of people-helping-people.

". . . at our meeting today we recognize our Fifty Golden Years and look forward to Shaping Tomorrow Together."

New Board of Directors table officers elected at the meeting included: *Paul Mitchell,* president, Food Industries FCU, Houston, chairman of the Board, Texas Credit Union League; *Clyde Choate,* president, Enserch FCU, Dallas, first vice chairman, TCUL; *Delton Moore,* president, Texaco PAW Employees FCU, Nederland, chairman, Members Insurance Companies; *Bea Herod,* president, Cicost FCU, Sherman, chairman, TCUL Services, Inc.; and *Melody Lowery,* president, Cal-Com FCU, Point Comfort, secretary/treasurer.

New directors elected to the League and Affiliates Board include: *David Dowell,* president, Sears Employees FCU, Dallas; *Larry Hertell,* president, Austin Teachers FCU; *Mike Marshall,* president, TCR Federal

CU, Texas City; *Artilla Patton,* manager, Sanpat Community CU, Portland; *Janice Ruyle,* president, IASA CU, Austin; *George Studdard,* treasurer/manager, Fort Worth Star Telegram Employees FCU; and *Sue Wilkerson,* manager, Cooperative Teachers CU, Tyler.

A Preamble
to the
Constitution and By-Laws
of the
Texas Credit Union League

Because of the eternal significance of the basic purposes of cooperative credit as first established by Frederick William Raiffeisen in Germany
in 1848 and as perfected by Luzzatti in Italy and Desjardins in Canada and
by the great credit union leaders all the world around, we do first seek to
understand those principles.

"Raiffeisen," notes Myron T. Herrick in his book on credit unions,
"was a layman preacher, teaching brotherly love, who strove to
make each credit union a center of educational and moral
influence as well as a source from which members might obtain
credit . . . he permitted loans for provident and productive
purposes only . . . he was the first man to realize that cooperation
could not attain its full usefulness without combination, and that
there had to be cooperation among credit unions as close as that
among the individual members." "According to Raiffeisen (notes
Donald S. Tucker in his book on the same subject) the cooperative
movement was a means of elevating the moral tone of economic
life." Notes Desjardins, another great cooperator and disciple of
Raiffeisen, "It is of even higher importance to educate and
enlighten the farmer and the workingman so that they may be in
position to protect themselves; to teach them to manage their own
business . . . in this high conception of social duty lies the real
reward of those who have labored to help the movement of credit
unions. Success for the young democracies of this continent
depends upon the prosperity and the worth of life to the millions
of working men who compose them." We recall also that the first
national association of credit unions was organized at Weimar in
Germany in 1859 at a meeting of twenty-nine credit unions
attended by thirty-eight delegates.

The credit union brings these higher conceptions of service to our
national economic life at a time when it has been determined that there can
be no permanent prosperity based upon greed; when we know at last that
we must comprehend these higher conceptions if eventually in America we
are to attain to that perfection of our economic life which will be truly for
the people and of the people and by the people.

CONSTITUTION
Article I
Name—How Constituted

Section 1. The name of this association of credit unions shall be the Texas Credit Union League.

Section 2. Any credit union organized under state or federal law in the State of Texas shall be eligible to membership in said League upon complying with the By-laws thereof.

Article II
Its Purposes

Section 1. The purposes of said League shall be to promote in every way the credit union movement within said State.

Article III
How Managed

Section 1. The said League shall be managed by a Board of Directors and by Officers chosen in the way and manner in the By-laws provided.

Article IV
How Financed

Section 1. The said League shall be financed in the way and manner by the By-laws provided.

Article V
Affiliation With The Credit Union National Association

Section 1. The said League shall, upon its organization, affiliate with the Credit Union National Association in the way and manner provided by the Constitution and By-laws of said Association.

Article VI
Amendments

Section 1. This Constitution may be amended in the way and manner provided for amendments to the By-laws of said League.

BY-LAWS
Article I
Primary Purpose

Section 1. The primary purpose of this League is, by direct action and by active cooperation with every agency now existing or which may hereafter be created, to increase in this State the number of credit unions organized in compliance with good credit union practice in accordance with State and Federal credit union laws.

Section 2. At each regular or special meeting of its members or of its Board of Directors hereinafter provided for, the first order of business shall be a statement by the President of this League of the number of credit unions organized in this State since the previous meeting of the members of the League or its Board of Directors, at which time the names of the new credit unions shall be read. The second order of business at all such meetings shall be a discussion of the then status of credit union development in this State. The third order of business at

342

all such meetings shall have to do with the development of ways and means of increasing credit union organization activity in the State.

Article II
Other Purposes

Section 1. Other purposes of this League shall include all matters pertaining to the advancement of the credit union development in this State and the effective operation of credit unions therein including (1) adequate legislation and the protection of existing laws; (2) protection from unfair taxation; (3) improvement of operating methods; (4) development of local credit union chapters; (5) affiliation with and cooperation with the Credit Union National Association; (6) establishment and maintenance of highest operating standards.

Section 2. In such way and manner as the Board of Directors may from time to time determine, this League shall serve as the State agency in this State for all central activities developed by the Credit Union National Association.

Section 3. When by State or Federal statute authorized so to do this League shall, at such time and in such manner as its Board of Directors may determine, set up and maintain such central financial agencies within this State as may by said State or Federal statute be authorized.

Article III
Membership

Section 1. Any credit union organized and operating in accordance with the State or Federal credit union law within this State shall be eligible to membership in this State League if (A) the Board of Directors is satisfied that said credit union is in good financial condition and that it is operating in accordance with standard credit union principles and operating practices and if (B) it meets with all of the requirements of this Constitution and these By-laws, Admission shall be on application in writing to the Board of Directors and upon a favorable two-thirds vote by said Board.

Section 2. The Credit Union National Association shall be ex-officio a member of this State League and shall be entitled to representation at all meetings of said League by its President and its Managing Director with full power to vote and to participate in discussions.

Section 3. Honorary members may be admitted to this State League upon unanimous vote of its Board of Directors; they shall have the power to participate in discussions but shall have no power to vote.

Section 4. Each member credit union of this League shall be entitled to two voting delegates at all meetings and two alternates who shall be designated by said member credit union at its annual meeting and shall serve until the next annual meeting of said member credit union thereafter. The Managing Director of this League shall be notified of the names and addresses of the delegates and the alternates so elected within ten days of their election.

Article IV
Directors

Section 1. At the annual meeting of this League there shall be chosen by the delegates there present from the membership of member credit unions a board of twelve Directors, six of whom chosen by lot at the first election shall serve for two years and six for one year; thereafter all elections shall be for two years. They together with Directors elected by chapters as hereinafter provided shall constitute the Board of Directors of this League. *The organization meeting shall be called the first annual meeting.* No Director may serve for more than two consecutive terms. No member credit union shall be entitled to more than one Director on said Board.

Section 2. Directors shall meet monthly at the call of the President who may call special meetings of said Board and shall call such meetings upon written request of at least three Directors. The secretary shall give at least three days' written notice to each member of said Board prior to any regular or special meeting. Seven Directors shall constitute a quorum. Notice of a special meeting shall contain the purpose of the meeting and the business of the special meeting shall be confined to that.

Article V
Officers

Section 1. The Directors at their first meeting and at each annual meeting thereafter shall elect from their own number a President, a Vice President, a Treasurer and a Secretary and from the credit union membership a Managing Director, all to serve for one year. No officer except the Managing Director shall serve for more than two consecutive terms.

Section 2. The President, Vice President, Treasurer and Secretary shall perform the usual functions of their respective offices. All checks, notes and other obligations of the League shall be signed by the Treasurer and counter-signed by the President. The Treasurer shall manage the finances of the League under the direction of the Directors; he shall be adequately bonded.

Section 3. The Managing Director shall manage the business of the League under the Board of Directors. His first and primary function shall be the organization of new credit unions. At each meeting of the Directors and of the members he shall read two reports: having to do with (1) new credit unions organized since the last meeting and their affiliation with the State League and (2) all other matters.

Section 4. It is a major objective of this League to maintain a full-time Managing Director at the earliest possible time. It is therefore stated to be the purpose of the League to raise sufficient funds for that purpose and to become completely operative as soon as said funds may be raised which shall not be later than that time when there are one hundred credit unions organized and operating in the State.

344

Article VI
Finances

Section 1. This League shall be financed by dues assessed against its members on the basis of ¼ of 1% of the assets of said credit unions per annum payable one-half in the month of January and one half in the month of June in each year unless said ½ of 1% of said assets would exceed 1/6 of the rate of dividend paid by said credit union during its previous full year in which case said dues shall be figured on the basis of 1/6 of said dividend rate. Said League shall pay from said revenue its dues to the Credit Union National Association.

Section 2. This League shall derive revenue from such central activities as it may maintain in accordance with the determination of the Board of Directors and resulting from its association in the Credit Union National Association.

Section 3. All salaries paid by the League shall be as established by the Board of Directors.

Article VII
Chapters

Section 1. This League shall cooperate from time to time in the organization of local chapters of credit unions in accordance with such rules and procedure as the Board of Directors may from time to time determine.

Section 2. Each Chapter shall, at its annual meeting, elect a Director to the Board of Directors of the League to serve until the next annual meeting of the Chapter when a successor shall be chosen. No Director so chosen may serve on the Board of Directors of the League for more than two consecutive terms.

Section 3. Said Chapters shall carry on such common services of an educational and inspirational character as may be consistent with the rules for Chapters as determined by the Board of Directors.

Article VIII
Fiscal Year—Meetings

Section 1. The fiscal year of this League shall end December 31 of each year.

Section 2. The *annual meeting* of this League shall be held at such time and place *in the month of January in each year* as the directors may determine.

Section 3. All member credit unions shall be entitled to at least one month's written notice prior to any regular meeting and two weeks' written notice prior to any special meeting of the members.

Section 4. The Board of Directors may, by a two-thirds vote, call a special meeting of the members and shall call such meeting on written request of ten member credit unions. The notice of a special meeting shall contain a statement of its purpose and no other business shall be transacted at it.

Article IX
Amendments

Section 1. This Constitution and these By-laws may be amended by vote of four-fifths of the delegates present at any regular or special meeting of the members, providing the notice for the meeting has contained a copy of the proposed amendment and a statement of its purpose.

IN WITNESS OF our acceptance of this Constitution and these By-laws and of our intention to operate the Texas Credit Union League in accordance herewith we, representatives of credit unions in this State in general meeting assembled, do affix our signatures this sixth day of October 1934.

NAME	CREDIT UNION
W. Hughes Knight,	Dallas Municipal Employees.
J.E. Meador,	Postal Employees Texarkana.
L. Roy Prescott,	Farm Credit Administration Houston.
James C. Ely,	Postal Employees Amarillo.
W.M. Vick, (W.U.Co.)	Public Service Employees Dallas.
C.W. Thomas,	Postal Employees Tyler.
T.J. Ford,	Postal Employees Port Arthur.
Preston Lockhart,	Postal Employees Dallas.
W.O. Freeman,	Armour & Company Employees Ft. Worth.
J.H. Hines,	Conoco Employees Ft. Worth.
A.L. Hoopingarner,	Ft. Worth Poultry & Egg Co. Ft. Worth.
W.C. Deaton,	Postal Employees Beaumont.
C.H. Bodine,	Postal Employees Wichita Falls.
J.G. Thach,	Armstrong Packing Co. Dallas.
F.S. Reed,	C.R.I.&P Ry (R.I.L.) Ft. Worth.
Joe Guinn,	Pollock Paper & Box Co. Dallas.
S.J. Smith,	Postal Employees Ft. Worth.
Adolph S. Anderson,	Postal Employees San Antonio.
Thomas Vannerson,	La France (Morten Milling Co.) Dallas.
J.S. Henry,	Public School Teachers Dallas.
Frank J. Matula,	Swift & Co. Houston.
G.W. Elder,	Postal Employees Houston.
B.S. Wallace,	Postal Employees Waco.
W.E. Suddarth, (Texas)	Rural Letter Carriers Tahoka.
G.E. Sisk,	Railway Postal Houston.
D.W. Mckee,	Armour & Co. Houston.
Adolph Geue,	Postal Employees Austin.
H.C. Michael,	Municipal Employees Ft. Worth.
F.E. Record,	Conoco Employees Wichita Falls.
W.H. Wehman,	Swift & Co. San Antonio.
J. Fred Hoffman,	Morris Sheppard #1. Texarkana.
W.M. Crawford,	Denver Ry Clerks Ft. Worth.
Paul H. Scott,	Postal Employees Abilene.

Act of Incorporation of
Texas Credit Union League
Dallas, Texas

The undersigned citizens of the State of Texas hereby voluntarily associate themselves for the purpose of organizing a corporation under the laws of the State of Texas:

First. The name of said corporation shall be the "TEXAS CREDIT UNION LEAGUE."

Second. Said corporation is organized for the purpose of promoting thrift and saving among the people of Texas in general and among the members of Texas Credit Unions in particular; to disseminate information and educational material relative to thrift and savings, and to assist through educational activities and programs in the organization and operation of credit unions having for their purpose the encouragement of thrift and saving in this state, such corporation to be a non-profit organization for strictly educational and benevolent purposes, without power directly or indirectly to declare, pay or distribute dividends, money or other things of value among its stockholders as earnings.

Third. The principal office and place of residence of such corporation shall be in Dallas, Dallas County, Texas.

Fourth. The number of directors shall be 12, and the names and residence of those persons selected as directors to serve until the first annual meeting of stockholders are as follows:

W.D. Turbeville	Southern Pacific Depot	San Antonio, Texas
Jos. A. Collerain	Humble Building	Houston, Texas
Phil Harvey		Pampa, Texas
Robert E. Miller	Box 2024	Fort Worth, Texas
O.F. Burgdorf	1716 W. 18th Street	Texarkana, Texas
C.W. Hudson	Interurban Building	Dallas, Texas
C.E. Burdick		Longview, Texas
H.B. Yates	Sanger Hotel	Dallas, Texas
H.G. Turner	Box 2628	Houston, Texas
H.W. Mecklenburg		Newgulf, Texas
G.V. Anderson	Tribune-Herald	Waco, Texas
E.E. Young	715 N. Jackson	San Angelo, Texas

Fifth. Said corporation shall have no capital stock, and is not the owner of any property or asset.

Sixth. Said corporation shall exist for a term of fifty (50) years.

IN TESTIMONY WHEREOF we have hereunto set our hands,
this the 5th day of September, 1945.

STATE OF TEXAS   )

COUNTY OF DALLAS   )

Before me, the undersigned authority, a notary public in and for Dallas County, Texas, on this day personally appeared

W.D. Turbeville,   Robert Miller,   C.E. Burdick,   H.W. Mecklenburg
Jos. A. Collerain, O.F. Burgdorf,   H.B. Yates,   C.V. Anderson
Phil Harvey,   C.W. Hudson,   H.G. Turner,   E.E. Young
known to me to be the persons whose names are subscribed to the foregoing instrument, and each acknowledged to me that he executed the same for the purposes and consideration therein expressed.

GIVEN UNDER MY HAND AND SEAL this 5th day of September, 1945.

S.M. Glazener, Notary Public
in and for Dallas County,
Texas.

Index